VIETNAM

NATIONS OF THE MODERN WORLD: ASIA

†*Vietnam: Revolution in Transition,* Second Edition, William J. Duiker

†*The Philippines: A Singular and a Plural Place,*
Third Edition, David Joel Steinberg

Japan: Profile of a Postindustrial Power,
Third Edition, Ardath W. Burks

Taiwan: Nation-State or Province? John F. Copper

*The Republic of Korea: Economic Transformation
and Social Change,* David I. Steinberg

Pakistan: A Nation in the Making, Second Edition, Shahid Javed Burki

†Available in hardcover and paperback

SECOND EDITION

VIETNAM

Revolution in Transition

William J. Duiker
PENNSYLVANIA STATE UNIVERSITY

Westview Press
BOULDER • SAN FRANCISCO • OXFORD

Nations of the Modern World: Asia

Published in 1995 in the United States of America by Westview Press, Inc., 5500 Central Avenue, Boulder, Colorado 80301-2877, and in the United Kingdom by Westview Press, 12 Hid's Copse Road, Cumnor Hill, Oxford OX2 9JJ

Library of Congress Cataloging-in-Publication Data
Duiker, William J., 1932–
   Vietnam : revolution in transition / William J. Duiker. — 2nd ed.
     p.   cm. — (Nations of the modern world: Asia)
   Includes bibliographical references and index.
   ISBN 0-8133-8588-1.—ISBN 0-8133-8589-X (pbk.)
   1. Vietnam—History.   I. Title.   II. Series.
DS556.5.D85   1995
959.7—dc20   94-36485
                                                    CIP

Printed and bound in the United States of America

10   9   8   7   6   5   4   3   2

To the memory of my sister Mary

Contents

Illustrations

Acknowledgments

I would like to thank the editors of *Vietnam* pictorial for granting me permission to reproduce several photographs from issues of their journal. I would also like to reiterate my gratitude to the Institute for the Arts and Humanistic Studies and to the College Fund for Research of the College of Liberal Arts at The Pennsylvania State University for providing financial assistance in support of the first edition of this book.

William J. Duiker

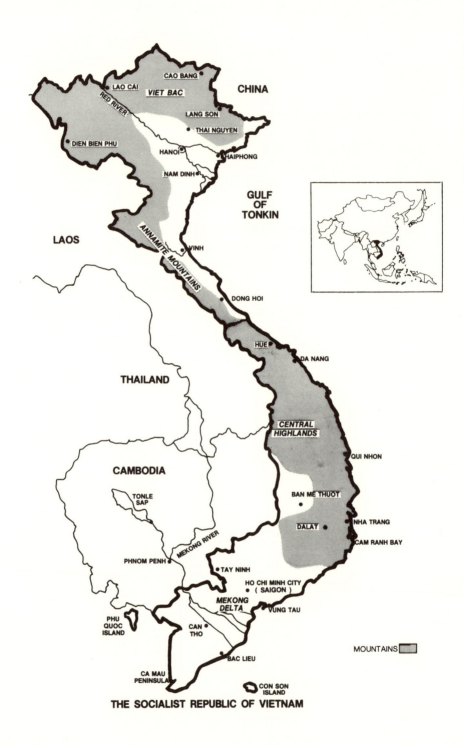

THE SOCIALIST REPUBLIC OF VIETNAM

1

Land and People

THE GEOGRAPHICAL SETTING

Vietnam lies along the eastern edge of the peninsula of mainland Southeast Asia. Shaped like an enormous letter *S*, the country extends from the border of China in the north to the tip of the Ca Mau peninsula in the south, a total distance of slightly more than 1,000 miles (1,600 kilometers). Bordered on the east by the South China Sea, it is separated from its neighbors on the west for much of its length by mountains that extend from the Chinese border in the north to the extensive plateau of the Central Highlands. South of Saigon the country flattens out into the vast marshy delta of the Mekong River, which flows into the South China Sea after a journey from the mountains of Tibet nearly three thousand miles away. At the southern tip lie the dense mangrove swamps of the Ca Mau Peninsula. Of a total land area of 127,259 square miles (329,556 square kilometers), only about 16 percent is under cultivation. The remainder consists of mountains or dense forests.

Vietnam is often described metaphorically as two baskets of rice separated by a bamboo pole. In the north lies the crowded triangle of the Red River delta, the ancestral homeland of the Vietnamese people; in the south, the flat, waterlogged delta of the Mekong River, one of the great river systems of the world. These two rich alluvial plains, separated from each other by several hundred miles, provide the major source of food for the population. Here live more than two-thirds of all Vietnamese, now numbering more than 75 million. The vast majority are rice farmers, living in villages and hamlets scattered like mushrooms over the flat green plains. Linking these two deltas is the narrow waist of Central Vietnam. In some areas, a flat coastal plain separates the mountains on the western horizon from the South China Sea. In others, the mountains thrust directly up from the surf, as at the Pass of the Clouds, just north of Da Nang, where the border is less than 30 miles (48 kilometers) from the sea. Along this central coast, farmers struggle to eke a living out of the sandy soil. Conditions here, however, are not as favorable as in the deltas to the north

1

Ha Long Bay. (Photo property of the author.)

and south. The coast is frequently buffeted by typhoons, and much of the land is sandy and subject to periodic invasion by salt water.

The other prominent feature of Vietnam is the chain of mountains that stretches from the Chinese border to a point less than 100 miles (160 kilometers) north of the Mekong River. The most extensive range is located to the north and west of the Red River delta and extends southward from the southern Chinese provinces into northern Vietnam and Laos. These mountains are rugged and heavily forested and frequently reach a height of more than 9,000 feet (2,800 meters). Further to the south lies the Annamite chain (in Vietnamese, Truong Son, or Central Mountains), which stretches nearly 800 miles (1,300 kilometers) from the Vietnamese panhandle, just south of the Red River delta, to a point about 50 miles (80 kilometers) north of the city of Saigon. For most of its length, the Annamite cordillera forms the border between Vietnam and its neighbors to the west, Laos and Cambodia. At its southern extremity, it broadens into a high plateau known as the Central Highlands (Tay Nguyen), an area of more than 20,000 square miles (51,500 square kilometers) lying between the Cambodian border and the South China Sea.

For the most part, the mountainous regions are thinly populated and are inhabited mainly by non-Vietnamese tribal groups who live by hunting and fishing or by primitive agricultural techniques. Historically, the Vietnamese people, living in the deltas or along the central coast, considered the mountains dangerous, disease-ridden, and inhabited by barbarians (*moi*); for centuries the mountains formed an almost impregnable barrier between the Vietnamese along the coast and their Southeast Asian neighbors to the west. In recent years, however, Vietnamese governments have attempted to encourage settlement by lowlanders in the higher regions to promote the cultivation of cash crops and reduce population density in the more crowded provinces.

The climate of Vietnam ranges from the tropical to the subtropical. In the Red River delta, temperatures vary from 41°F (5°C) in winter to more than 100°F (38°C) in summer. In the flat, steaming plains of the south, the temperature varies little, ranging from 79°F to 85°F (26°C to 30°C), and seasons are marked only by the division of the year into the dry season and the monsoon season, with the latter beginning in May and lasting until early fall. In general, there is plentiful rainfall over most of the country, permitting the cultivation of wet rice in all lowland areas. The mountainous regions have traditionally been relatively unproductive; favorable topography and a temperate climate in the Central Highlands permit the growing of cash crops like coffee, tea, vegetables, and in the lower regions, rubber.

THE PEOPLES OF VIETNAM

From an ethnic and cultural point of view, mainland Southeast Asia is one of the most heterogeneous regions on earth. Several of the major families of *homo sapiens* can be found within its borders. Most of the world's great religious and philosophical systems, including Buddhism, Confucianism, Hinduism, Islam, and Christianity, have been practiced there. It has been estimated that there are more different languages and dialects spoken in mainland Southeast Asia than in any other area of comparable size on the face of the earth.

This diversity is a product of geography and history. Chains of mountain ranges thrusting like giant fingers southward from China divide the peninsula into a series of isolated river valleys, from the Salween and the Irrawady in the west to the Red River and the Mekong in the east. Tribal groups migrating into the area from China or, some scholars maintain, from the Indonesian archipelago competed for control of the fertile lowlands, driving weaker peoples into the heavily forested and malaria-ridden mountains in between.

These topographical features have affected the dynamics of mainland Southeast Asian history and produced two distinct forms of human habitation. Constrained by their environment, the hill people have lived for centuries in isolated and frequently primitive conditions. Living on the slopes of mountains where water is scarce and erosion leaches the soil of

Rice farmers. (Photo property of the author.)

precious nutrients, they turned in order to survive to a seminomadic existence marked by food gathering or slash-and-burn (swidden) agricultural
techniques. Population was stagnant, cultural development was limited
(few of such peoples, for example, possessed written languages), and political organization was usually rudimentary, often consisting of no more
than a kin group organized in the form of a mountain village. By contrast,
the lowland peoples typically represented the most dynamic force in
premodern Southeast Asia. Plentiful water and an ever-fertile soil, en-
riched by the constant flow of rich nutrients in the sediment carried down
from the mountains, made the river valleys attractive regions for the
growth of human civilizations. Wet rice is one of the most productive
grain crops known to man. It is nutritious and can be used as a staple food
in a limited diet. Under proper conditions, it produces more food per unit
area than almost any other grain crop. At the same time, the cultivation of
wet rice presents serious challenges to societies for which it has become a
staple commodity. First, it requires an extensive expenditure of human labor and thus places constant upward pressure on the level of population
growth. Second, it requires a relatively equitable distribution of water and
thus the development of a system of canals and dikes to ensure the rational distribution of water throughout the region. The effects of these conditions on wet-rice societies are well known: Societies based on the control
of water to assure an abundant harvest tend to expand to the limit of the

irrigable land and to develop an administrative bureaucracy above the village level in order to control the distribution of water.

The Vietnamese

The population of Vietnam is a reasonably accurate reflection in microcosm of the population mix in the region as a whole. According to one estimate, there are as many as sixty different ethnic groups within the country. As throughout the region in general, these various ethnic groups can be classified broadly into lowland valley or hill-farm peoples. By far the most dominant, in terms of numbers and political importance, are the ethnic Vietnamese. Comprising more than 85 percent of the entire population of the country, they are a lowland people who today inhabit both major river delta areas and much of the coastal plain. Throughout history, the vast majority of ethnic Vietnamese have been rice farmers. Relatively few would venture in to the mountains, not only because of the insalubrious climate in upper regions but because of fear of hostile tribesmen. As a result, the distinction between lowland Vietnamese and upland peoples in neighboring mountains has been a fairly clear one throughout history, with the Vietnamese viewing the hill dwellers as barbarians and the latter fearing the intrusion of the Vietnamese on their ancestral lands.

The ethnic origins of the Vietnamese people have been the subject of dispute among scholars. In their physiographic makeup, they appear to represent an amalgam of at least two of the major ethnic groups that inhabited East and Southeast Asia in the Neolithic era. Some scholars speculate that they may be a mixture of Australoid peoples already in the region with Mongoloid and Indonesian peoples who migrated from neighboring areas. Linguistics is of little assistance in solving this mystery. Although the Vietnamese spoken language is tonal, and thus similar to those of the Sino-Tibetan language family spoken by most of the peoples of China, it possesses many similarities in syntax and vocabulary to non-Chinese languages spoken elsewhere in Southeast Asia. Some specialists classify it as a branch of the Sino-Tibetan language family; others identify it as a member of the Mon-Khmer family or even as a distinct language group.

The Overseas Chinese

The Vietnamese are by no means the only ethnic group inhabiting the lowland areas of contemporary Vietnam. The ethnic Chinese are the most numerous of the other groups. Unlike most of the present-day inhabitants of Southeast Asia, the Chinese are relatively recent arrivals. Most arrived as part of a continuing migration of Chinese into southeast Asia during the seventeenth and eighteenth centuries. Some came in pursuit of commerce; others were Ming loyalists who sought refuge from the Manchu conquest of China in the mid-seventeenth century. In Vietnam, as elsewhere in Southeast Asia, most Chinese were urban dwellers and played a dominant role in commerce and manufacturing. In South Vietnam, the ethnic Chinese achieved prominence in foreign trade or in some handicrafts and often performed the role of middlemen in the rice trade. In the North, most were involved in commerce in Hanoi and Haiphong, but some were fishermen, dockworkers, or coal miners, and a few engaged in rice farming. Like its counterparts elsewhere in Southeast Asia, the Chinese community was itself not homogeneous. They came not only from the coastal provinces of Fukien and Kwangtung, but also from the island of Hainan, all areas that had a long history of trade with Southeast Asia. By the middle of the present century, the Chinese population of Vietnam numbered approximately 1.5 million.

During the precolonial period, the ethnic Chinese were permitted to retain their separate existence within the larger body of Vietnamese civilization. Under Vietnamese rule, most Chinese lived in separate communities called "congregations" (bang) and did not have the duties and privileges of their Vietnamese counterparts. They served above all as merchants or artisans and were treated as a separate administrative unit by Vietnamese authorities. This policy was continued under French colonial rule and even, to a degree, under the independent governments that emerged in the North and South after the Geneva Conference in 1954. The Saigon government of President Ngo Dinh Diem attempted with only limited success to assimilate the Chinese in South Vietnam into the larger society by prohibiting noncitizens from entering into commercial or manufacturing activities. The Communist regime in the North was initially more tolerant of Chinese distinctiveness. Although its ultimate objective was to assimilate the Chinese into Vietnamese society, it temporarily permitted members of the local Chinese community, numbering about 200,000, to retain Chinese nationality if they so chose. According to an agreement reached with the People's Republic of China (PRC) in 1955, the process of integration was to be gradual and voluntary. In the meantime, those who elected to remain Chinese citizens were permitted to retain a certain degree of autonomy, including exemption from the draft and separate Chinese schools, and a small private commercial sector dominated by ethnic Chinese was tolerated. This cautious treatment undoubtedly reflected the need of the Communist government in Hanoi to obtain support for government policies from the local Chinese community and from the Chinese government in Peking.

With the end of the war in 1975 and the unification of the South and North, the situation rapidly changed. Although in the immediate aftermath of the fall of Saigon, the new revolutionary leadership in the South permitted private businesses to stay in operation, a number of wealthy merchants, most of whom were Chinese, were criticized for their disruptive economic activities and had their property confiscated. Reportedly, a few, such as the infamous "barbed wire king," were publicly executed. Thousands of petty merchants and artisans within the Chinese community in Saigon's sister city of Cholon were pressured to settle in the New Economic Areas that were being built with government funds in the countryside. In 1978, the regime issued regulations calling for the abolition of large-scale private commerce throughout the country. Official sources denied that the policy had racial motivations, but the clear consequence of the new policy was to deprive the majority of ethnic Chinese of their livelihood, and many were convinced that the regime was preparing to crack down on Chinese nationals in order to integrate them forcibly into Vietnamese society. In desperation, many sought to flee abroad, either on foot to South China or by sea to other countries in Southeast Asia. An accurate count of the numbers who fled is not available, but observers have estimated that two-thirds of the more than 500,000 refugees who left Vietnam in the early 1980s were ethnic Chinese. For those who stayed in Vietnam, the future is uncertain.

The Cham and Khmer

Two of the remaining major ethnic minority groups in Vietnam, the Cham and Khmer, can be classified as lowland peoples. Both represent the remnants of former kingdoms overrun by the Vietnamese in the course of their historic expansion south from their original homeland in the Red River delta. The Cham, a people of Malay extraction, trace their history to the kingdom of Champa, which flourished along the central coast of Vietnam from the early first millennium A.D. until its final destruction at the hands of the Vietnamese in the eighteenth century. Today there are slightly more than 50,000 people of Cham extraction living in Vietnam. Cham communities can be found throughout lowland areas of South and Central Vietnam, but most are located along the Central Coast near the port cities of Nha Trang and Phan Rang. Many are fishermen, and some are engaged in farming.

Like the Cham, the Khmer in Vietnam are the remnants of an empire that fell victim to Vietnamese southward expansion. During much of the traditional period, the Mekong delta was under Cambodian rule, and the lower delta, then consisting primarily of swampy marshland, was only sparsely inhabited. In the seventeenth century the Vietnamese seized the area from its Cambodian rulers and absorbed it into Vietnam. The descendants of those Khmer who remained live today in settlements scattered throughout the lower provinces of the delta. Most are rice farmers like their Vietnamese neighbors, but they have retained their own customs and language and are Theravada rather than Mahayana Buddhists. Today there are more than half a million ethnic Khmer living in Vietnam, virtually all in the provinces south of Saigon.

Mountain Peoples

The vast majority of non-Vietnamese ethnic groups living in Vietnam today can be classified as hill peoples. Some, like the Thai, the Nung, the Meo, and the Yao, are Sinitic peoples who gradually migrated from the southern Chinese provinces during the last several centuries and settled in the mountain highlands adjacent to the Red River delta. Others, like the Rhadé and the Jarai peoples in southern Vietnam, are Malay peoples, probably the descendants of Malayo-Polynesian-speaking settlers who migrated into Southeast Asia in the third and second millennia B.C. and were forced by more aggressive later arrivals to move from the lowlands into the mountainous Central Highlands.

The most numerous are the Tho (Tay), a Sino-Tibetan people who today inhabit the mountains north of the Red River delta, an area frequently called the Viet Bac (northern Vietnam). They are closely related to the Nung, a mountain people numbering slightly more than 300,000, who have settled near the Chinese border. Most are rice or swidden farmers. Other major groups are the Muong, a mountain people closely related to the Vietnamese, who inhabit the mountains adjacent to Hoa Binh, on the fringe of the Red River delta, and several tribal groups who live in the isolated mountains of the far northwest, like the Thai (nearly 500,000), the Meo (about 220,000), and the Yao (called Man by the Vietnamese, and numbering about 200,000). In the South, the mountain peoples live in the Central Highlands. The largest numerically are the Rhadé and the Jarai, numbering more than 100,000 each. Residing in the higher elevations of the Central Highlands, the Rhadé and Jarai are related to the Cham. For the most part they live by the methods of slash-and-burn agriculture.

Traditionally, the relationship between highlanders and lowlanders in Vietnam has been an ambivalent one. Although trade and alliances against outside aggression have been characteristic of the relationship since the formation of the original Vietnamese state before the Chinese conquest, the mountain peoples were usually suspicious of the Vietnamese and frequently resisted their occasional encroachments on tribal territories. A few, like the Muong and the Tho, who are themselves closely related ethnically and linguistically to the Vietnamese, absorbed some measure of Vietnamese influence. Those living further in the mountains, like the Thai and the Nung in the North and the Malay peoples in the Central Highlands, maintain their separate cultural and religious traditions and had few historical contacts with the lowland population.

Under colonial rule, this tradition of autonomy was retained. Although the French extended their rule into the highlands, such areas were administered separately from the remainder of Vietnam. Most tribal groups kept their cultural and linguistic autonomy and were permitted to retain their traditional leadership at the local level. After independence in 1954, this system was abandoned in the South, where the new government in Saigon, in an effort to achieve centralized control over the entire country, abolished the autonomous structure set up by the French and attempted to make the tribal areas an integral part of the new republic. Lands traditionally viewed as under tribal rule were seized by the government and transformed into Rural Development Centers for the settlement of refugees from the Communist regime in the North. Vietnamese administrators were posted to the area and unrest was summarily quelled. By the late 1950s, tribal discontent had led to rebellion and the formation of a new multitribal alliance to press for autonomy, the Front Unifié pour la Lutte des Races Opprimées (FULRO). In the mid-1960s, under pressure from the United States, the Saigon government began to devote increased attention to the tribal areas in order to reduce the likelihood that minority peoples would side with the Communists in the civil war then raging in the Central Highlands.

By contrast, after 1954, the new regime in Hanoi dealt with the minority problem along the lines of the classical Leninist pattern established in Soviet Russia. Cultural autonomy was combined with political control and a policy of gradually integrating the minority areas into North Vietnamese society. Separate autonomous zones were established in the Viet Bac and the Northwest. In these areas, tribal cultural traditions were retained, schooling was given in the local language, and administrators (often trained at a new minority institute in Hanoi) were selected from among the local population. Separate seats were assigned to minority representatives in the national legislature. In recognition of the relatively primitive level of social and political development in tribal areas and the sensitivity of minority peoples to domination by arrogant lowlanders, the central government did not compel the tribal areas to advance quickly along the road to socialism but permitted them to adopt at a slower pace. At the same time, the regime adopted a program to persuade mountain peoples gradually to abandon their tribal way of life, to adopt settled farming, and to exchange traditional feudal practices for a modern socialist outlook.

For the Communists, control of the Central Highlands was an essential component of their strategy to establish liberated areas from which to advance gradually into lowland areas and eventual power in the cities. The party leadership in Hanoi adopted a moderate program calling for cultural and administrative autonomy in the expectation that this would assist local revolutionary leaders in the South to mobilize the tribal population in support of the revolution and to transform the Central Highlands into a key liberated base area against the Saigon regime.

With victory in the South in 1975, the Communist regime in Hanoi began to implement its minority policy in the mountainous areas of the Central Highlands. But the regime's efforts to integrate mountain minority peoples gradually but inexorably into the mainstream ran into difficulties. Dissident activity against the government began to increase beginning in the late 1970s, and there were reports that FULRO had been revived. Significantly, signs of tribal discontent began to emerge in the North as well. Official reports from Hanoi accused China of attempting to subvert the loyalty of the mountain peoples near the Sino-Vietnamese border. In tacit admission of official concern over the loyalty of tribal peoples north and northwest of the Red River delta, two leading party veterans of minority extraction, Chu Van Tan and Le Quang Ba, were reportedly relieved of their posts in 1978 and placed under house arrest. By the mid-1980s, however, the unrest had apparently subsided, and the FULRO organization in the Central Highlands had been effectively eliminated.

The Catholics

Not all minorities in Vietnam are identifiable by their racial or linguistic distinctiveness. As in most Southeast Asian societies, some of the most prominent minority groups in Vietnam are a product of religious preference rather than ethnic origin. The largest and undoubtedly the most influential are the Catholics. The conversion of Vietnamese to Roman Catholicism began in the seventeenth century, when French missionaries organized by the Société des Missions Etrangères (Society of Foreign Missions) became active in the area. At first, such proselytizing was tolerated by the Vietnamese monarchy, and by the end of the century, according to some estimates, more than 200,000 Vietnamese had been converted to the new faith. In time, however, the Vietnamese monarchy came to view the spread of Christianity as a threat to the regime and its Confucian institutions, and the practice and propagation of Christianity were declared illegal. Missionaries were expelled, and a few who persisted were executed. Christianity survived, however, and after French rule was imposed in the late nineteenth century the number of Catholics rapidly expanded, particularly in the South. At the granting of independence in 1954, there were approximately 2 million Catholics in the country. With the division of Vietnam into two zones at Geneva, many Catholics in the North, fearful of persecution under the new Communist regime, fled to the South. By some estimates, of the 900,000 who left the North in the months following the conference, nearly two-thirds were Catholic.

Catholicism prospered under the new Saigon regime in the South. The first president, Ngo Dinh Diem, was himself a Catholic, and he viewed the Christian community as a primary bulwark of his regime against the Communist threat to South Vietnam. Catholics were given prominent positions in the government and in the armed forces. Many played a major role in commerce, the professions, and in cultural life. Catholic refugees from the North were settled in the suburbs of Saigon and in new Rural Development Centers in the Central Highlands to provide the basis of support for the anticommunist government.

In the long run, Diem's effort to build a strong constituency among Vietnamese Christians in the South backfired. The country's Buddhist majority grew increasingly restive at the government's apparent favoritism toward the Catholic population, and in the early 1960s lay and religious Buddhist groups increasingly voiced their discontent at alleged Catholic domination of the country. That discontent ultimately led to the overthrow of the Diem regime and the rise to power of the military.

In the North, the Communist regime, anxious to win the allegiance of those Catholics who had not departed for the South, as well as to avoid alienating Catholic opinion in the South and throughout the world, adopted a moderate position with regard to the church and its followers in the Democratic Republic of Vietnam (DRV). The local Catholics were permitted to practice their religion, and relations with the Vatican were retained. Church activities were restricted, however, and some Catholics who attempted to emigrate were reportedly persecuted. In 1956, villagers in a heavily Catholic district along the central coast rioted against government policies and had to be subdued by North Vietnamese troops. In general, however, there was little evidence of open discontent over official policies among the Catholic community in the North, and spokesmen for the regime maintained that Catholic communities had been successfully integrated into the new socialist Vietnam and were as loyal to the regime's goals as their non-Christian compatriots. Foreign visitors to Catholic areas were assured that Catholics had willingly joined collective organizations and that many were even loyal members of the Vietnamese Workers' party (VWP).

How have the Catholics in the South fared since the unification of Vietnam in 1976? Undoubtedly many of the more anticommunist members of the Catholic community fled in the days immediately prior to the fall of Saigon. Of those who remained in the South, many reported later that because of their Catholic background, they were viewed with suspicion and were harassed by the new revolutionary authorities. According to one source, who later fled the country, "My family fled from the north in 1954 because they were Catholics. After 1975, freedom of religion was very restricted, although we attend church. Certain church activities, such as the youth organization, were not allowed. The Communists also started to use movies and other propaganda with an anti-religious theme."[1]

It seems likely that the party viewed the southern Catholics with a certain degree of suspicion and had some reservations about their willingness to assimilate into a new socialist Vietnam. Many were of middle-class origin and highly Westernized and had fled communism once before, in 1954. The regime therefore probably watched Catholics closely and attempted to restrict their activities, while permitting churches to continue in existence. There were periodic press reports that Catholic priests had been arrested and charged with carrying on activities against the state. Given the tense relations between the regime and the Catholic community, it is not surprising that a high percentage of refugees who fled Vietnam after 1978 were Catholics. In recent years, the authorities have taken steps to reduce the mutual suspicion between the government and the Catholic community, but press reports of the arrest and conviction of Catholic activists suggest that the problem has not yet been resolved.

The Sects

Two other religious minorities, the Cao Dai and the Hoa Hao religious sects, have played a significant role in the history of modern Vietnam. Both emerged in South Vietnam during the interval between the two world wars. The Cao Dai movement appeared in 1925 among urban intellectuals in Saigon but soon took root in rural districts to the west and south and eventually established its headquarters in Tay Ninh province. The religion (the name Cao Dai itself means "high tower") was based on an amalgam of Buddhist, Christian, Confucian, and Taoist beliefs. Although the movement had originated for religious and social reasons, it eventually took on a more political orientation in opposition to French rule in Vietnam. During World War II, its leaders supported the Japanese in the conviction that the occupation authorities would grant Vietnam independence from French rule. After the war, its anticolonial orientation continued, and for a while Cao Dai leaders were tempted to join the Communists against the French, but clashes between the two movements soon erupted in the Mekong delta, and in late 1946 its leaders agreed to an alliance with the French against the forces of social revolution.

The Hoa Hao sect was founded in 1919 by the so-called mad bonze, Huynh Phu So. So, a mystic from Hoa Hao village in Rach Gia province, founded the movement as a type of reformed Buddhism, with emphasis on simplicity and social justice. It prospered in rural areas in the southernmost provinces of the delta and along the Gulf of Thailand. As with the Cao Dai, its followers soon came to number more than a million, and after a brief period of flirtation with the Communists, its leadership turned to the French after clashes with Communist forces operating in the vicinity led to growing hostility and the assassination of Huynh Phu So, allegedly by order of the party leadership. After independence, the leadership and the bulk of the membership of the two sects continued to oppose the Communists, although a few dissident members joined the revolutionary movement when revolutionary war resumed in the late 1950s. At the same time, relations with Saigon were never close, particularly during the Diem era, because of the government's persistent efforts to bring sect areas under central rule. Like the Cao Dai, the Hoa Hao was a regional organization with parochial concerns rather than a full-fledged nationalist movement, and the political influence of both groups in South Vietnam has been limited and sporadic. Perhaps their primary importance was their resistance during the war to domination both by the Communists and by the Saigon government and their attempt, with varying degrees of success, to preserve a maximum of autonomy in areas under their control.

Like the Catholics and the overseas Chinese, the sects were undoubtedly viewed with some suspicion by the new revolutionary regime that took power in the South in 1975. Sect areas had persistently resisted attempts to encroach on districts under their influence, by either the Saigon government or the liberation army forces, and resented efforts by any regime to integrate them into a centralized state. Hanoi was aware of such attitudes and attempted to minimize problems by handling the sects with delicacy. When the collectivization of agriculture got under way in the late 1970s, for example, sect areas, where the percentage of prosperous private farmers was higher than elsewhere in the South, were given special consideration, and the process of forming collectives was slower and emphasized voluntary means. Nevertheless, hostility to the new regime was high in areas controlled by the Hoa Hao, and eventually its priesthood was disbanded. Resistance was lighter among the Cao Dai, whose "Holy See" is still permitted to operate.

CONCLUSION

From the above discussion, it is clear that, from an ethnic point of view, Vietnam is a relatively homogeneous society with about 85 percent of the total population belonging to the dominant Vietnamese culture. Nevertheless, the existence of several religious minorities, along with the ethnic minorities, has created difficulties for any government determined to create a centralized, highly integrated society. For the Saigon government, this was a serious problem that impeded its efforts to unify the South Vietnamese people against the Communist-led insurgency movement. In the years since reunification, it has been a source of continuing difficulties for the party leadership in Hanoi.

One further aspect of this problem merits brief mention here. Although a sense of common national identity is strong among all ethnic Vietnamese, history, politics, and geography have promoted the emergence of regional attitudes even within the majority culture. Vietnamese tend to recognize three separate regional groupings, each with its distinctive character: northerners, southerners, and Central Vietnamese. Best known, of course, because of recent history, are the distinctly different attitudes of northerners and southerners toward politics, social organization, and behavioral patterns. The peoples of the North are viewed as hardworking, serious, community-oriented, formal in their habits, and conservative in their resistance to change. Southerners are often described as easygoing, informal, rebellious, and individualistic. Centrists are often traditionalist and conservative in their outlook and tend to oppose both the Westernized bourgeois culture to the south and the social radicalism represented by Communist rule to the north. Some of these contrasts are undoubtedly a consequence of climate and geography. Where the North is densely populated, short of arable land, and relatively traditional in its social patterns, the South is considered a "frontier area," with excess land, a higher level of social mobility, and a more informal attitude toward social relationships. Not only was the recent civil war a product of such attitudes, but it also tended to accentuate them. Today the Communist regime is attempting, with considerable difficulty, to reduce such differences and create a more homogeneous population by assimilating the easy-going Southerners into the relatively regimental system in existence in the North.

NOTES

1. Quoted in Bruce Grant, *The Boat People: An "Age" Investigation* (Harmondsworth: Penguin, 1979), p. 102.

2

Precolonial Vietnam

PREHISTORY

The origins of the Vietnamese people are shrouded in mystery. It has sometimes been asserted that their ancestral homeland was not in the Red River delta, where they first appear in history, but elsewhere, probably in South China. At present, there is little evidence to confirm this view. Archeological evidence indicates that human habitation in the area of the delta and the adjacent mountains extends back at least several hundred thousand years to the early Paleolithic era. Recent finds by Vietnamese archeologists at Mount Do in Thanh Hoa province have confirmed that early human beings lived in the area at roughly the same time as the famous earliest examples of Peking Man and Java Man, about 500,000 years ago.

Unfortunately, there is little to link such scattered evidence to present-day inhabitants. The first clear signs of the probable ancestors of the modern-day Vietnamese and their neighbors in the adjacent mountains recently appeared as the result of archeological finds in the vicinity of the modern cities of Hoa Binh and Lang Son, suggesting the emergence of Mesolithic and Neolithic cultures in the vicinity of the delta at least 8,000 to 10,000 years ago. Available evidence suggests that the earlier stages were characterized by hunting and food gathering; the later stages show signs of the cultivation of agriculture and the domestication of animals—an indication that the inhabitants of the area had mastered primitive agricultural techniques as early as 9,000 years ago. If this is the case, the Vietnamese were among the first peoples to practice settled agriculture.

By 1300 B.C., the Stone Age civilization had clearly passed into the Bronze Age. Concrete evidence for this transformation appeared with the discovery of finely crafted bronze drums at an archeological site at Dong Son in Thanh Hoa province. Bronze work of this type has been found in neighboring areas in Southeast Asia and in China, and some archeologists have speculated that the technique of bronze working was imported into Vietnam from the north. Others, noting the sophistication of the work-

15

manship, have suggested that the technique may have been first mastered by the inhabitants at Dong Son and later spread throughout the region. Whatever the case, other evidence at the site confirms that, by the end of the second millennium B.C., the inhabitants in the vicinity of the Red River delta had created an advanced civilization based on foreign trade and the cultivation of wet rice.

THE ORIGINS OF VIETNAMESE CIVILIZATION

Were the inhabitants of these Neolithic and Bronze Age sites ancestors of the present-day Vietnamese? At this point, evidence is too scanty to permit firm conclusions, although some experts suggest that the peoples who inhabited these Neolithic sites probably belonged to the Australoid-Negroid group, early inhabitants who may later have combined with arriving elements from South China to form the ancestors of many of the current peoples of mainland Southeast Asia, including the Vietnamese. What seems clear is that sometime during the last millennium B.C. the ancestors of the present-day Vietnamese had emerged as a significant force in the lowland and upland regions in the vicinity of the Red River delta. This was a period of rapid change throughout the area. During the previous several centuries, Chinese civilization had been gradually expanding from its origins along the banks of the Yellow and Yangtze rivers in China. By the late third century, this dynamic culture had begun to expand among the proto-Chinese peoples in the hilly regions south of the Yangtze River. With growth, however, had come instability and a long period of internal civil war (called, in Chinese history, the period of the Warring States) that was brought to an end only in 221 B.C. with the creation of the first centralized Chinese empire of the Ch'in, under the dynamic ruler Ch'in Shih Huang Ti.

Among those peoples who were affected and later absorbed by the new empire of the Ch'in were the so-called Yüeh (in Vietnamese, Viet) peoples then living throughout the southern coastal provinces of China and down into mainland Southeast Asia. Among the southernmost of these Viet peoples were the so-called Lac Viet, who lived in the lowland marshy areas of the Red River delta. Sometime during the third century B.C., the Lac Viet united with other Viet peoples (sometime called the Tay Au, or Hsi Ou in Chinese) living in the nearby mountains to found the small state of Au Lac with its capital at Co Loa, not far from the present-day city of Hanoi. What little is known about the kingdom of Au Lac comes largely from Chinese sources. The state was primarily agricultural, and the people tilled the fields with polished stone hoes. Most of the arable land was owned by feudal aristocrats; there may have been some slavery. By Chinese standards, Lac Viet was undoubtedly rather small and unexceptional. According to Vietnamese historical sources, however, the small state had a distinguished ancestry; it was descended from a semimythical Hong Bang dynasty, which had ruled over an ancient kingdom of Van Lang for more than two thousand years, beginning in 2879 B.C. The historical accuracy of such records is difficult to determine, and certainly those parts relating the origins of the Vietnamese peoples to the marriage of a dragon, Lac Long Quan, and a fairy, Au Ca, are apocryphal. Yet historians believe that Van Lang may have been an actual state, and it is not unlikely that the origins of the kingdom of Au Lac can be found in the Dong Son Bronze Age civilization a thousand years earlier.

THE CHINESE CONQUEST

Whatever its origins, the infant kingdom of Au Lac was not destined to survive. In 206 B.C. the short-lived Ch'in dynasty collapsed. In the chaotic situation that ensued, one of the Ch'in military commanders in South China, General Chao T'o (in Vietnamese, Trieu Da), founded a new kingdom of Nam Viet (South Viet, or Nan Yüeh in Chinese), with its capital at Canton. In the process of consolidating his rule, Trieu Da defeated the armies of Au Lac and assimilated the lands of the Red River delta into his own empire. Trieu Da was able to maintain control over his kingdom until his death, but his successor soon ran into conflict with the new Han dynasty that had risen from the ashes of the Ch'in in China, and in 111 B.C. Chinese armies defeated Nam Viet and incorporated it into the growing empire of the Han.

The Chinese conquest had lasting consequences for Vietnam. At first Chinese rulers were willing to apply the principle of indirect rule and governed the peoples of the delta through local tribal chieftains. During the early years of the first century A.D. however, Chinese efforts to assimilate the area politically and culturally into the Han empire intensified. Chinese settlers began to immigrate into the area in increasing numbers, and some were selected to assume a major role in administration. Chinese institutions and customs were introduced as Chinese authorities sought to transform what they considered a semibarbarian society into a more civilized reflection of parent China to the north. This policy of Sinification undermined the social status and political authority of the native feudal magnates, however, and in 39 A.D led to a revolt by the famous Trung sisters (Hai Ba Trung). Trung Trac and her sister, Trung Nhi, were widows of Vietnamese noblemen who had allegedly died fighting the Chinese. Now they hoisted the banner of rebellion against foreign rule. The revolt was briefly successful, and Trung Trac declared herself ruler of an independent kingdom. But Han armies under General Ma Yüan soon returned to the attack and reincorporated the rebellious areas into the Chinese empire. In despair, the Trung sisters committed suicide by throwing themselves into a river.

For the next several centuries, Vietnam was a part of China, exposed to a concentrated policy of political and cultural assimilation. Chinese administrators replaced local aristocrats in positions of authority, although a few Vietnamese were permitted to occupy subordinate positions in the bureaucracy. The Chinese written language was introduced and became the official language of administration and literary expression. Chinese rituals and customs replaced the relatively informal social mores practiced by the local Vietnamese. The Confucian classics became the foundation of the educational system in Vietnam. Chinese art, architecture, and music were imported and served as models for Vietnamese creative workers.

From the Chinese standpoint, the effort to integrate Vietnam into the broader world of Chinese culture was simply an extension of the historic attempt to pacify the outer frontier of the Chinese world and bring culture to the allegedly barbarian peoples living beyond the bounds of Confucian civilization. As such, the conquest and absorption of the Red River delta was not only a security problem but a consequence of the cultural dynamism and moral imperatives of the Chinese state. For most of the proto-Chinese peoples living in South China, the effort was a success, and the provinces south of the Yangtze River are today an integral part of the cultural world of modern China (although it should be noted that cultural differences between North and South China remain, and even today, Vietnamese intellectuals are occasionally prone to comment on the cultural and ethnic similarities of Vietnamese and South Chinese). In the case of Vietnam, the effort failed. Why this occurred is both a matter of intense pride to the Vietnamese and a source of dispute and fascination among historians. Whatever the reasons, several centuries of Chinese rule were not able to erase the memory of Vietnamese independence, and revolts broke out sporadically in abortive efforts to drive out the foreign invader.

INDEPENDENCE RESTORED

In the early tenth century, the T'ang dynasty, one of the most powerful and advanced in Chinese history, began to disintegrate. Taking advantage of the chaos, a revolt led by Ngo Quyen drove out the Chinese and restored the independent state of Nam Viet, with its capital at the ancient city of Co Loa. But Ngo Quyen died in 944, and for the remainder of the century the country was shaken by civil war. Only the weakness of the new Sung dynasty prevented a reconquest of the area by Chinese troops. In 1010, however, a new Ly dynasty rose and soon proved to be one of the stablest and most glorious in the history of the Vietnamese nation. Under

Chinese ancestral temple at Hoi An. (Photo property of the author.)

the leadership of several dynamic emperors, notably the founder Ly Thai To and his successor Ly Thanh Ton, the Vietnamese state, now renamed Dai Viet (Great Viet), consolidated its independence and began to expand beyond the confines of the Red River delta. In that undertaking, the new state learned quickly the benefits of relying on Chinese experience. The political institutions and ideology of Confucian China were retained and put to use in building a centralized state.

Like China, and like most of its neighbors throughout the region, Vietnam was an agricultural society, based primarily on the cultivation of wet rice. In terms of landownership, the system in some ways resembled the feudal system in medieval Europe. In theory, the king owned all land, but much of it was normally awarded to top officials or nobles who were thus able to amass vast feudal manor holdings. Most of these manor holdings were tilled by serfs or, in some cases, slaves, but there was also a class of freeholding peasants based on small plots of land in countless villages throughout the Red River delta or along the coast.

If agriculture was the foundation of the state, commerce and manufacturing were not entirely neglected. Handicrafts flourished in the major cities (mainly textiles, ceramics, and wood and metal working), and a trading network developed not only within the country but with the mountain peoples and other states across the South China Sea as well. Like China, however, Vietnam under the Ly was not primarily a seafaring state, and commerce was distinctly secondary to agriculture in national priorities.

China had not abandoned its dream of ruling Vietnam. The Sung dynasty, which ruled until the late thirteenth century, lacked the military prowess to restore Chinese rule over the delta, although the rulers of Dai Viet, in order to avoid provoking imperial hostility, accepted tributary status with the court to the north. In the late thirteenth century, however, the Sung fell to the growing power of the Mongols, who established the new Yüan dynasty in 1279. Under the Yüan the old threat to Dai Viet rapidly revived. In 1285, the Tran ruler (the Tran dynasty had succeeded the Ly in 1225) refused permission for Mongol troops to cross Vietnamese territory to attack the state of Champa along the coast to the south. To punish such insolence, a Mongol army invaded Vietnam and sacked the capital. But the Vietnamese, under the inspired and astute leadership of one of their greatest national heroes, Tran Hung Dao, mobilized a national war of resistance against the invaders and, after several bloody battles, drove them back across the frontier. Two year later the Mongols returned to the attack but were again dealt a stunning defeat and eventually accepted a Vietnamese declaration of fealty to the Yüan emperor.

By the late fourteenth century, the Tran dynasty, plagued by famine, official corruption, land hunger, and almost constant war with the state of

Champa, had begun to decay. In 1400, Ho Quy Ly, the regent for a child emperor, seized the throne. In China, Emperor Yung Lo of the vigorous new Ming dynasty refused to recognize the new dynasty and in 1407 launched an invasion, bringing Vietnam once again under foreign rule. Chinese officials were again imported to fill all high-ranking posts, and a program of comprehensive sinification was adopted to replace all remaining native traditions.

This time, Chinese rule lasted only twenty years. Although early resistance, mounted by a claimant representing the Tran dynasty, failed, in 1418 a more serious threat was mounted by commoner from Thanh Hoa province. Le Loi, son of a prosperous landowner and a former official who had refused to serve under the Ming occupation, declared himself a new "pacifying king" and, with the aid of the astute Confucian scholar and military genius Nguyen Trai, launched a guerrilla movement in the hilly regions of Thanh Hoa province, south of Hanoi. By 1426, Le Loi felt strong enough to begin a major offensive against Chinese positions in the Red River delta and to lay siege to Chinese troops in the capital. The Ming court sent reinforcements, but they suffered a disastrous defeat. In the winter of 1427, Chinese forces surrendered and were permitted to withdraw. Like most founding emperors, Le Loi of the new Le dynasty set out immediately to solve one of the most persistent problems in Vietnamese society, the inequality of landholdings. Large landowners who had served the Tran or the Chinese were dispossessed by the state, and their land was redistributed among Le Loi's followers, while village commune lands were distributed to the poor. Legal restrictions on peasant rights were eased or eliminated, and rents were reduced. Major efforts were made to increase grain productivity.

The early Le dynasty can be considered a high point in the evolution of traditional society in Vietnam. A series of vigorous rulers reduced the power of the feudal magnates and issued decrees calling for greater equality of landholdings. The influence of Buddhist advisers at court declined, and a strengthened bureaucracy based on Confucian orthodoxy was established. The regime reached its apogee under Le Thanh Tong (1460–1497), during whose reign a new civil code, called the Hong Duc Code,, was promulgated to establish the rule of law and systematize the laws and regulations of the empire.

MARCH TO THE SOUTH

One major contribution of the Le dynasty was to solve a long-standing problem in relations with Vietnam's neighbor to the south, Champa. For centuries, the major foreign policy concern of the Vietnamese state had been the danger of invasion from the north. Under the independent

Cham temples at Nha Trang. (Photo property of the author.)

dynasties of the Ly, the Tran, and the Le, however, a new frontier opened up to the south. Here, along the central coast, lay the kingdom of Champa. Originally of Malay extraction, the Cham were a seafaring people who since the first millennium A.D. had inhabited the coastal areas of what is today central Vietnam and down into the Mekong delta. Unlike Vietnam, Champa had been exposed to influence not from China but from India and, after the eighth century, from Islam. If Dai Viet was a classic example of an Asian agricultural society, using its ability to exploit water resources to produce a food surplus, Champa was an active participant in the trading network establishing by Chinese and Arab traders throughout the region of the South China Sea. With the rise of the Ly dynasty in the eleventh century, tension between the two neighboring states began to increase and eventually led to conflict. On several occasion, Cham armies invaded the southern provinces of Dai Viet and once, taking advantage of the internal decay of the Ly, even sacked the Vietnamese capital. In general, however, the Vietnamese had the better of the struggle and, during the early Le dynasty, gradually advanced south, forcing the Cham to cede territory and move their capital southward. In 1471, Vietnamese troops occupied the Cham capital at Vijaya (in present-day Binh Dinh province) and reduced the state to a virtual dependency.

Vietnamese expansion to the south provided new lands for a growing population and extended the power of the state but also created new problems. With territorial expansion, combined with the gradual decline of the Le dynasty in the sixteenth century, tension arose at court and led to the rise of two powerful noble families, the Trinh and the Nguyen. Under weak rulers, land seizures by the wealthy and powerful and official corruption drove desperate peasants to rebellion. Rivalry between the Trinh and Nguyen led to the domination of the former in the North, while the latter were compelled to accept viceroyship over the newly conquered lands in the South, with their capital at Huê.

Internal dissension, however, did not end Vietnamese expansion in the South. On the contrary, the Nguyen completed their conquest of the Mekong delta and placed the entire area under Vietnamese rule. By now their main rival was the declining Khmer empire of Angkor in Cambodia. In earlier centuries, Angkor had been the most powerful state in mainland Southeast Asia and had held sway over much of the lower Mekong and the area around the Tonle Sap. By the mid-fifteenth century, however, its power was in decline, and when marauding Thai armies sacked the capital near the present-day market town of Siem Reap, the Angkor kingdom abandoned the area near the Tonle Sap and established a new capital at Phnom Penh. During the seventeenth century, Vietnamese settlers, frequently supplemented by armed force, gradually occupied lands from modern Bien Hoa down to the delta of the Mekong. Taking advantage of factionalism at the Khmer court, the Nguyen periodically intervened in internal politics and reduced the disintegrating Khmer state to a virtual dependency of Vietnam, while consolidating their control over the lower Mekong.

THE COMING OF THE WEST

The expansion of the Vietnamese state toward the south in the sixteenth and seventeenth centuries coincided generally with the appearance of a new political and cultural force on the Southeast Asian scene. In 1511, the first signs of the new age of Western adventurism emerged with the arrival of a Portuguese fleet under Admiral Alfonso da Albuquerque at Malacca, on the west coast of the Malayan peninsula. The Portuguese were followed by others, and by the end of the century the Indian Ocean and the South China Sea were teeming with ships flying the flags of Portugal, Spain, the Netherlands, France, and England.

The motives of the Europeans were diverse. While statesmen viewed the East in terms of imperial grandeur, control over the seas, and national wealth and power, merchants were lured by the promise of riches and a monopoly of the spice trade that had so long been dominated by Arab traders. Men of the cloth viewed the newly discovered lands as the home of millions of heathen souls to be saved. As the process accelerated, such motives often coalesced and intertwined. European governments subsidized the formation of joint stock companies, like the famous Dutch and British East India companies, to exploit the riches of Asia. Catholic missionaries accompanied Spanish, French, or Portuguese fleets on their voyages and frequently combined mercantile activity with their evangelical mission.

Vietnam's first direct exposure to the West came in 1535 when a Portuguese ship entered the bay of Da Nang on the central coast. Within a few years the Portuguese had set up a trading port at Faifo (now, Hoi An), a few miles to the south, which now became the main port of entry for foreign goods. The Portuguese were soon followed by others, and by early in the seventeenth century traders from several European nations were active at several ports along the Vietnamese coast.

The first Catholic mission to Vietnam came in 1615, when Jesuit missionaries from the Portuguese colony of Macao set up a small mission at Faifo. A similar mission was set up in the Trinh capital of Thang Long (today Hanoi) a decade later. The French, however, soon became the leaders in the effort. Under the vigorous sponsorship of an ambitious Jesuit scholar, Alexander of Rhodes, French Catholics set up the Society of Foreign Missions to train missionaries to propagate the Christian faith in Vietnam. A significant aspect of Rhodes' work was his desire to train native priests to serve the needs of Vietnamese converts. As a means of facilitating this goal, he devised the first transliteration of the Vietnamese spoken language into the roman alphabet. Although this written script (known as *quoc ngu,* or national language) did not at that time come into general use, French and later Vietnamese missionaries used to translate the Bible into Vietnamese. As a result of such dedicated efforts, thousands of Vietnamese were converted to the new faith.

Success, however, was short-lived. Missionary activities eventually antagonized Vietnamese authorities, who feared, with some justification, that Christian doctrine would subvert Confucian institutions and beliefs and undermine the loyalty of the population to the emperor. In 1631, the propagation of Christianity was barred in the South; thirty years later, a similar decree was issued in the North. European missionaries were expelled, and a few were executed. A similar decline occurred in commercial contacts. Although by no means a poor country, Vietnam had relatively little to offer in the way of spices and mineral resources. In 1697, the French closed down their small factory at Faifo. Others soon followed, leaving only the Portuguese with a small office.

THE TAY SON REBELLION

Throughout much of the eighteenth century, peasant rebellions had underscored rural unhappiness about mandarin corruption, land grabbing by the wealthy, and the general incompetence of the decrepit Le regime. Like peasant jacqueries everywhere, most were disorganized and quickly put down. But in 1771, a rebellion broke out that would eventually overthrow both the Nguyen and the Trinh and lead to the founding of a dynasty that united the country once again. The leaders of the revolt were three brothers from the village of Tay Son in Binh Dinh province in Central Vietnam, thus providing the so-called Tay Son rebellion with its name. Riding in the vanguard of such a widespread struggle by impoverished and land-hungry peasants in South to alleviate intolerable economic conditions, the Tay Son brothers, like Asian Robin Hoods, ravaged the countryside while seizing the wealth of the rich and giving it to the poor. For several years the rebellion was limited to the provinces of Quang Nam, Quang Ngai, and Binh Dinh. But in 1776, the Trinh took advantage of the chaotic situation and invaded the Nguyen domain. In the confusion, the Tay Son rebels seized Saigon. Many of the Nguyen lords were killed, but one, Prince Nguyen Anh, managed to flee to safety to an island in the South China Sea.

Flushed with success, the rebels now attacked the North and overthrew Trinh rule. Promising to restore power to the figurehead Le dynasty, the eldest and most capable of the brothers, Nguyen Huê, now married the daughter of the emperor and declared his fealty to the old dynasty. The emperor, however, distrusted the intentions of the Tay Son rebels and requested assistance from Chinese Emperor Ch'ien Lung. In 1788, a Chinese invasion force crossed the border and seized Hanoi, but Nguyen Huê deposed the Le ruler and declared himself the founding emperor of a new dynasty. In a bitter conflict near Hanoi, the Vietnamese achieved a decisive victory over Chinese forces, who fled in disorder back to China.

Following traditional fashion, the new emperor, under the reign title Quang Trung, set out to solidify his rule by improving conditions in rural areas. Common lands were returned to the poor peasants, and fields abandoned by their owners during the civil war were put back under the plow. Commercial activity was promoted and good relations were sought with China. But Emperor Quang Trung died suddenly in 1792 at the age of forty, and his two brothers proved to lack his acumen; the empire rapidly began to disintegrate.

The sudden decline of the power of the Tay Son came as a blessing to the remaining survivor of the Nguyen house in the South. After fleeing to Phu Quoc Island to escape the Tay Son, Nguyen Anh went to Thailand to seek assistance to recover his patrimony, but his first attempt to return was defeated in 1784. Then, however, he was befriended by Pigneau de Behaine, a French bishop stationed at Ha Tien on the Gulf of Thailand. Convinced that French help in restoring Nguyen Anh to power could create an opening for the revival of Catholic missionary activity in Vietnam, Pigneau promised to provide him with assistance. A trip by Pigneau to Paris in 1787 elicited a promise from the French government to support a naval expedition against the Tay Son in return for a promise of trade privileges and the cession of Poulo Condore Island and Da Nang harbor to France. The plan was scuttled by the French viceroy in India, however, who refused to provide the funds for the mission. Undeterred, Pigneau raised the money on his own to purchase two ships and provide weapons and volunteers for an expedition that was launched in the summer of 1789. After the death of Quang Trung in 1792, the insurgents began to make progress, and in 1802, Nguyen Anh seized Hanoi and declared the founding of a new Nguyen dynasty with its capital at Huê, in Central Vietnam. Pigneau, who died in 1799, did not live to see the victory of his protégé.

THE NGUYEN DYNASTY

Pigneau de Behaine's gamble that French assistance to Nguyen Anh would provide an opening for French commercial and missionary interests in Vietnam proved to be unjustified. The new emperor, assigning himself the reign title Gia Long, was reasonably tolerant and permitted French missionaries to operate in Vietnam during his lifetime. He refused to ratify the abortive treaty arranged by Pigneau in Paris, however, and French hopes for improved trade relations between the two countries were not fulfilled. After Gia Long died in 1820, his successor Minh Mang continued and in some ways extended this restrictive policy toward contact with the West. Bright and dedicated, the new emperor was a devout believer in Confucian orthodoxy, and although interested in mastering Western technology, he feared the effects of European ideas on traditional culture in Vietnam. During his reign, the propagation of Christianity was sternly forbidden and missionaries and their converts were persecuted. A few who persisted were executed.

The dynasty's effort to solve Vietnam's chronic social and economic problems had only indifferent success. Despite attempts to control land concentration and official corruption, conditions in rural areas did not improve significantly from the declining years of the Le, resulting in sporadic peasant unrest. Such problems were intensified by internal dissension at court and the widespread unpopularity of the Nguyen dynasty in the North, where memories of the civil war ran deep.

THE FRENCH CONQUEST

Throughout the first half of the nineteenth century, commercial, military, and religious circles in France had attempted to goad the French government into adopting a more active policy toward Vietnam. Such voices became even more vocal at mid-century, when periodic executions of French missionaries in Vietnam aroused a public outcry. For the most part, government leaders had resisted these pressures, but by the late 1850s it had become difficult to maintain such an attitude. Commercial interests, concerned at increasing British control over Burma and the possible loss to the British of the "China Market," agitated for an aggressive policy to bring Vietnam under French influence and to open up the "soft underbelly" of China to French economic exploitation. Religious organizations, angered over Huê's persecution of Catholic missionary activity, demanded protection for French missionaries and Christian converts in Vietnam. In 1857, the government dispatched a French fleet to seize the central Vietnamese port city of Da Nang and to compel the Vietnamese court to accept French demands.

The first attack, launched in the summer of 1858, did not achieve these objectives. A predicted revolt against the imperial government in the rural areas along the central coast did not materialize, and European troops were pinned down in the city and unable to advance northward to threaten the imperial capital. With his troops ravaged by disease, the French commander, Admiral Charles Rigault de Genouilly, decided to evacuate the city and resume the attack further south at Saigon, which the French seized the following February. In succeeding months, French troops extended their control into neighboring areas after bitter fighting. Defeat in the South, coupled with a spreading revolt led by Le pretenders in the North, led the court to seek peace, and in the spring of 1862, French and Vietnamese negotiators reached agreement on a treaty that ceded three provinces in the South and the island of Poulo Condore to France. Three port cities were opened to French commerce, and Christian missionaries were granted freedom to propagate their religion in Vietnam.

The seizure of three provinces in the South was only the first step in a process that led before the end of the century to the conquest of the remainder of the country and the creation of an Indochinese Union including Vietnam, Laos, and Cambodia. In 1867, French units under Governor Benoit de la Grandière seized the remainder of the South and transformed the area into the French colony of Cochin China. In the meantime, the French had assumed Vietnamese rights in Cambodia and turned it into a protectorate. For more than two centuries, Thailand and Vietnam had clashed repeatedly over dominance in Phnom Penh, with each relying for support on factions within the Khmer court. In the early nineteenth century, Vietnam had turned the disintegrating state into a virtual protectorate, but resistance to Vietnamese domination led to a revolt, and in 1846, an agreement between Vietnam and Thailand placed the area under their joint suzerainty. In the Treaty of Saigon, signed in 1862, the Nguyen court renounced its claims over Cambodia, claims that were assumed a few months later by France.

The seizure of Cochin China and Cambodia did not satisfy the dreams of French expansionists. Exploratory probes made it clear that the Mekong River did not offer a water route to the vast potential market of South China. Militant elements in Saigon and Paris agitated for vigorous action to bring the North under French rule and put France in a more advantageous position to dominate the China market.

In 1873, an opportunity to extend French influence to the north appeared when a French adventurer, Jean Dupuis, who had been running guns up the Red River into South China, encountered difficulties with local authorities. When the Vietnamese authorities attempted to control his activities, he mobilized a small military force of Europeans and Asians, seized parts of Hanoi, and then appealed to the governor of Cochin China in Saigon, Admiral Jean-Marie Dupré, for assistance. Dupré, who viewed the situation as an opportunity to compel the court to accept a French protectorate over the remainder of Vietnam and French authority in all of Cochin China, dispatched a small detachment of French troops under the command of a former naval officer, Francis Garnier. Ostensibly, Garnier's responsibility was to extract Dupuis from Hanoi, but Garnier—an imperialist in the mold of Cecil Rhodes—joined forces with Dupuis and seized the Hanoi citadel. Garnier himself was killed in a brief skirmish with imperial troops in December. In Paris, however, reaction to Saigon's unilateral effort to seize the North was hostile, and after the government had informed Saigon of its opposition to an occupation of the North, French troops were withdrawn in return for the court's recognition of French sovereignty over all Cochin China.

In the mid-1880s, the French completed their conquest of Vietnam. Pressure in France to adopt a more aggressive policy to counter British advances in Burma continued to rise, and in early 1882, reacting to the arrival in the North of Chinese troops in response to a plea for help from the court at Huê, Captain Henri Rivière was dispatched with 200 men to Hanoi. Arriving in April, he seized the citadel and consolidated French control over the entire lower delta. Rivière was later killed in a skirmish with pirates, but Paris had already decided to take further military action to bring the court to heel and to force it to accept French suzerainty. Taking advantage of the death of Emperor Tu Duc, Paris ordered additional troops to the delta. Resistance from Chinese and Vietnamese forces was soon broken, and in August 1883, the dispirited court acceded to French demands and signed a treaty establishing a French protectorate over the remainder of the country. In a separate treaty, China renounced its claims to a tributary relationship with Vietnam. Less than a decade later, the new

French "balcony on the Pacific" was completed by the establishment of a protectorate over the kingdom of Laos.

CONCLUSION

To those acquainted with the history of the Vietnamese people, the relative ease with which the Nguyen court succumbed to the French is somewhat puzzling. Why, after a tradition of centuries of staunch resistance to invasion from the north, did the Vietnamese so readily accept the new rulers from the West? One obvious factor is the military superiority possessed by the French, an advantage that marked virtually every confrontation between European and non-European societies at that time. But another was that Vietnam had the misfortune of encountering intense Western pressure at a time of serious internal weakness. Since the decline of the Le dynasty in the late sixteenth century, the country had faced serious internal problems. Expansion to the south had eased the heavy pressure on the land in the Red River delta, but it had not solved the problems of official corruption or concentration of land in the hands of the wealthy. Peasant unrest had become a familiar part of the political landscape and continued to cause internal instability well into the middle of the nineteenth century. Furthermore, expansion had led to a growing split within the ruling elite, resulting in the de facto division of Vietnamese society into two separate and mutually antagonistic regions in the North and South for several generations. The rise of the Nguyen dynasty had not brought a solution to this problem, and regional factionalism continued during the nineteenth century beneath the superficial unity of the Nguyen dynasty.

The internal divisions and tensions within Vietnamese society were exacerbated by the cultural challenge from abroad. Although the official attitude toward the West at court was tinged with hostility, fear, and at least initially, a whiff of Confucian contempt for barbarian ways, it did not take long for perceptive members of the ruling elite to observe that Western civilization was equal or perhaps in some respects even superior to Sino-Vietnamese civilization in Vietnam, particularly as the latter was facing a severe internal crisis. For many Vietnamese intellectuals concerned over the fate of their nation, fear of the West was soon tempered by the realization that, in order to survive, Vietnam might be compelled to abandon its traditional heritage and adopt many of the attributes of Western culture.

3

The Colonial Experience

THE FRENCH "MISSION CIVILISATRICE"

By the end of the nineteenth century, the colonial edifice in Indochina was firmly in place. The Indochinese Union comprised five separate territories: protectorates in North Vietnam (known as Tonkin, from the Vietnamese phrase "eastern capital"), Central Vietnam (known as Annam, a Chinese historical term for Vietnam and translated as the "the pacified South"), Cambodia, and Laos, and the colony of Cochin China. At the top of the administrative hierarchy in the new union was a governor-general appointed from Paris to make policy for the entire region. To assist him were lower-ranking officials responsible for each of the five territories—French *résidents supérieurs* in each of the protectorates and a governor in Cochin China. In addition, French *résidents* were placed at the provincial level in the protectorates to provide advice to native administrators. In the central provinces of Annam, the emperor and his bureaucracy were permitted to retain a modicum of their quondam administrative authority. But in the North, the authority of the emperor was emasculated by making the *résident supérieur* the official representative of the court.

From the beginning, there was little question that the primary objectives of French colonial policy in Indochina were economic. For commercial interests, of course, the main purpose of colonialism was simply to register economic gain—to exploit the natural resources of the area and to open up new markets for the manufactured goods of the home country. For government officials in Paris, Hanoi, or Saigon, the perspective was somewhat more complicated, but not markedly at variance with the mercantile view. Although they were not blind to the seductive lure of commercial profit, for officials in Paris the main purpose of the French colonial venture in Southeast Asia could only be to enhance national security and prestige. There was no necessary contradiction between such objectives. In the prevailing wisdom of the day, nations, like living species, operated by the law of natural selection. Only the fittest nations survived, and those that could not adapt to changing conditions would be left behind in the brutal struggle for survival. For turn-of-the-century Europeans, national survival was directly linked to the possession of a colonial empire, which provided not only political and military power and influence but also the economic wealth that was itself the foundation of national strength.

But if there was no question of the ultimate objectives behind the French colonial effort, the purpose of the colonial enterprise that was presented to the public was quite another matter. Like most other contemporary practitioners of the colonial experiment, the French placed considerable emphasis on the moral aspect of colonialism—what in English-language countries was often summed up in the well-known phrase the "white man's burden." The lure of economic profit was, all things considered, the most crucial factor in provoking the French imperialist effort in Asia, but for millions of ordinary French citizens the primary justification for colonial rule was the civilizing mission (*mission civilisatrice*)—the obligation of the advanced peoples of the world to bring the benefits of modern civilization to the primitive peoples of Asia and Africa. In an earlier age, this sentiment had usually been cloaked in religious terms—to bring the word of the one true God to the heathen. By the end of the nineteenth century, the civilizing mission of French colonial rule could as easily be couched in secular terms: Commercial exploitation would bring Asian societies into the world market. This would lead not only to their economic enrichment but ultimately to the development of a modern society based on the concepts of representative government and individual freedom. The fact that such beliefs were smug and self-serving did not necessarily diminish the conviction with which they were held.

It was one thing to proclaim the existence of a French civilizing mission in Indochina. It was quite another to know how to carry it out. What were the responsibilities of the colonial power in Indochina? Were the colonial peoples to be exposed to the full panoply of Western values and institutions? Or should they be allowed to pick and choose in order to produce a viable synthesis of foreign and indigenous concepts? Could, indeed, the Vietnamese be transformed into—in the picturesque French phrase—"*français de couleur*"? Such questions were of more than academic interest. They went to the heart of the question of the nature of man. Was human nature universal? Were Asian peoples destined to repeat the path to industrial development and democracy now being trod in the West? Or, as Rudyard Kipling had proclaimed, were East and West divided by irreconcilable cultural and philosophical cleavages?

Moreover, there were potentially serious contradictions between the publicized goal of the white man's burden and the more pragmatic objective of exploiting the economic resources of the colonial territories for the benefit of the home country. How could the interests of the colonial peoples be adequately protected when the primary objective of the colonial regime was to serve the commercial needs of the metropole? Would the colonial government promote the growth of an indigenous manufacturing and commercial sector in Indochina when the products of such a sector might compete against manufactured goods imported from France? Could the social and economic welfare of Indochinese workers and peasants be served when it was clearly in the interests of the French economy that prices of raw materials imported from Indochina be kept to a minimum? Finally, why should the French promote the capacity of the peoples of Indochina to create and operate democratic institutions when, in the end, such a society must inevitably wish to restore its independence?

Such questions underlined the ambiguities in French colonial policy and ultimately caused its undoing. From the beginning, French colonial strategy was marked by ambivalence and a coherent statement of political and social objectives in Indochina was never realized. From the outset, too, the civilizing mission was subordinated to the more immediate goal of commercial profit. The result was that most explosive of political combinations: heightened expectations followed by disillusionment.

Early colonial administrators in Cochin China, motivated primarily by the practical objective of facilitating the economic exploitation of the area, had attempted to minimize the impact of the French presence on the native population of Indochina. Where possible, the support of local elites was solicited to create the necessary conditions for efficient exploitation of the economic resources of the colony.

By the early years of the twentieth century, this policy, known in French colonial parlance as the philosophy of "association," had come increasingly under criticism. The attack came from diverse sources. In part it came from France, where liberal elements contended that the policy of association simply milked the colonies for their economic resources without in turn providing them with the benefits of Western civilization. A similar charge came from within Vietnam, where some intellectuals complained that the French were not living up to their promise to bring the benefits of Western civilization to the native population. The most vocal of such critics was probably the Confucian intellectual Phan Chu Trinh, who in a highly publicized letter to the French Governor-general Paul Beau called on the colonial government to live up to its civilizing mission and introduce Western institutions and values to Vietnamese society. Unfortunately, Trinh was arrested shortly afterward for taking part in peasant antitax riots in Central Vietnam. After a short period in prison, he was sent to live in exile in France.[1]

Ultimately, such criticism led to a change in colonial policy. In the early twentieth century, the position of governor-general was occupied by a number of progressive colonial administrators who expressed French determination to carry through its *mission civilisatrice* in Indochina. Under the guiding hand of such enlightened governors-general as Beau and Albert Sarraut, the French government began to devise reforms designed to introduce the local population to the benefits of Western civilization and to establish, as one of them declared in a moment of exuberance, a "politics of collaboration." The results were somewhat less than the early promise. The colonial regime set up legislative assemblies at the provincial level in Annam and Tonkin (a Colonial Council, dominated by French *colons* and limited in its authority, had already been established in Cochin China before the end of the century). These bodies, however, were only consultative and restricted in their membership and franchise and hardly represented a serious effort to initiate the Vietnamese people into democratic practices. Although some consideration was given to setting up a legislative body to provide political representation for the entire population of the Indochinese Union, the proposal never left the drawing board.

Similar problems plagued French policy in the field of education. Although liberal administrators attempted to set up a new system to introduce the native population to the values and institutions of the modern West, the system was haphazard and often contradictory in both theory and practice. The small colonial elite received an education in the French language and based roughly on the Western model, but the mass of the population received only a rudimentary exposure to Western culture and institutions, and for lack of funds, many young Vietnamese in rural areas received virtually no education at all. If education was a measure of the seriousness of the colonial effort, French practice fell far short of promise. According to historian Huê-Tam Ho Tai, during the mid-1920s there were slightly less than 200,000 Vietnamese students in the school system, with only about 17,000 of these in secondary schools. There were an additional 3,000 students registered in *lycées* and a handful at the University of Hanoi, created by Governor-general Paul Beau in 1902. According to her estimates, that meant that only about 10 percent of school-age children actually attended school.

The results were hardly what the apostles of the *mission civilisatrice* would have wished. As the patriotic Confucian intellectual Duong Ba Trac wrote in the journal *Nam Phong*, those students who failed to graduate from elementary school became the "shock troops of rebellion," while their counterparts at the secondary level became "frustrated talents" angry with the status quo.[2]

Above all, performance of the colonial regime was judged in the area of economic and social progress. The primary objective of colonialism, of course, was to provide financial profit to the home country and to its citizens operating in Indochina. On the other hand, one of the major justifications of French colonial rule was that it would improve the standard of

living of the local population and thus increase the productive capacity of
society and its ability to compete effectively within the international economic order. As one French colonial administrator, Paul Reynaud, remarked in the early 1930s, it was quite obvious that most Vietnamese
would prefer independence. The best way for the French to justify their
presence was to demonstrate that economic and social benefits resulted
from colonial rule.

The centerpiece of the colonial argument was that French colonial
rule would create a modernized commercial and manufacturing sector,
improve transport and communications, and generally improve the local
standard of living. Along these lines, apologists for the colonial regime
pointed out that under French rule there was general economic progress
in Vietnam. In the big cities of Hanoi, Haiphong, Saigon, and Da Nang, as
well as in smaller provincial capitals and market towns like Vinh, Nam
Dinh, and Qui Nhon in the Center and My Tho and Can Tho in the Mekong delta, a young and vigorous commercial and manufacturing sector
gradually emerged. Most of this activity was in the area of light industry:
textiles, paper, sugar, matches, bicycle assembly, and food processing.
There was little in the way of heavy industry, although the coal mines
along the coast north of Haiphong are worthy of note. Defenders of the regime also pointed with pride to progress in transport and communications. Under French rule, bridges were built over the major waterways,
railroads were constructed from Hanoi to Saigon and from Hanoi north to
the Chinese border and thence on to Kunming, and what many described
as the best system of metalled roads in all of Southeast Asia was established.

Perhaps the greatest contribution made by the French in rural areas
was the expansion of the amount of land under cultivation. Swampy and
frequently inundated by salt water, the lower Mekong delta was generally
unfit for the cultivation of wet rice during the precolonial period. The
French drained many of the marshlands and built a series of canals that
put thousands of acres under cultivation for the first time. They were also
active in piedmont areas and in the *terre rouge* (red lands) along the Cambodian border. Here new cash crops for the export market, like coffee, tea,
and rubber were cultivated in plantations owned by the French but
worked by Vietnamese laborers hired from the crowded villages of the
North. In the early years of the twentieth century, rubber became, after
rice, the second major source of export earnings in Indochina.

How effective such measures were in increasing the productive potential of the economy and raising the standard of living of the native population is a matter of dispute. Defenders of the colonial regime frequently
pointed to the steady growth in rice exports as an indication that the
French presence had a beneficial impact on the living standard of the mass

of the rural population. At the height of the export boom, in the mid-1930s, as much as 300,000 metric tons of milled rice were exported from Vietnamese ports each year. Critics charged, however, that such statistics were seriously misleading and that in actuality living conditions in rural areas may have declined during the period of colonial rule. Higher taxes, French monopolies on the production and sale of salt, alcohol, and opium, and the creation of a market economy that led to rising land concentration and rural tenancy all combined to make life more difficult for many peasants and to drive many below the level of subsistence.

This is not the place to attempt a definitive assessment of the question, for statistics can often be misleading. There are indications that rural standards of living, at least in Cochin China, may have risen between 1900 and 1930 but then declined during and after the Great Depression in the 1930s.[3] And although thousands of acres of new land were opened up by drainage of the marshy areas in the Mekong delta, much of this land was held by absentee landlords who leased out small parcels of land to poor peasants from Annam and Tonkin for high rents, sometimes as much as 50 percent of the annual harvest. For those who left their lands to seek employment in the cities, on the plantations in southern Indochina, or in French colonies abroad, a new environment often did not bring an improvement in circumstances. For many it was undoubtedly far worse. Living conditions on the rubber plantations in Cochin China were harsh, and frequently led to disease or even to the death of the worker. Although in principle recruitment was voluntary, in practice it was often coercive and accompanied by violence. The situation for workers in factories or in the coal mines was little better. Working hours were long, and pay scales were low and housing was abysmal.[4]

This, of course, is a pattern familiar to all societies in an early stage of capital and industrial advancement. The commercialization of agriculture forces excess laborers from the villages into the cities in a desperate search for jobs. The fortunate ones obtain employment in factories or in plantations or coal mines. Others, living adjacent to the cities, keep one foot in the village, the other in the factory, working the fields at harvest time and seeking jobs in the cities during the off-season.

This process had occurred during the early stages of the industrial revolution in Europe and has been repeated in other parts of the world recently. In Europe, the process of agricultural modernization, although tragic enough in its consequences for those who suffered personal hardship as a result of it, eventually led to the rise of industrial societies based on the concepts of representative democracy. Land concentration and capital investment in rural areas led to a more efficient system of agriculture. Surplus workers in the cities provided the cheap labor that, combined with the increase in capital and technological advancement, fueled the

emergence of modern capitalism. Unfortunately, in Vietnam the consequences were not so beneficial. In good part, this was a direct result of colonial policy. The French did not encourage the development of an indigenous commercial and manufacturing sector. To the contrary, commerce
and manufacturing in colonial Vietnam tended to be dominated by European interests or by foreign immigrants such as the Chinese and Indians.
Moreover, government policy attempted to discourage the development
of local industries that might compete with French goods by a tariff policy
that encouraged French imports. In effect, Vietnam was forced to undergo
the painful stresses of agricultural modernization without the benefit of
rapid industrial growth in the cities.

Here, of course, was one of the fundamental weaknesses of colonialism as a vehicle for the modernization of preindustrial societies. The implied or stated promise of colonial policy was to undertake needed measures to bring about social and economic change and political democracy,
but such objectives frequently conflicted with the economic priorities of
the ruling power and its citizens. When such conflicts took place, of
course, the latter normally took precedence. France, like most colonial
powers, was a democracy that was ultimately responsible to its domestic
constituency in France and the European population in Indochina. Because the interests of the Vietnamese were inadequately represented in
Paris, these interests tended to be ignored.

SOURCES OF NATIONALISM AND COMMUNISM

The Vietnamese response to the French conquest had been surprisingly weak in view of the long tradition of national resistance to foreign
aggression. That is not to say, however, that resistance to foreign rule was
totally lacking. In fact, a relatively substantial movement of opposition to
the French emerged at the grass-roots level, among civilian and military
officials, urban residents, and even among peasants in the village. Much
of this was disorganized and sporadic, however, and suffered from lack of
support from the court. Indeed, after the Treaty of Saigon, the emperor,
fearful of French wrath, expressly forbade resistance activities and attempted to quell them in areas under his control. In some instances, local
elite groups raised the flag of rebellion despite lack of approval from the
court. The most worthy of mention was the guerrilla movement organized by the patriot leader Phan Dinh Phung in the hills of central Vietnam, a movement that was not finally quelled until Phung's death in 1896.
In general, however, such spontaneous resistance was ineffectual and,
lacking either organization or the capacity to counter the technological superiority of French firepower, was put down by the French with relatively
little difficulty.

By the opening of the twentieth century, then, the French colonial regime was firmly in place. Some Vietnamese managed with few compunctions to live with the new situation. A new class of native "collaborators" sprang up to cooperate with the foreigners and facilitate the operations of their new regime. Some became low-level functionaries of the bureaucracy—clerks, translators, village officials, and mandarins in areas still ruled by the imperial court. Others became members of a new class of economic middlemen—local employees of the colonial enterprises, foremen in the rubber plantations and coal mines. Others, while not directly tied to the regime or to the enterprises of the Europeans, nevertheless benefited directly from their presence—lawyers, agronomists, engineers, architects, and the members of that small but vocal group, the affluent commercial and manufacturing bourgeoisie.

For such elements, of course, the colonial presence represented their livelihood. Many of them were attracted to the glittering quality of Western civilization and adapted quickly to it, learning the French language, dressing in French clothes, eating French food, and if they could afford it, living in French-style houses. Collectively, this class would perform the role of middlemen between the French colonial regime and the mass of the population and would be the most visible evidence to apologists of colonialism that the *mission civilisatrice* was succeeding.

Although some members of the small but influential Vietnamese elite came to terms with the new circumstances, others did not and attempted to carry on the struggle of Phan Dinh Phung and other opponents of the French conquest, albeit by different means. Most prominent of this new generation of patriots was the well-known scholar Phan Boi Chau. Born in Central Vietnam in 1867, Chau was exposed to classical learning as a child and later gained local renown for his achievement in the Confucian civil service examinations. But even as a boy, he had ardently opposed the French conquest, and after early attempts to organize resistance in his village had failed, he was quick to conclude that new methods were required in new conditions. After reading a number of books by leading progressive intellectuals like K'ang Yu-wei and Liang Ch'i-ch'ao, he formed the Modernization Society (Duy Tan Hoi) in 1903 to evict the French and build a new Vietnamese society based on the Western model. Then he went to Japan to establish a training institute for Vietnamese patriots and write propaganda for the cause of national independence.

Some scholars have pointed out that Phan Boi Chau, like so many Asian intellectuals of his generation, was not truly a modern man. It is true that Chau was strongly influenced by Confucian ethics and the Confucian worldview, and even his arguments for reform were often couched in Confucian teachings. The expressed goal of his Modernization Society was to create a constitutional monarchy, and he selected a member of the royal family, Prince Cuong De, as the titular head of his movement. But in many ways Phan Boi Chau broke sharply with the past, and there was nothing insincere or contrived about his conversion to modern values and modern ways. In *New Vietnam (Tan Viet Nam)*, a short pamphlet that he wrote while living in Japan, he sketched an outline of a new society strikingly modern in its characteristics.

Phan Boi Chau also had a surprisingly modern understanding of the concept of a nation. On one occasion he remarked: "When I read the books of Asian Confucian scholars I learned the words 'loyalty to the king' (*trung quan*). But later I read many foreign books and discovered that the word 'patriotism' (*ai quoc*) was stronger than the phrase 'loyalty to the king.'" Chau had obviously read a number of Western books on the subject. In *An Outline History of the Vietnamese Nation (Viet Nam Quoc Su Khao)*, he noted that a nation must have three things: people, territory, and a government. Of the three, he emphasized, the people are the most important. Only with people can a nation (*nuoc*) exist, and if the power of the people is lost, then the nation itself is lost.[5]

Phan Boi Chau heeded these words in his efforts to organize a popular movement to evict the French. In his writings from Japan and later from China, he called for all Vietnamese, regardless of age, sex, ethnic origins, or religious preference, to rise up in a common effort against the invader. He was refreshingly free from gender or class prejudice, and appeared to give as much weight to the participation of women and the poor as to that of his own class of scholar-patriots. It was to the latter, however, that he turned for leadership of the movement, and most of the leading members of his organization were members of the scholar-gentry class.

Although Phan Boi Chau spent much of his active life writing tracts in defense of his cause, his approach to the task of evicting the French was essentially activist. "To know and not to do," he remarked, "is the same as not knowing." By his own admission he was possessed of a passionate temperament, and during his long life he frequently vacillated between periods of optimism and deep despair. "I feel," he once said, "like a blind boy riding a blind horse."[6]

Indeed, his disappointments were many. Efforts at revolt by his followers inside Vietnam were pitilessly crushed by the French. When in 1908 he was ordered to leave Japan because of a change of policy in Tokyo, he sought support from Sun Yat-sen's revolutionary movement in China. Sun had told him when the two had met in Japan in 1905 that after the Manchus were overthrown, all the efforts of the Chinese people would be utilized to help other nations of Asia achieve their own independence. To Phan Boi Chau, the 1911 revolution that brought an end to the Ch'ing dynasty and the establishment of the first Chinese republic must have seen like an act of deliverance. The Chinese revolution, he remarked, was like "an explosion and an echo vibrating among the people of many nations." An explosion it was, but its shock waves did not reach Indochina. Preoccupied with their own problems, Sun Yat-sen and his followers paid little attention to Phan Boi Chau's appeals, and in 1914, his efforts to promote rebellion in Vietnam aborted, he was arrested by Chinese authorities. Although he was released a few years later, he had lost much of his rebellious spirit and most of his followers.[7]

While Phan Boi Chau was breaking his lance on the solid rock of the French colonial edifice, others took a longer view and focused their attention on the ineluctable fact that national liberation would signify little unless the Vietnamese people were introduced to the changing realities of the new century. It was this conviction that had inspired Phan Chu Trinh to appeal to Governor-general Paul Beau in his public letter of 1906, and a similar view had motivated a number of Trinh's contemporaries when they founded the famous Tonkin Free School (*Dong Kinh Nghia Thuc*) in Hanoi on 1907. The founders of the school were Confucian scholars who, like Phan Boi Chau, had been influenced by the reformist writings of progressive intellectuals in China and hoped to introduce young Vietnamese to the ideas of the modern West. Classes at the school taught practical subjects such as mathematics and the social sciences and introduced students to *quoc ngu,* Alexander of Rhodes' transliteration of the Vietnamese language in the Roman alphabet that was now being popularized as a replacement for the cumbersome Chinese characters.

The distinction between reformists and revolutionaries was a classical example of a pattern that was seen in anticolonialist parties throughout early-twentieth-century Asia, and would later present a major obstacle to cooperative efforts to drive out the French. But at the beginning of the century the differences between the two approaches were somewhat blurred. Phan Boi Chau encouraged the work of the founders of the school, and they in turn often spoke and wrote favorably about his activities. One reason for this collaborative attitude was that leading elements of both factions were Confucian intellectuals who had been influenced by reformist writings in China as well as the Meiji Restoration in Japan. All shared the common goal of building a modern and independent Vietnam. Phan Boi Chau and Phan Chu Trinh were childhood friends whose exchanged letters, some of which have been published, offer a personal flavor to the political debate.[8]

Ultimately, the reformist approach had no more success than had Phan Boi Chau in shaking the foundations of the colonial regime. The Free School was closed down by the French after only eight months in operation, and Phan Chu Trinh, one of the school's most prominent supporters, was arrested on charges of sedition and later exiled to France. The first stage in the rise of modern nationalism in Vietnam had thus achieved few concrete results. But Phan Boi Chau, Phan Chu Trinh, and their scholar-gentry collaborators had aroused the sympathy of much of the nation. When Trinh died of cancer shortly after his return to Vietnam in 1925, his funeral became the of occasion of mass mourning throughout the country. Phan Boi Chau had been arrested and returned to Hanoi for trial the same year, and his conviction had aroused widespread outrage and sympathy from his compatriots.

In particular, the writings and activities of the generation of scholar-patriots had touched the hearts and minds of young intellectuals who had been raised in the shadow of colonial rule.

The quickening pace of commerce and industry in the cities led to the rise of a new urban class. Composing this new petty bourgeoisie were shop clerks, petty functionaries in the bureaucracy, schoolteachers, journalists and students. Throughout the colonial world it has characteristically been among this class of urban intelligentsia that the first signs of serious resistance to colonial rule have begun to appear. Such was the case in Vietnam. Living in the cities, educated in the new Franco-Vietnamese school system, this class made up the first generation of Vietnamese to have a first-hand understanding of the nature of Western culture and its impact on Vietnamese society. Having absorbed the doctrine of progress, certainly one of the primary attributes of the modern Western outlook on life, many of them had developed rising expectations about their personal futures and were quick to discern the yawning gap between the promise and the realities of the colonial experiment. Many, indeed, had come from families of elite status within the traditional society and soon sensed the frustration of blocked access to positions of wealth, prestige, and influence.[9]

For most, the Western concepts of democracy, science and technology, and material affluence had considerable appeal. Few indeed wished to return to the now discredited doctrines and practices of traditional Sino-Vietnamese society. Their reaction to Western culture was thus inevitably somewhat ambivalent. Admiration for the progressive aspects of Western society, and a firm desire that the future of Vietnam should follow a similar path, were colored by the conviction that the path to that bright future (in both personal and national terms) was obstructed by the colonial presence.

The emotional and intellectual outlet for the frustrations and aspirations of Vietnamese educated youth was thus focused on a new and heightened sense of nationhood based on the vision of a democratic and economically advanced society. The first clear sign of this new sense of nationalism began to appear during and immediately following World War I. In all three regions of Vietnam, small factions dedicated to the eviction of the colonial regime began to appear among radical youth in the cities.

In some cases, such groups were little more than student organizations agitating for economic or political reforms, or small coteries of urban intellectuals vacillating between reformist agitation and violent revolution.

The French authorities were quick to respond to such agitation, and demonstrations in Saigon and other major cities were broken up and their perpetrators placed in jail. When student riots took place, schools were closed. Publications considered hostile to the regime were shut down, and all others were exposed to vigorous official censorship. For a while, such preventive efforts appeared to take the heart out of the opposition. But in the last years of the 1920s a sense of professional commitment began to emerge with the formation of political organizations dedicated to the achievement of total independence. Even at this early stage, however, the nascent nationalist movement showed signs of incipient weakness. Most nationalist organizations were factions rather than parties; often they were identified with a region or an individual rather than imbued with a sense of common national interest. Some, like the sects in the South, sought regional autonomy more than the eviction of the French. There was disagreement, too, over ultimate goals. Although the majority of participants undoubtedly sought independence, some were dedicated to violent revolution while others hoped to achieve their goals through reformist measures. A few would tolerate or even seek a continuing tie with France.

Perhaps a more serious obstacle to the effectiveness of the nationalist movement was its inability to build a base among the mass of the population. Whereas the generation of scholar patriots like Phan Boi Chau and Phan Chu Trinh had their roots in the village, the nationalist parties in the 1920s were composed primarily of radical urban youths, with a sprinkling of older patriotic figures; few had close ties with peasants and workers. As a result, such parties suffered from the typical weaknesses of elite groups. For the most part, their goals reflected the aspirations of the educated middle class—increased political rights, equal pay for equal work, democratic freedoms, female emancipation, and so on. Although not unsympathetic to the poor—many of their programs called for lower taxes, equality of landholding, and the right of collective bargaining—they tended to concentrate on political issues that had little meaning to the average Vietnamese. And in the tradition of fledgling revolutionary organizations, they tended to see the final uprising as an affair of a few rather than the result of a patient mobilization of the force of the mass of the population.

The failure of the nationalist parties to prepare for a mass struggle to overthrow the colonial regime was not simply a consequence of inadequate understanding or execution by patriotic intellectuals. Until the late 1920s, neither peasants nor workers had become politically aroused in the nationalist cause. Rural discontent had broken out sporadically in the years since the French conquest—notably a series of peasant riots against high taxes and mandarin corruption in the provinces south of Huê in 1908—but on the whole peasant discontent had been focused on economic rather than on political issues. The situation was similar with the small Vietnamese working class. A Vietnamese proletariat had begun to appear early in the century in the factories, the shipyards, and the coal mines run by the French and by the decade following World War I numbered nearly 200,000 men and women. The first signs of worker organization appeared in the early 1920s when Ton Duc Thang, a radical nationalist recently returned from France, began to organize secret labor unions in the factories and on the docks in Saigon. For a few years overt activity was quelled, but with the onset of the Depression in the late 1920s, worker strikes became increasingly frequent. Most were staged primarily for economic objectives—higher salaries, shorter hours, paid vacations, and improved working conditions—but they were a sign of increasing activism within the growing laboring class.

It was in these conditions that the Indochinese Communist party (ICP) made its appearance in Vietnam. The founder of the party was the young patriot Ho Chi Minh, then known under the earlier pseudonym of Nguyen Ai Quoc (Nguyen the Patriot). Son of a patriotic official in Nghe An province in Central Vietnam, Ho Chi Minh was educated at the prestigious National Academy in Huê but apparently left school before graduation and took employment on a French ocean liner as a cook's helper. After several years at sea, he settled in Paris after the end of World War I and became active in radical circles. In 1920 he joined the French Communist party (FCP) and three years later was summoned to Moscow to receive training as an agent of the Comintern. In late 1924, he returned to South China and formed a proto-communist organization among Vietnamese radicals in exile called the Revolutionary Youth League. Fiercely dedicated, an astute organizer with a seductive and charismatic personality, Ho Cho Minh had good success in winning support from the radical youth in Vietnam, and by the end of the decade, membership in the organization had reached more than one thousand. In 1930, after a brief split caused by policy disagreements, the league was transformed into the ICP.

The party appeared at a significant juncture in the colonial era. After several decades of relatively peaceful conditions, in 1930 serious disturbances took place in both urban and rural areas. The immediate cause of the unrest was the Great Depression. Plant closings exacerbated existing anger over salaries and working conditions and led to strikes in several factories in cities throughout Vietnam. Similar unrest broke out at rubber plantations near Bien Hoa in Cochin China. By midsummer, the agitation had spread to rural areas in the central provinces of Nghe An and Ha Tinh. In September, rioting peasants seized power in local villages, terrorized local officials, and, incited by Communist activists, set up so-called soviets and in some cases distributed commune land to the poor. The French reacted swiftly, dispatching a unit of legionnaires to the rebellious districts and bombing a procession of angry peasants marching toward the provincial capital of Vinh. By the spring and summer of 1931, the revolt had been quelled, and thousands of participants, including most of the leadership of the ICP, were in prison. To the Comintern leadership in Moscow, the so-called Nghe-Tinh revolt must have seemed the harbinger of revolution throughout Asia, as the impoverished masses rose to overthrow their colonial masters. If so, the hope was to be seriously disappointed. With most of their leadership dead or in prison and their apparatus within Vietnam a shambles due to government repression, the ICP and other radical nationalist parties were unable to pose a serious threat to French rule for a decade. The masses were quiet if sullen. For several years, the resistance movement in Vietnam came to a virtual standstill.

THE COMING OF WORLD WAR II

The suddenly precarious stability of the French colonial regime was further shattered by the Pacific crisis and the expansion of Japanese power into Southeast Asia at the end of the 1930s. Since early in the century, many Japanese politicians had felt a mild proprietary interest in the anticolonial movements in Southeast Asia and particularly in Vietnam. Between 1905 and 1908, Japan had permitted Vietnamese and other Southeast Asian radical groups to establish headquarters in exile in Japan, and some politicians had implied that Tokyo might encourage revolutionary struggles for independence in colonial areas. In 1908, however, Japanese policy shifted when Tokyo reached an agreement with France and the United States on mutual spheres of influence in Asia, and radical anticolonialists such as Phan Boi Chau were ordered to leave Japan.

In the late 1930s, Japanese interest in Southeast Asia revived. Expansion into Soviet Siberia had been thwarted by the pact signed by Tokyo's ally Germany with the Soviet Union in August 1939. Plans for domination of China had been sidetracked by unexpectedly strong resistance from Chiang Kai-shek and his government, now holed up in its mountain capital of Chungking. Anxious to put the "China incident" to an end and lured by the promise of rich mineral resources in colonial Southeast Asia, Japanese military strategists in 1940 adopted a new southward strategy directed at incorporating the European colonies in Southeast Asia into a new Japanese-directed "Greater East Asia Co-prosperity Sphere."

The first impact of the new policy was felt in Indochina in the summer of 1940, when Tokyo demanded that the French government prohibit the shipment of goods to China from Tonkin and provide Japan with military and economic privileges in the northern provinces of Indochina. After some hesitation, during which time Governor-general Georges Catroux sought in vain the promise of military assistance from the United States to counter a possible Japanese invasion of the area, the colonial regime eventually acceded to the Japanese demands. By the summer of 1941, Japan had expanded its presence into Cochin China and, under the cover of the now intimidated French Vichy government, seized control of the area. The fiction of French sovereignty was temporarily retained, but in fact the Japanese had become masters of Indochina.

In the last analysis, the primary benefactors of the Japanese occupation of Indochina were the Communists. The nationalist parties were divided over how to respond to the new situation. A few, like the Vietnamese Nationalist party (VNQDD), which had been a significant force in Tonkin since 1927, declared their hostility to both the Japanese and to the French and maintained their headquarters for the duration in South China. Others, including several smaller nonviolent parties in Saigon and the Cao Dai sect, accepted Japanese promises to bestow independence on colonial peoples in Asia and decided to cooperate with the new rulers. For the Communists, there was no question that the Japanese, along with the French, were to be treated like an enemy. Indeed, to Ho Chi Minh, recently returned to the area after several years in the Soviet Union, the war and its consequences in Indochina represented a great opportunity. If, as Ho predicted, Japan went to war with the United States and eventually lost, its defeat could create a vacuum in Vietnam at the end of the war that the ICP might hope to fill before the arrival of Allied occupation forces to accept the surrender of Japanese troops.

In the spring of 1941, the ICP Central Committee met in a small mountain village near the Chinese border and inaugurated a new revolutionary strategy to seize power at the end of the Pacific war. The political centerpiece of the new approach was the establishment of a new united front, called the League for the Independence of Vietnam, Vietminh for short. In order to attract patriotic elements from all social classes the Communist direction of the new front would be disguised. Radical social measures, such as the nationalization of industry and the collectivization of agriculture, would be avoided, and a moderate program would be adopted calling for social reforms and democratic freedoms. The primary focus of the new front would be on the struggle for independence.

Supplementing the new political approach was a new military strategy. Borrowing from the experience of its fraternal party in China, the ICP turned to the strategy of people's war to mobilize support from peasants and workers, set up liberated base areas in isolated areas of the country, and then, through a combination of guerrilla tactics and popular uprisings, seize power in both rural and urban areas at the end of the war. For the next four years, the Communists painstakingly built up the new Vietminh Front in villages throughout North Vietnam. Guerrilla forces were created in the mountains adjacent to the Chinese border and, in 1944, the Vietminh leadership set up the first units of what would eventually become the Vietnamese Liberation Army.

In March 1945, the Japanese occupation authorities, suspicious of growing support for the Gaullist Free French movement among French civilian and military officials in Indochina, deposed the French colonial regime and granted a spurious independence to a pro-Japanese puppet government under the puppet emperor Bao Dai. The Japanese coup improved Communist prospects for victory at war's end. Not only was the French regime now dismantled, but the Japanese did not bother to fill the vacuum left by the destruction of the French administrative apparatus in rural areas. Into that vacuum, the Vietminh would be free to move.

THE AUGUST REVOLUTION

On August 14, 1945, Japan surrendered to the Allies. At approximately that moment, the Communists appealed to their supporters to rise and seize power in Vietnam. Within two weeks, forces under the Vietminh Front had seized control of most rural villages and cities throughout the North, including Hanoi, where President Ho Chi Minh announced the formation of the Provisional Democratic Republic. In the Center, forces under Communist direction seized the imperial capital of Huê and compelled the abdication of Bao Dai. In Cochin China, the Vietminh combined with other nationalist parties in forming a Committee of the South, which claimed to voice the legitimate aspirations of the population.

It had been a masterful performance. With an army of only a few thousand poorly armed guerrillas, the Communists had seized control of most of the country under the noses of the Japanese occupation authorities. The keys to success, as Ho Chi Minh had pointed out to his colleagues, were the elements of initiative and surprise. Power would have to be seized in the interval between the surrender of the Japanese and the arrival of Allied expeditionary forces (the British in the South, the Nationalist Chinese in the North) as called for by the Potsdam conference in August. If the Vietminh could present the Allies with a fait accompli, the new provisional republican government might obtain recognition as the legitimate representative of the wishes of the Vietnamese people.

The Communists came within an eyelash of succeeding. The August Revolution was a brilliant success. In less than two weeks, the North and Center were almost entirely in Communist hands, in a virtually bloodless takeover. The Japanese were lured into taking a neutral attitude toward the situation, and the noncommunist nationalists, for the most part, were

Crowds listening to Ho Chi Minh declare Vietnamese independence in September 1945. (Source: *Ho Chu Tich Song Mai Trong Su Nghiep Chung Ta.*)

ineffective or still in South China. Only in Cochin China was the Vietminh forced to share power. Here, where the influence of moderate nationalism and the sects had been high since before the war, the Vietminh played an influential but not a dominant role in the Committee of the South.

In September, Allied occupation troops began to arrive in Vietnam. In the North, the Chinese military command had relatively little interest in the political situation and proved willing to deal with Ho Chi Minh's new government, although it pressed Ho to broaden its base by including in the cabinet members of rival nationalist parties. This Ho Chi Minh was willing to do, and in late autumn an agreement was reached calling for the formation of a coalition government with Ho as president and a prominent nationalist, Nguyen Hai Than, as vice-president. National elections were scheduled to be held in January 1946. A constitution for the new state, to be known formally as the Democratic Republic of Vietnam, was promulgated early in 1946. In the meantime, at Ho Chi Minh's insistence the social and economic policies of the new government were basically moderate—only major industries and utilities were nationalized, taxes were reduced, and a mild program of land reform was instituted.[10]

The Communists were less successful in the South. Not only did local nationalist groups and French residents pose greater resistance to Vietminh domination of the new Committee of the South, but the commander of the British expeditionary forces, General Douglas Gracey, was sympathetic to the restoration of French colonial rule and, in defiance of the agreement at Potsdam to avoid intervention in the local political situation, disarmed the Vietminh and other nationalist groups and turned power over to the French,, whose military units began to arrive in October. During the fall, the Vietminh were driven forcibly from the city into the countryside, where French troops gradually pacified most of the area and returned the villages to French administration. For the moment, local Vietminh forces were unable to counter French moves and were reduced to sporadic guerrilla action. In effect, within three months of the end of the war, Vietnam had been divided into two hostile zones—a Communist North and a French South. The ultimate shape of a generation of conflict had begun to take form.[11]

For several months, the French and the Communist-dominated government in Hanoi attempted to avoid full-scale war. In March, Ho Chi Minh signed a preliminary agreement with the French representative in Indochina, Jean Sainteny, calling for French recognition of Vietnam as a "free state," with its own army, parliament, and finances. In return, the Vietnamese government would agree to accept a continuing French cultural, economic, and political presence in Vietnam and to join the projected French Union. French troops could be stationed in the North to protect French interests and residents. Because the two negotiators could not agree on whether to include Cochin China in the new free state, a plebiscite was called for to allow the local population to determine the future status of the colony. Ho Chi Minh had only with difficulty persuaded the ICP Central Committee and the cabinet (which included a number of militantly anti-French nationalists) of the need for a compromise. In the end, however, Ho's arguments were undoubtedly persuasive. The Vietnamese government in Hanoi was now isolated on the global scene (the United States, which had earlier expressed some reservations about the return of the French, had now moved perceptibly toward the French position, while the Soviet Union, the Vietminh's major potential supporter, was preoccupied with events in Europe and inclined to counsel the ICP to moderation) and not yet strong enough to achieve its ultimate goal of independence by armed force. While a free state was considerably less than the Communists wanted, it would give them time to consolidate their strength and prepare for a further advance in the near future.

In June, full-scale negotiations began at Fontainebleau, outside of Paris, to work out remaining differences and reach a final settlement. By then, however, the preliminary agreement itself was in peril. Each side accused the other of bad faith, but the major source of difficulty emanated from Saigon, where pro-French elements within the colonial community, encouraged by the new high commissioner for Indochina, Admiral Thiérry d'Argenlieu (the new title replaced the prewar position of governor-general) set out to sabotage the Ho-Sainteny Agreement, which d'Argenlieu had publicly labeled a "Munich." In April, d'Argenlieu convened a separate conference consisting of pro-French and anticommunist elements in Cochin China in the mountain resort town of Dalat. Predictably, the conference rejected membership in the projected free state governed from Hanoi and declared its preference for the establishment of a separate republic of Cochin China that would make its own arrangements with Paris.

In the meantime, a new government had taken office in France that showed itself less receptive to a compromise in Indochina. When formal negotiations got under way at Fontainbleau in June, the French position had hardened. Despite pleas from Ho Chi Minh, who warned that failure to achieve an agreement would only strengthen the hand of militants in the Hanoi government, French delegates took a hard-line position at the talks, and in late summer the negotiations broke down and the Vietnamese delegation returned to Hanoi. Ho Chi Minh, convinced that the Vietminh was not yet strong enough to risk war, remained in Paris and in September signed a "modus vivendi" that called for a cease-fire and a resumption of talks early the following year.

During the fall it became increasingly apparent that war could not be avoided. As tensions rose, bloody clashes broke out in the North between local Vietnamese forces and French troops stationed in the area. Ho Chi Minh, who had returned to Hanoi in October, attempted to keep the channels of negotiation open while strengthening the Communist role in the government and ordering preparations for military conflict. In November, disagreement over control of customs authority led to a brutal French bombing of the native quarter at Haiphong. As incidents increased in December, the French military and command in the North demanded that French troops be given responsibility for law and order. Convinced that war was unavoidable, the Vietminh launched a surprise attack on French installations in Hanoi on December 19. While local forces engaged in a holding operation, main force Vietminh units gradually withdrew to prepared base areas in the countryside and prepared to resume guerrilla war.[12]

THE FIRST INDOCHINA WAR BEGINS

As the Franco-Vietminh conflict began, the Communists were not in an enviable position. Their military forces were small and lacked the firepower to pose a serious challenge to the French. Aid from their socialist allies would be limited. The U.S.S.R. was distant and more concerned over the prospects of a Communist government in Paris than those of a successful revolutionary struggle in far-off Indochina. The Chinese Communist party (CCP) was fully occupied in North China with its own civil war against the forces of Chiang Kai-shek. Even within Vietnam, the situation was ambiguous. Increasing evidence that the Communists were the dominant force behind the Vietminh Front and the DRV had alienated many moderates and made them reluctant to support the front in its struggle against French colonialism. In an effort to take advantage of this situation, the French negotiated with former Emperor Bao Dai (in late summer 1945, he had, with some reluctance, caved in to Vietminh pressure and abdicated the throne, accepting in its stead the sinecure of supreme political adviser to the provisional republican government) to accept the position of chief of state in a new French-supported "Associated State of Vietnam." In 1949, Bao Dai accepted this arrangement, although, according to the Elysée Accords, the new state possessed only limited powers. Vital issues dealing with both internal and foreign policy remained in the hands of the French. The "Bao Dai solution" did provide an alternative to Ho Chi Minh's government, but most nationalists viewed it as simply a creation of French colonialism.

During 1947, the Vietminh were reduced to a struggle for sheer survival. Guerrilla units hid in the mountains of the Viet Bac, or in the Central Highlands or the Plain of Reeds further to the south, while the party leadership urgently concentrated on building up the strength of the revolutionary forces. By 1948, Vietminh strategists felt sufficiently confident to move cautiously into highly populated lowland areas, to intensify recruitment efforts, and to launch sporadic attacks on French military outposts and exposed villages and district towns. Gradually, Vietminh forces were beginning to approach parity in numbers with the French.[13]

VIETNAM ENTERS THE COLD WAR

The year 1949 was of pivotal significance for the future course for the war. On the battlefield, signs of stalemate were beginning to appear. The momentum of French military attacks on Vietminh strongholds was beginning to ebb, and French military strategy increasingly concentrated on protecting populated areas from Communist attacks. Public support for the war in France was beginning to slacken, and voices calling for an end to the war were on the increase. On the other hand, the Vietminh, although undoubtedly stronger than at the beginning of the conflict, still lacked the firepower to pose a significant military threat to French rule in Vietnam. Moreover the formation of the Bao Dai government had weakened the Vietminh claim to represent the legitimate national interest of the Vietnamese people. While the Associated State hardly attracted enthusiastic support in nationalist circles, it did provide a potential alternative to Ho Chi Minh's movement, which was now increasingly viewed as dominated by the Communists.

Under such circumstances, both sides groped for a breakthrough that would give them an advantage in the lengthening conflict. For the Vietminh, the communist victory in China in the fall of 1949 brought a surge of optimism through the ranks. Since before the Pacific war, the CCP had given some assistance to its Vietnamese comrades. During the civil war in China, however, ties were limited. But the victory of the forces of Mao Tse-tung in the fall of 1949 raised hopes for a vast increase in Chinese support for the Communist cause in Vietnam. The following January, Vo Nguyen Giap, commander of Vietminh forces and a top party member, traveled secretly to Peking for arms aid talks with the new People's Republic of China (PRC), and two months later Ho Chi Minh signed a formal agreement providing for Chinese military assistance to the Vietminh. The PRC formally recognized the DRV as the sole legitimate government in Vietnam. A few days later, the Soviet Union followed suit.

Preparations to take advantage of the new opportunity were soon in evidence. During the summer of 1950, French intelligence reported an ominous buildup of Vietminh forces along the Chinese border. In the fall, the insurgents launched a major offensive against French border posts in the area. The attack resulted in the first major French defeat of the war. The French decided to abandon a string of bases along the frontier and concede Vietminh control over the entire Viet Bac, thus giving the Vietminh easy access to China and possession of a liberated base area adjacent to the densely populated and strategically critical Red River delta. Any hopes that the French had of destroying Vietminh power were now virtually eliminated.

The French response to the communist victory in China and the heightened threat from the Vietminh was to seek increased aid from the United States. Since the end of World War II, the Truman administration had stayed aloof from the conflict in Vietnam. At first, admiration for Ho Chi Minh and for the Vietminh as an anti-Japanese guerrilla force and traditional antipathy to French colonialism had made some Americans (including a number of military officials on the spot) sympathetic to the Vietminh cause. The Truman administration was unwilling to risk antagonizing or weakening the French, however, and refrained from placing pressure on Paris to abandon its claim to Indochina. By 1947, the communist complexion of Ho's government had become increasingly apparent, and sympathy gradually gave way to hostility in Washington. Still, it was viewed as a French, not an American, problem.

The rise of the Cold War in Europe and concern over the regional impact of a communist victory in China began to change minds in Washington. In 1950, the administration approved a military assistance program for Indochina. Although the bulk of the aid was designed to go to the Vietnamese National Army, recently created by Paris as a means of transferring some of the burden of the war from France to the Vietnamese, at French insistence U.S. aid was channeled through the French. U.S. officials expressed some vocal criticism of the French failure to perfect Vietnamese independence under the Bao Dai government but refrained from exerting strong pressure on Paris for fear that the French would abandon what was now increasingly viewed as a Cold War struggle between the forces of communism and those of the free world.

The indirect entry of China and the United States into the Franco-Vietminh conflict not only brought the struggle into the vortex of the Cold War but also led to an increasing militarization of the war. In early 1951, Vietminh forces, now strengthened by rising quantities of arms from China, launched a major military offensive against French posts on the fringes of the Red River delta with the apparent hope of breaking though to Hanoi. Vo Nguyen Giap, however, had underestimated the resourcefulness and determination of the new French military commander in Indochina, General Jean de Lattre de Tassigny. De Lattre, who had won respect for his military prowess during World War II, had been appointed high commissioner and commander in chief of French military forces in Indochina in December 1950. Newly arrived when the Vietminh offensive broke, de Lattre reacted quickly, ordering air strikes against advancing Vietminh troops and transferring units from other areas to the beleaguered city of Vinh Yen, in the upper Red River delta. De Lattre's action salvaged the situation for the French and blunted the force of the Vietminh attack. Later offensives north and south of Hanoi had no greater success, and by spring, the Vietminh had abandoned their campaign.

NEGOTIATIONS AT GENEVA

For the next two years, Vietminh strategists avoided the risk of open confrontation with French units in Indochina, preferring instead to launch small-scale attacks on isolated French posts in the Northwest, in Laos, and in the Central Highlands. Such tactics were hardly a recipe for total victory, but they enabled Vietminh leaders to build up their forces for a future offensive in lowland areas. Moreover, by maintaining pressure on the battlefield, Vietminh strategists hoped to provoke growing public discontent in France with the war. The logjam began to break in the fall of 1953. For years, the French had spurned Ho Chi Minh's offer of peace talks. Now officials in Paris sought not to win the war but to find an honorable way to end it. When government sources in Paris suggested a negotiated settlement to end the conflict, Ho Chi Minh responded. In a November interview with the Swedish newspaper *Expressen*, he declared a willingness to explore proposals for peace with the French. Early the following year, the two sides agreed to discuss the Indochina issue at an international conference to be held at Geneva in May. Joining the French, the Bao Dai government, and the DRV at the conference table would be representatives of the great powers, including the PRC, the Soviet Union, Great Britain, and the United States, as well as representatives from Vietnam's neighbor states in Indochina, the kingdoms of Laos and Cambodia.

The DRV attitude toward a negotiated settlement has long been a matter of dispute. It has frequently been asserted that the Vietnamese were pressured to come to the conference table by the Soviets and the Chinese, each anxious for its own reasons to end the conflict. There is probably some truth to this contention, since information from several sources confirms that many party officials were unhappy at the decision to accept a compromise settlement. Realism, however, prevailed. Not only would the Vietminh find it difficult to achieve a military victory without active Soviet and Chinese diplomatic and material support, but without a settlement, U.S. military intervention was likely. The ever practical Ho Chi Minh probably persuaded his colleagues that a compromise settlement was the best that could be hoped for at the moment. The Vietminh did not enter the negotiations from a position of military weakness; on the eve of the conference, after a six-week siege, the French post at Dien Bien Phu in the mountainous Northwest fell to a Communist assault. The Vietminh attack had been made possible by massive shipments of arms from China; it is probable that such aid was Ho Chi Minh's price for accepting negotiations.

With their morale drained by the long conflict and the tragic fall of Dien Bien Phu on the eve of the conference, the French had no heart for continuing the war, and in June Pierre Mendès-France became prime minister on a pledge to bring the conflict to an end within thirty days. A month later, French and DRV representatives agreed on a cease-fire dividing Vietnam into two separate regroupment zones, the Vietminh in the North, the French and the supporters of the Bao Dai government in the South, with the two zones divided at the Ben Hai River, on the seventeenth parallel. Vietnam was to be neutralized, and neither zone was permitted to join a military alliance. The size of the military forces in the two zones was to be restricted to existing levels, and an International Control Commission (ICC), composed of Canada, India, and Poland, was to supervise the provisions of the agreement.

Neither the DRV nor the Bao Dai government, however, was willing to accept a permanent division of the country into two separate states divided by ideology. To resolve that problem, the conference delegates drew up a political declaration declaring that the cease-fire line was a provisional one and "should not in any way be interpreted as constituting a political or territorial boundary." The declaration called for general elections to be held in both zones in July 1956 in order to obtain an expression of the national popular will on the issue of the future of Vietnam. Consultations on such elections were to be held between representatives of the two zones in July 1955. The DRV delegation agreed to these arrangements, but that of the Bao Dai government did not.

The Geneva Conference settlement was designed to permit an honorable withdrawal of the French from Indochina, to remove the area from the arena of great power competition, and to permit a political settlement of the crisis. Only the first goal was attained. One reason for this was the attitude of the United States. The Eisenhower administration had been reluctant to take part in the negotiations from the beginning. Secretary of State John Foster Dulles had attempted to persuade Great Britain and France to join with the United States in a grand alliance to fight and win the war, but London and Paris preferred to await the results of the Geneva Conference. Washington had then agreed to participate in the talks with some reluctance. At Geneva, Dulles reluctantly acceded to the division of Vietnam into separate zones but made it clear that the United States could not accept a solution that provided for the possibility of a total takeover of Vietnam by the Communists. Unhappy with the provisions of the political declaration, Secretary Dulles indicated that Washington could take no more responsibility for the conference. In the end, the United States refused to sign, or even verbally consent to, the political declaration, and the U.S. delegation merely "took note" of it and promised "to refrain from the use of force to disturb" it. It reiterated its position that the unity of Vietnam should be sought through elections supervised by the United States.[14]

Agreements on Laos and Cambodia settled the conflicts in those areas and established the independence of the new royal governments in those countries. In Laos, the Communist Pathet Lao movement, a front group allied with the Vietminh, was granted two provinces in northeastern Laos as a regroupment zone, and the two sides were instructed to negotiate a political settlement to integrate the Pathet Lao area into the royal Lao administration. The small Communist movement in Cambodia, popularly named the Khmer Rouge (Red Khmer), received no recognition or regroupment zone, and final agreement simply called for the departure of foreign troops from Cambodian soil.

In later years, the failure to activate the political provisions of the Geneva Agreements was the source of considerable controversy with respect to the issue of responsibility for the later resumption of the conflict. Some blamed the agreement itself for its vagueness and legal ambiguity. Did the agreement specifically require that national elections promised by the ICC be carried out? Was the Bao Dai government, which had publicly indicated its disagreement with several of the provisions and would later refuse to be held to them, legally bound to carry out the political protocol? Had in fact the conference really intended elections to take place, or was the political declaration merely a polite fiction (as some U.S. observers contended) to save the face of the DRV? To what degree was the United States bound by the agreement? Indeed, if the United States was not bound by them, how could the area be isolated from the Cold War?

This is not the place for a definitive evaluation of the agreement and its legal standing, but a few brief points are in order. There is no doubt that the ambiguity of the agreement sowed the seeds of future disagreements and ultimately led to renewed conflict. Under the circumstances, however, it may well have been the only way to end the war and indeed to avoid a widening conflict. It is often the essence of diplomacy to use ambiguity in order to obtain an agreement that otherwise would not be possible. The French were willing to depart but would not have been willing to accept a total defeat. The Communists were willing to accept a compromise but not to give up all their objectives. The United States had threatened to take matters into its own hands if not satisfied that the negotiations provided an opportunity for the development of a Vietnam free from Communist control. Although the results, from Washington's standpoint, were not entirely satisfactory, the Eisenhower administration appeared willing to live with them. In such circumstances, the agreement was a gamble that with the removal of foreign troops and the establishment of cease-fire, political factors would take effect and lead to an internal solution. That they did not is less an indication of the failure of the delegates than a measure of the depth of the ideological and political bitterness that had marked the conflict from its earliest years and would continue to fan the fire of discontent well into the future.

NOTES

1. Phan Chu Trinh's letter to Paul Beau was printed in the *Bulletin de l'Ecole Frànçaise d'Extrême Orient* (March–June 1907).

2. Duong Ba Trac, *Nam Phong,* no. 167 (November 12, 1931), quoted in Nguyen Anh, "Vai net ve giao duc o Viet Nam tu sau dai chien the gioi lan thu I den truoc cach mang thang tam" (Vietnamese education from the end of World War I to the August Revolution), in *Nghien Cuu Lich Su,* no. 102 (September 1967), pp. 38–39 (hereafter NCLS).Also see Huê-Tam Ho Tai, *Radicalism and the Origins of the Vietnamese Revolution* (Cambridge: Harvard University Press, 1992), pp. 34–35.

3. Robert L. Sansom, *The Economics of Insurgency in the Mekong Delta of Vietnam* (Cambridge: MIT Press, 1970), pp. 41–42. Sansom contradicts the prevailing wisdom that farm income dropped steadily under the French, but remarks that the

government paid little attention to improving rice yields and tended to favor large landholders. See p. 57.

4. The French author Paul Monet, in *Les Jauniers* (Paris: Gallimard, 1930), was only one of many of his compatriots who reported critically on conditions on the plantations. French officials tended to deflect such charges as exaggerated, although Governor-general Pierre Pasquier, in a speech to the French-sponsored Council of Economic and Financial Interests of Indochina in October 1929; conceded that if there was a problem in regard to the plantations, it was in the "methods of recruitment." See ibid., p. 279. For an extended discussion of the problem by a contemporary historian, see Ngo Vinh Long, *Before the Revolution: The Vietnamese Peasants under the French* (Cambridge: MIT Press, 1973).

5. Phan Boi Chau, *Viet Nam Quoc Su Khao*, in *Van Tho Phan Boi Chau Chon Loc* (Collected Writings of Phan Boi Chau) (Hanoi: Van Hoc, 1967), p. 121. The word "nuoc" is a native Vietnamese word for the country and appears to be etymologically related to the same word "nuoc," meaning water. The previous quote is from Dang Thai Mai, *Van Tho Phan Boi Chau* (Hanoi: Van Hoa, 1960), p. 33.

6. Nguyen Duc Su, "Chu nghia yeu nuoc cua Phan Boi Chau" (The Patriotism of Phan Boi Chau), in NCLS, no. 83 (January 1966), pp. 28–36).

7. The quote is from Chuong Thau, "Moi quan he giua Ton Trong Son va Phan Boi Chau," (the relations between Sun Yat-sen and Phan Boi Chau), in NCLS, no. 93 (October 1966), p. 21. Phan Boi Chau's early relations with Sun are also briefly mentioned in S. L. Tikhvinskii, "The foreign policies and views of Sun Yat-sen from 1905–1912," in *Sin'khaiskaya Revoliutsia v Kitae* (The 1911 Revolution in China) (Moscow, 1962), pp. 246–271.

8. There have been a number of studies on the Tonkin Free School. For a lengthy treatment in English, see Vu Duc Bang, "The Dong Kinh Free School Movement," in Walter F. Vella (ed.), *Aspects of Vietnamese History* (Honolulu: The University Press of Hawaii, 1973), pp. 30–93.

9. John T. McAlister, Jr., in his *Vietnam: The Origins of Revolution* (New York: Doubleday, 1971), has provided a provocative analysis of the personal and emotional motivations of early revolutionaries in Vietnam.

10. The most comprehensive account of this period is King C. Chen's *China and Vietnam, 1938–1954* (Princeton: Princeton University Press, 1969). For a more recent view, see Stein Tonnesson, *The Vietnamese Revolution of 1945: Roosevelt, Ho Chi Minh, and de Gaulle in a World at War* (London: Sage Publications, 1991).

11. For a recent defense of General Gracey's role in Vietnam, cf. Peter M. Dunn, *The First Vietnam War* (New York: St. Martin's Press, 1985). Dunn points out that Gracey's actions provided the South Vietnamese people with three decades of independent existence. See the preface, vii.

12. The debate over which side was primarily responsible for the outbreak of war has never been resolved. Stein Tonnesson, in his *1946: Déclenchement de la Guerre d'Indochine* (Paris: l'Harmattan, 1987), speculates that hard-line elements within the ICP or other anti-French parties may have forced Ho's hand, but solid evidence is lacking.

13. For an extensive discussion of the buildup of Vietminh forces during the early stages of the Franco-Vietminh conflict, see Greg Lockhart, *Nation in Arms:*

The Origins of the People's Army of Vietnam (Sydney: Allen & Unwin, 1989), Chapter 6.

14. A copy of the Geneva Accords is available in George Mct. Kahin and John Wilson Lewis, *The United States in Vietnam*, revised edition (New York: Delta, 1969), appendix 2.

4

A Nation Divided

The Geneva Agreement did not end the Vietnamese conflict. It merely served as a watershed between two phases of the conflict—the anticolonial and anti-French phase before 1954 and the civil war and the anti-American phase afterward. The political and ideological chasm between the two sides was probably too deep and too bitter to be resolved through a purely political solution. To make it worse, the Vietnam question had now increasingly become a part of the Cold War and could not be resolved without affecting, in one way or another, the interests of the great powers and the international power balance. If and when the conflict resumed, it would do so on a more intense and dangerous level.

In the South, the Geneva Agreements led to the departure of the French and their replacement by the United States. During the negotiations in Geneva, John Foster Dulles had stated at a press conference in Washington that once the accords had been concluded, the United States could begin to held build up the noncommunist regimes in South Vietnam, Laos, and Cambodia. Although the U.S. attitude toward the projected national elections was apparently somewhat ambiguous, there is little doubt that policymakers in Washington soon came to view the new Government of Free Vietnam (as it termed itself) in the South as a keystone in the emerging U.S. strategy for the defense of Southeast Asia from communist aggression and feared the possibility of a Communist victory in those elections. Washington's options were limited. The two zones of Vietnam, plus Laos and Cambodia, were prohibited from joining alliances and limited in the size of their military force levels. The United States could thus not formally incorporate the new noncommunist states into the defense alliance system formed at Manila in September, the Southeast Asia Treaty Organization (SEATO). To circumvent this legal restriction, the SEATO pact members created a so-called umbrella clause, according to which the three noncommunist Indochinese states could be protected by the provisions of the alliance even though they were not officially members of the organization.[1]

THE DIEM REGIME

The de facto integration of the Government of Free Vietnam into the SEATO alliance system was only a formal confirmation of the fact that the United States was now committed to stabilizing the situation in South Vietnam in an effort to create a viable state that could halt the further expansion of communism in Indochina. For the moment, the nature of that effort would be primarily political. The key to success, above all, would depend on Washington's ability to locate new political leadership that could provide a measure of stability and direction and the basis for the rise of a strong and viable new noncommunist society in the South. Bao Dai, the chief of state, was considered by many U.S. officals to be lacking in competence, too pro-French, and tainted by his imperial past. Francophile elements in Saigon were viewed as hopelessly addicted to the characteristic French political disease of factionalism and lacking an adequate commitment to nationalism and democracy. To save South Vietnam, a new political leadership with a strong commitment to a noncommunist nationalism would be required.

The result of that effort was the emergence of Ngo Dinh Diem. Descended from an elite family with connections at the old imperial court in Huê, Diem had been active in Vietnamese politics prior to the Pacific war and had briefly served in Bao Dai's first cabinet in 1933 as minister of the interior. Diem was viscerally anti-French, however, and resented Bao Dai's willingness to collaborate with the colonial regime; he had resigned his position after a few months and refused further cooperation with the emperor. Diem, a devout Catholic and an admirer of Confucianism, was equally opposed to the Communists. He refused an offer by Ho Chi Minh in 1945 to cooperate with the Vietminh and during the Franco-Vietminh conflict abstained from involvement with either government, spending much of the war abroad, including a stay at a Catholic seminary in the United States. Here he came to the attention of the Eisenhower administration.

It would be too much to describe Diem as a creature of the United States. Diem was headstrong and independent and noted for his integrity and dedication to Vietnamese nationalism. Moreover, many U.S. officials considered him too "monkish" and stubborn to be an effective political leader, and there is no evidence that the Eisenhower administration exerted pressure on Bao Dai to appoint him prime minister of his associated state of Vetnam. According to Bao Dai himself, he appointed Diem a month before the conclusion of the Geneva Conference in the hope that his firm anticommunist credentials would induce the United States to provide assistance to his government after the departure of the French.[2]

Still, the relationship between Bao Dai and his new protégé was not an easy one. Diem's contempt for Bao Dai and the pro-French politicians around the head of state led quickly to mutual antipathy, and in 1955 he arranged for a plebiscite between the two of them for chief of state. In the vote, in which there was considerable suspicion that Diem's supporters had stuffed the ballot boxes, he won an overwhelming victory.

Diem also moved decisively against the sects and other pressure groups that might challenge his authority and soon centralized power in his own hands. At first, the Eisenhower administration took an ambivalent view of Diem's hard-line approach to his potential political rivals and appeared nervous that he would alienate important sectors of Vietnamese opinion. On the other hand, the vigor of his efforts earned admiration, and by the summer of 1955, Washington was firmly on his side. Because of the new restrictions on military force levels and foreign involvement, the U.S. commitment was a limited one, contained in a personal letter dated October 1, 1954, from President Eisenhower to Diem. In that letter, Eisenhower promised assistance to help the new government, which had placed its capital in Saigon, in "developing and maintaining a strong, viable state, capable of resisting subversion or aggression through military means." It was qualified by the statement that the United States would expect that the aid "would be met by performance on the part of the Government of Vietnam in undertaking needed reforms."[3]

President Eisenhower's letter to Diem had emphasized the U.S. desire to see the creation of a strong and viable state in South Vietnam. There had been considerable pessimism in U.S. intelligence circles regarding the capacity of the Saigon government to survive a concerted onslaught by the Communists in the postwar period, and Diem's rapid and vigorous assertion of power was gratifying. Yet more would be needed to transform South Vietnam into a bastion of the free world than mere force. Diem would need to establish a regime able to respond to the collective aspirations of the population and to earn international recognition as a legitimate representative of Vietnamese nationalism. And he would have to move with dispatch to resolve some of the social and economic problems that had plagued Vietnam since before the imposition of French rule nearly a century earlier. To assist him in this effort, U.S. advisers were sent to Vietnam to help the new regime in building a political system based on democratic Western traditions. A constitution was approved calling for the creation of a republican government based on a combination of the presidential and parliamentary models.

Diem, of course, remained president of the new Republic of Vietnam (RVN). During the next few years, he continued to consolidate his control.

As a mainstay of his regime, he relied to a considerable degree on the 2 million Catholics in the South, and many were selected for positions of influence and responsibility within the government. Catholic villages (Catholics composed more than two-thirds of the approximately 900,000 refugees who fled south after the Geneva Agreements) were built in the suburbs of Saigon to provide the capital with a protective belt against possible attack by Communists in the countryside. Others were settled in Rural Development Centers established in the piedmont areas adjacent to the Central Highlands. To maintain loyalty to the regime, Diem's brother Ngo Dinh Nhu was charged with setting up Leninist-style progovernment organizations such as the secret Can Lao (Personalist Labor) party and mass front organizations to enlist the support of and participation of the population. To strengthen the government's hold over rural villages, the tradition of local autonomy in electing village officials was abolished and village leaders were appointed by and responsible to the central government.

Through such techniques, Diem attempted to consolidate his control over the government in the South in order to begin to tackle the deeper and more intractable problems in the economy. Arguably, the most serious problem was the unequal distribution of arable land. Policies adopted under the colonial regime had resulted in the concentration of land in the rich Mekong delta in the hands of a few landlords, many of them absentee owners living in Saigon and charging exorbitant rents to their tenants. According to generally accepted statistics, throughout the country as a whole, 2.5 percent of all landowners owned approximately 50 percent of all the cultivable land. Some of this land had been confiscated and distributed to poor peasants in areas where the Vietminh had established a revolutionary administration before the Geneva Conference. After peace was restored, the landlords returned and seized their land, often charging the peasants back rents. With U.S. assistance, Diem launched a land reform program to reduce inequities in land holdings and thus win the support of the rural population. The program, however, was faulty both in design and in implementation. In many cases, peasants were asked to buy land that had previously been given to them under Vietminh occupation. In others, landlords ignored provisions in the law restricting rents to 25 percent of the crop and continued to charge high rents, with peasants too intimidated to protest. Most damaging of all was that the government program was not sufficiently rigorous. Landlords were allowed to retain up to 100 hectares (about 250 acres) of rice land under their ownership—in a society where the average peasant holding was less than one hectare. In the end, less than one-third of the land that had been earmarked for transfer was actually purchased by the peasants.

By the end of the decade, the promise engendered by the early years of the Diem regime had rapidly dissipated. Although a man of personal integrity and decency, Diem found it difficult to act as the head of a democratic government. Intolerant of criticism, Diem, with the active assistance of his brother Nhu, cracked down on all potential sources of opposition within South Vietnamese society. Newspapers were censored and politicians hostile to the regime were harassed and sometimes arrested. Diem was particularly fearful of the Communists. A "denounce the Communists" campaign was inaugurated, and roving tribunals moved from village to village trying and convicting these charged with collaboration with the Vietminh. Many of those convicted of treasonous activities may actually have been followers of the Communists (several thousand had remained in the South to maintain the revolutionary apparatus), but there were widespread reports that the campaign suffered from corruption and that many innocent Vietnamese were forced to pay bribes to avoid prosecution or were falsely accused by others seeking personal revenge.

The regime's heavy-handed suppression of all resistance and its intolerance of potential sources of opposition soon led to widespread alienation. Southerners resented alleged domination over society by northern and central Vietnamese; the sects and the mountain minorities resented Saigon's efforts to place their areas under the administrative control of the central government; the overseas Chinese resented attempts to compel them to adopt Vietnamese citizenship; Saigon intellectuals disapproved of the regime's suppression of free speech; peasants were antagonized by the false promises of the land reform program; and Buddhists resented Diem's policy of favoring the nation's minority Catholic population. In effect, Diem's potential base of support among the population was gradually eroded; increasingly he, and his regime, were isolated.

THE SECOND INDOCHINA WAR BEGINS

After the close of the Geneva Conference in 1954, there was strong concern in Saigon and in Washington that the Communists would shortly resume the revolutionary war to complete their takeover of all of Vietnam. In fact, contrary to general belief at the time, the Communists had no plans to return to a policy of armed violence in South Vietnam, at least in the years immediately following the restoration of peace. In the first place, the party needed time to recover from the war and to begin the long and arduous march to socialism in the North. The final months of the war, including the attack at Dien Bien Phu and related attacks in Laos and in the Central Highlands, had been costly and exhausting, and it would undoubtedly take time before the Vietminh armed forces and the new "rear base" in the North could be transformed into an effective instrument for the liberation of the South. An equally persuasive reason for avoiding an early return to military conflict was the attitude of the DRV's foreign allies. Both Moscow and Peking, each for its own reasons, had been anxious to end the struggle in Indochina. The new post-Stalin Soviet leadership under Nikita Khrushchev wished to minimize the risks of military confrontation with the United States and to put competition on a new economic, political, and ideological basis. China had embarked on a major effort to modernize the economy and needed time to prepare for socialist construction. A resumption of war in Vietnam would threaten the security of China and could force it into a direct confrontation with the United States. It is likely that both Moscow and Peking warned Hanoi that their support would be limited if war resumed.

Given such circumstances, it seems probable that the Communist leadership in Hanoi placed its hopes in the mechanism created by the Geneva Agreement, which called for unification through elections in 1956. Although it is not improbable that there was some skepticisim in Hanoi that the elections would ever take place (there were frequent references in the world press to the possibility that Saigon would refuse to hold consultations as called for by the accords), DRV leaders adopted a public attitude of optimism that the provisions of the Geneva Agreement would be adhered to. If not, party strategists appeared to believe that, given the intrinsic weakness of the noncommunist nationalist forces in Vietnam, the Saigon regime would eventually collapse of its own accord or be compelled to accept a coalition government that would include the Communists and their supporters. To handle such contingencies, the party left a small apparatus of supporters in South Vietnam to prepare for elections, for political agitation, or for the possibility of a return to armed struggle. The remainder, perhaps numbering between 50,000 and 100,000, went to the North. Many were youths, often the sons and daughters of Vietminh supporters who, on arrival in the North, were enrolled in cadre schools, where they were trained in guerrilla and propaganda techniques for a possible future return to the South.

In the summer of 1955, Ngo Dinh Diem announced that the Saigon government would not hold consultations on elections with the DRV, claiming that any elections held in the North would not be fair and, furthermore, that as the RVN had not signed the accords, it could not be held responsible for them. The Eisenhower administration, although somewhat concerned at the possible propaganda backlash from such an outright refusal to abide by the agreement, supported Diem's position. Saigon's refusal to hold talks on elections did not immediately change Communist strategy toward the South, and for the next few years, North Vietnamese leaders continued to take the official position that a peaceful solution to the problem of national unification needed to be found. For the moment, no major shift in strategy took place, and the slogan of the day was to "build the North, and look to the South."

But as the new decade approached, two related factors combined to force a reappraisal of this position. First, the efforts of Diem's security forces to eradicate the Communist menace in the South led to heavy losses of personnel and in some key areas to the virtual destruction of the revolutionary apparatus. Second, it was becoming increasingly clear that Diem's policies were creating serious discontent among key groups in the South. By the late 1950s, local party leaders in the South were pleading to the central leadership in Hanoi that Saigon was ripe for the plucking if only the party would take the lead in focusing the unrest. Otherwise, the revolutionary movement might be too weakened by Diem's repressive policies to take action.

In early 1959, the Central Committee, after several months of hesitation, approved a policy calling for a more active strategy in the South. Party leaders were still reluctant to return to armed struggle, not only because they were not certain that it was required, but also out of concern over the possible U.S. reaction. To avoid provoking Washington, a policy combining political activity with low-level armed struggle was adopted. The key was to use the "political force of the masses" in demonstrations and protests against RVN policies. In selective cases, the assassination of "enemies of the people" was approved, while intensive efforts began to build up the revolutionary forces for a possible return to war.

One way to minimize the risk of U.S. involvement and to maximize the revolutionary appeal in the South, was to disguise the leading role of the Communists and of the DRV in the anti-Diem struggle. For that reason, a maximum effort would be needed to give the impression that the movement was composed of and directed by southerners. In actuality, the movement would be directed from Hanoi. To provide such guidance, several party officials of Central Committee rank were assigned to direct the movement in the South and to communicate periodically with the Politburo. To provide additional direction, a number of southerners who had been trained in the DRV after Geneva were infiltrated into the RVN to serve as leading cadres in the movement.

To create a vehicle for the new resistance movement, the party turned to the technique that had been used with such success against the French. A broad alliance called the National Front for the Liberation of South Vietnam (NLF) was established in the winter of 1960–1961. The presidium of the front was to be composed of representatives of a wide variety of groups opposed to the Diem regime in the South, including peasants, workers, intellectuals, the sects, the Buddhists, and the mountain minorities. There was no hint of northern involvement in the new organization, and its program, carefully avoiding any identification with Marxist doctrine, stressed such popular concerns as democratic freedoms, "land to the tiller," independence (from U.S. imperialist domination), and a policy of neutrality leading to peaceful unification with the North.

In general, the party's strategy was relatively successful. During the early 1960s, the Diem regime, under the pressure of rising political discontent and a series of low-level attacks by the revolutionary forces (labeled by their opponents the Viet Cong, or Vietnamese Communists), continued to weaken. Characteristically, Saigon overreacted. In an effort to increase government control over rural villages and thus dry up the sea in which the guerrilla fish must swim, the RVN forced unwilling peasants to leave their home villages and to settle in so-called agrovilles, develpment centers in rural areas designed to concentrate the rural population in a secure environment and provide the basis for sustained economic growth. The crackdown on all forms of political opposition against the Diem regime was intensified, particularly in the cities, increasing the restiveness of the country and leading to an abortive coup launched by rebellious elements in the armed forces.

But if the Communists had correctly foreseen the growing weakness of the Diem regime, they were less perceptive in their estimate of the U.S. reaction. Hanoi had hoped that Diem could be overthrown without increased U.S. involvement. But the new Kennedy administration, which had come into office in January 1961, did not follow the Communist script. Anxious to impress the Kremlin leadership with an image of U.S. toughness after the Bay of Pigs fiasco in Cuba, Kennedy deliberately chose to adopt a tough stand in Vietnam even while recognizing the growing weakness of the Diem regime. During Kennedy's first year in office, several high-level officials from the new administration visited South Vietnam to evaluate the situation on the spot and discuss future strategy with Vietnamese leaders. By the winter of 1961–1962, Kennedy had committed the United States to increase aid to the RVN, but only on condition that Diem's own performance improve.

A crucial element in the Kennedy strategy was the adoption of a new approach to the growing insurgency in South Vietnam. Where the Eisenhower administraton had tended to interpret the threat to the RVN primarily in terms of a possible armed attack across the demilitarized zone similar to what had taken place a decade earlier in Korea (thus leading to the assumption that the South Vietnamese armed forces—Army of the Republic of Vietnam [ARVN]—should be organized in conventional main force units), leading elements in the Kennedy administration countered that Siagon needed to adopt a counterinsurgency strategy to deal with the problem of a local war waged by guerrillas at the village level. The plan called for a breakdown of ARVN forces into smaller units trained in counterguerrilla techniques in order to protect the rural population from the insurgency. The keystone of the program was the so-called strategic hamlet. Similar in concept to the agrovilles but smaller in scope, the strategic hamlets were to be based on existing village organizations, which were to be strengthened to provide security against Communist attacks. In order to provide guidance in carrying out the new program and to boost South Vietnamese morale, the Kennedy administration also approved an increase in the number of U.S. advisers in South Vietnam. By 1963, the number of Americans in South Vietnam had risen to more than 15,000.

In theory, the Kennedy program was well conceived and sensitive to the realities of the situation in Vietnam. It had corrected past misconceptions of the nature of the problem and attempted to fashion a new approach that dealt with the real threat from within the country. It attempted to provide assistance and guidance to the Saigon government without actually Americanizing the war (a proposal in 1961 to introduce a division of U.S. combat troops was rejected by the president). It focused on the need of the Diem regime to improve its own capacity to deal with the threat of insurgency and to meet the needs of the population. But the program could be effective only if the Saigon regime demonstrated its ability and willingness to carry it out. In fact, this was the weakest link in the entire program. In the early 1960s, the RVN leaders became increasingly isolated from the population. As opposition grew, the government reacted with ferocity. Harassment of the opposition was intensified, and several anti-Diem figures were arrested. In rural areas, the strategic hamlet program was characterized by corruption, official arrogance, and sloppy execution, and soon ran into difficulties. Peasants were frequently forced to join the new organizations against their will and to provide labor without compensation. The new hamlets were often just existing villages surrounded by barbed wire. Security was difficult to maintain, and many were attacked and destroyed several times by insurgent forces. By 1963, the program, initially worrisome to the Communists, had lost momentum and was being widely criticized.

By the summer of 1963, the Diem regime was beginning to disintegrate. Alleged government favoritism to Catholics had alienated Buddhist elements, and public protests, sometimes organized by professional Buddhist associations in Huê and Saigon, were put down with brutality by the police. Unrest even reached into the upper ranks of the armed forces, where plotting against the government reached epidemic levels. In Washington, the Kennedy administration was increasingly dismayed at the rapid deterioration of the Saigon regime and warned Diem that U.S. support could not continue unless the situation improved. Diem responded by expelling U.S. reporters, whose accounts of conditions in the South were increasingly critical, and by threatening to make a separate peace with the Communists.

By now, many policymakers in Washington were convinced that the war could not be won unless Diem was replaced. When in late summer dissident elements within the armed forces privately queried U.S. officials in Saigon as to whether the United States would support an overthrow of the Diem regime, Washington, after some hesitation, gave an affirmative answer. Although the administration did not wish to become openly involved in a coup, it promised privately that it would support a new government that would agree to continue the war effort. In November, a coup launched by several high-ranking military officers overthrew the Diem regime. Diem refused an offer of asylum at the U.S. embassy and, with his brother Nhu, sought refuge in Saigon's neighboring city of Cholon. When his hideout was discovered, he surrendered but was assassinated with his brother on the way back to Saigon.

Washington's decision to support the coup d'état against the Diem regime represented a gamble that a new government would be able to unite the country more effectively against the threat of the insurgency. In the beginning, there was a glimmer of hope. A Military Revolutionary Council was formed under the leadership of a popular general of southern origin, General Duong Van "Big" Minh. The new government was greeted with an outburst of popular enthusiasm by a populace relieved at the fall of the increasingly detested Diem regime. The new regime rejected overtures from the Communists to explore a negotiated peace and declared its determination to continue the struggle against the insurgent forces in cooperation with the United States.

But the buoyant optimism soon evaporated. Duong Van Minh, although affable and personally popular, appeared to lack leadership ability, and the new government soon fell prey to internal squabbling and factionalism. Violent riots between Catholics and Buddhists groups erupted in the streets of Saigon. In the field, combat operations suffered as military commanders, responding uneasily to the chaos in Saigon, refrained from aggressive operations against the insurgent forces.

The Communist leadership in Hanoi reacted to the overthrow of the Diem regime with caution. Uncertain of the intentions of the new government in Saigon, it tentatively offered negotiations. When these were rejected, Viet Cong forces increased military pressure in the countryside to test the mettle of their new adversary. By December, it had become apparent that the new regime intended to pursue the struggle with continued and perhaps enhanced support from Washington. At a plenary session that month, the Central Committee approved a proposal to escalate the level of conflict in the South in the hope that the new Saigon government could be toppled rapidly before it was stabilized with U.S. help. The level of infiltration from the North was significantly increased, and in late 1964, the first main force units of the People's Army of Vietnam (PAVN) began to stream south. For the first time, the struggle in South Vietnam began to take on the signs of an open military confrontation. Hanoi's main risk was that a further deterioration of security in the South would lead to increased U.S. involvement, something neither Hanoi nor its allies in Moscow and Peking desired. In a circular to other communist parties, the Central Committee contended that U.S. intervention was improbable, but worth risking.

The rising level of Communist activity led to a further crumbling of the RVN position in the South and to growing concern in Washington. The military council of "Big" Minh was overthrown by a military coup led by General Nguyen Khanh. But he too was unable to stabilize the situation. Reflecting the anarchy in Siagon, security in rural areas deteriorated, and by the winter of 1964–1965 most of the countryside was in Communist hands. U.S. officials in Saigon were predicting that without significantly increased U.S. involvement, South Vietnam would fall in less than a year.

It was the misfortune of President Lyndon Johnson, who assumed office in November 1963 after the assassination of John Kennedy, to be faced with the problem that had been feared but avoided by three of his predecessors: What should be done if the Saigon regime could not hold? Party leaders in Hanoi hoped and predicted that, faced with a deteriorating situation, the United States would withdraw its advisers or negotiate a settlement, as it had done in China in the late 1940s, in Korea in 1953, and in Laos in 1962. Yet here, as in 1959 and 1960, Hanoi had misread U.S. intentions. Unlike his predecessor, Lyndon Johnson apparently gave little serious consideration to the possibility of a U.S. pullout and reacted to the crisis by raising the level of U.S. involvement. In August 1964, on the pretext of a North Vietnamese attack on U.S. naval craft off the North Vietnamese coast, Johnson ordered air attacks on Communist military installations along the northern coast and then requested a resolution from both houses of Congress giving him the right to take action to protect U.S. forces in the area.

Armed with the powers provided by the Tonkin Gulf Resolution, Johnson now responded vigorously to the deteriorating situation by expanding the U.S. military role in the conflict in South Vietnam. When insurgent units attacked a U.S. advisers' camp at Pleiku, killing several U.S. servicemen, the administration announced a program of retaliatory bombing of vital targets in North Vietnam. Eventually this policy of tit-for-tat attacks turned into a series of sustained bombing raids throughout the North under the name Operation Rolling Thunder. American dependents were evacuated, and during the spring and summer, U.S. military units began to arrive in South Vietnam and for the first time took part in combat operations against insurgency forces in the Central Highlands and along the central coast. The primary objective of the U.S. units, according to the strategy of commanding general William Westmoreland, was to undertake "search and destroy" operations to blunt the momentum of the insurgency and to drive the guerrillas back from the lowland villages into the mountains and along the frontier, thus depriving them of recruits and provisions. In the meantime, ARVN forces could be released for pacification operations to secure local areas and clean out pockets of guerrillas in the heavily populated provinces in the Mekong delta and along the central coast.

Critics charged that, by approving an escalation of U.S. military involvement, Lyndon Johnson had ignored the primarily political character of the war. Administration spokesmen retorted that they were only responding to a military escalation already undertaken in the South by Hanoi. Both sides had now decided that success on the battlefield would have a lot to do with determining the political realities in South Vietnam. Washington policymakers were not blind to the importance of political factors, however, and were aware that the determination, cohesiveness, and capacity for leadership of the RVN would be crucial in determining victory or defeat.

To respond to that challenge, in 1966 the administration began to try to bring some order to the political and economic situation in the South. Since the fall of the Diem regime in 1963, the political situation in Saigon had been in virtual chaos. Over a period of less than two years, several governments had arisen and quickly collapsed. Finally, in the early summer of 1965, a new regime composed of younger military officers under Generals Nguyen Cao Ky and Nguyen Van Thieu came to power in Saigon. Somewhat to Washington's surprise, the new government began to demonstrate an ability to stabilize the situation.

After an initial period of hesitation and doubt about the capacity of the new leadership, the Johnson administration attempted to take advantage of the promise of renewed stability in Saigon. In 1966, a conference of top officials from Washington and Saigon convened in Honolulu to discuss measures to increase political stability in Saigon and to win popular support for the new government. U.S. officials promised more assistance to help the RVN solve its burgeoning economic and social problems. The Saigon generals promised to move with dispatch toward the creation of a representative government with the trappings of Western democracy. A constituent assembly was to be elected in 1966 to write a constitution and schedule national elections. In these elections, held in 1967, Nguyen Van Thieu was chosen president, with Ky as his vice-president. Similar reforms were undertaken in the area of economic and social policies. Per-

haps the most pressing problem was that of land reform. For years the issue had lain dormant, as officials in Washington and Saigon refused to
concede that peasant economic discontent was at the root of Communist
popularity at the village level. By the late 1960s, the importance of the land
question was more widely recognized, and in 1969 the RVN pushed
through a "land to the tiller" law that in effect assigned ownership of
farmland to the tenant without payment. Owners were to be compensated
by the government.

The main objectives of the new U.S. strategy were twofold: (1) to
strengthen the RVN so that it could gradually develop the capacity to defend itself and (2) to demonstrate to the Communists in Hanoi (and to as-
piring insurgent movements elsewhere) U.S. capacity and resolve to prevent successful national liberation struggles throughout the Third World.
The success or failure of the first objective would be determined only after
the U.S. departure from Vietnam. The validity of the second assumption,
however, would soon be put to the test. The U.S. escalation did not result
in a major change in Hanoi's strategy in the South. Indeed, Hanoi's war
planners concluded that the U.S. challenge must be met head-on and defeated. To back down, to retreat to a defensive posture of sporadic guerrilla war—as was apparently advised by Peking—would only cause the
revolutionary forces to lose their momentum and suffer a decline in morale and would make a future victory that much more difficult. To defeat
the U.S. strategy, the Communists would be compelled to maintain the
pressure on the battlefield and to maximize U.S. casualties in order to reduce public support for the war in the United States.

The strategy was an extremely costly one. Because the liberation
armed forces could not hope to match the enemy in firepower (despite increased military assistance from Moscow and Peking) they would have to
rely on the power of numbers and the advantages of stratagem and surprise. For several months, Hanoi strategists attempted to maintain the initiative on the battlefield. U.S. "head count" figures of more than 300,000
Communist casualties a year were probably exaggerated, but there is no
doubt that Hanoi's losses were high. To maintain force levels, Hanoi
found it increasingly necessary to introduce regular force units from the
North, and infiltration rates reportedly reached more than 100,000 a year.
Because access to the villages in the South was increasingly restricted by
U.S. and ARVN sweep operations, the local apparatus was unable to recruit effectively and had to use fillers from the North. This in turn led to
morale problems and growing antagonism between northerners and
southerners within the movement. Because revolutionary units had been
driven from the rich lowlands into the mountains and along the Cambodia border, provisions were short and had to be imported from the North.
U.S. bombing raids along the Ho Chi Minh Trail (as the transportation

network from North to South Vietnam was popularly called) through southern Laos made overland shipments difficult, and supplies were increasingly brought in through the new Cambodian port of Sihanoukville.

Hanoi could hardly hope for a clear-cut military victory over the United States and ARVN forces in the South. Its best hope was to achieve sufficient military success to destabilize the Saigon government and force a change of government that could produce leaders willing to pursue a negotiated settlement. Alternatively, battlefield failures might undermine public support for the war effort in the United States and force Washington to withdraw or seek peace. Signs of disenchantment with the war in the United States were increasingly apparent in 1967 as university campuses erupted in hostility to the conflict. To intensify such discontent, the Communists would require a major success on the battlefield.

TET

Planning for a major military offensive apparently began in the late summer or early fall of 1967. At approximately the same time, U.S. observers noticed heightened enemy activity in the northern provinces just below the demilitarized zone (DMZ) where Westmoreland had ordered the construction of a string of U.S. firebases to interdict Communist infiltration across the border between the DRV and the RVN. Throughout the remainder of the year, Communist pressure in the area grew in intensity, resulting in a prolonged attack on the U.S. firebase at Khe Sanh, a rocky hill a few miles south of the DMZ. General Westmoreland ordered the base reinforced, and it was able to hold despite a lengthy siege.

There was considerable speculation at the time that the Communist buildup near the DMZ signaled an attempt to create a U.S. "Dien Bien Phu" in the north. Other observers suggested that it might have represented an effort by Hanoi strategists to divert U.S. attention from areas more vital to the South. In all likelihood, Communist strategy was flexible and designed to take advantage of whatever opening U.S. moves created, although Hanoi's primary objective was to bring down the government in Saigon. In any event, in late January 1968, during the annual Tet (New Year's) holiday, Communist forces throughout the country attacked major cities, provincial and district capitals, and rural villages in a nationwide offensive. Approximately 80,000 troops took part in the assault. The most prominent areas of attack were Saigon and the imperial capital of Huê. In Huê, the attacking forces seized most of the city and the imperial citadel and held on to it for three weeks until finally driven out after street-by-street attacks by U.S. and South Vietnamese forces. In Saigon, Communist sapper units and suicide squads assaulted several vital military and government installations. Communist success was brief but had maximum psychological impact. One squad managed to penetrate the grounds of the walled U.S. Embassy compound in downtown Saigon and occupied the ground floor of the chancery for several hours before they were killed. Other units managed to hold out for several days in Cholon before they were suppressed.

In the countryside, the impact of the offensive, although less spectacular, was longer lasting. Attacks on several provincial capitals were driven back only after heavy U.S. bombardments, which in some cases caused considerable damage and loss of life. In rural areas, the pacification program was seriously disuprted and RVN control over many areas was reestablished only several months later.

Some Western observers claimed that the Tet Offensive had been a failure. General Westmoreland, citing heavy Communist losses, contended that Tet had been a severe defeat for Hanoi's forces, who did not achieve their goal of destroying the Saigon regime. Others, however, pointed to the psychological impact of the offensive on public opinion in the United States and to the ultimate effect on U.S. policy as an indication that the offensive had been a striking success. The truth was probably somewhere in between. Communist casualties in the attack were indeed heavy—by some estimates up to one-half of the entire assault force—and it would be several years before Hanoi would be able to recoup its losses to launch a second offensive of similar size. Moreover, revolutionary successes in rural areas turned out, for the most part, to be ephemeral. Within a year, ARVN troops had seized most of the areas lost to the insurgent forces and resumed pacification operations. But there is no question that Tet resulted in a significant shift in U.S. war strategy. By mid-spring, the Johnson administration had become persuaded that further military escalation in pursuit of total victory was not worth the cost either on the battlefield or on the domestic scene in the United States and had reluctantly decided to seek a negotiated settlement. It remained only to find a means of coming to the conference table.

The route to the conference table had been a tortuous one. Diplomatic exchanges about possible peace talks had been in the air throughout the early 1960s, but without concrete results. In effect, neither side had wanted to begin negotiations until relatively favorable military and poolitical conditions had appeared, leading to the possibility of a diplomatic victory. Since 1965, both sides, while wishing to appear willing to begin peace talks, had refused to make the necessary concessions to bring the other to the conference table. Washington had rejected Hanoi's Four Points, which appeared to require the resignation of the Thieu regime. The DRV, on the other hand, had refused to open talks without a cessation of the U.S. bombing of the North. After the Tet Offensive, both sides modified their positions, and when President Johnson agreed to stop the bombing (although he refused to put the commitment in writing), the last stumbling block was removed and talks could begin.

In the presidential elections of 1968, Republican Richard Nixon won a narrow victory over the Democratic candidate, Hubert Humphrey. Nixon's election did not significantly change the direction of U.S. policy in Vietnam, despite the new president's claim that he had a "secret plan" to end the war. In fact, the policy of the new administration toward the war was substantially a continuation of that adopted by President Johnson after the Tet offensive, with some elaborations. Nixon's strategy, in effect, was to attempt to find a compomise settlement to the war while strengthening the South Vietnamese government and armed forces so that they could defend themselves if negotiations did not succeed. In negotiations, Nixon would offer the Communists a legitimate political role in the South, provided that they withdrew their PAVN units to the North and accepted the presidency of Nguyen Van Thieu. In the meantime, U.S. combat units would be gradually withdrawn over a four-year period (the target date for full withdrawal was June 1972, only a few months prior to the next presidential elections), while ARVN forces would be strengthened to take over the primary burden in the war. The process of "Vietnamization" would begin slowly but would accelerate as conditions permitted. It was, indeed, a clever strategy, provided that the American public had the patience to permit the war to continue for several more years. In the last analysis, of course, its ultimate success would be based on the assumption that, at some future date, Saigon would be able to stand on its own.

Such a compromise settlement was a step forward from the hard-line position taken by the Johnson administration before the Tet Offensive, but it had little immediate appeal to Hanoi. The removal of U.S. forces was of little benefit so long as Thieu remained president and North Vietnamese units were called upon to withdraw from the South. A better settlement could be achieved by waiting for the departure of the bulk of the U.S. troops and then launching a second major offensive to destroy or at least seriously weaken the Thieu regime. During the months following the opening of peace talks in Paris, then, no significant progress was registered, as both sides concentrated on strengthening their military and political positions in South Vietnam. With Communist forces weakened by the losses suffered at Tet and U.S. strategy shifting perceptibly from an offensive to a defensive posiion, the level of conflict gradually subsided, although military operations continued on both sides.

THE INVASION OF CAMBODIA

In March 1970, the neutralist Cambodian regime of Prince Norodom Sihanouk was overthrown and replaced by a new military government, under General Lon Nol, more sympathetic to the United States. The sudden change of government significantly affected the situation in neighboring Vietnam. For the Communists, it represented both opportunity and danger. For years, the revolutionary forces fighting in the South had used the eastern border provinces of Cambodia as a sanctuary and as a conduit for the shipment of weapons, men, and supplies into South Vietnam. The Sihanouk government had reluctantly tolerated such activities in order to placate Hanoi, whose power and ultimate intentions were greatly feared in Phnom Penh. There was a small communist movement, the Khmer Rouge, in Cambodia, but under Hanoi's guidance it had refrained from a policy of armed struggle in order to avoid provoking Sihanouk to revoke his tacit toleration of Vietnamese use of the border area. But the new government was unsympathetic to Communist use of the border provinces. Less than a week after seizing power, Lon Nol demanded that all Vietnamese forces be withdrawn.

For the Nixon administration, the new situation offered temptation. For several years Washington policymakers, reluctant to antagonize Sihanouk, had rejected appeals by General Westmoreland in Saigon to permit U.S. and ARVN forces to launch attacks to clean out the sanctuaries. Now the situation had changed, and in April, Nixon approved a proposal to launch an invasion of the Cambodian eastern provinces. The invading forces, consisting of both U.S. and South Vietnamese units, met with little resistance and advanced virtually unmoleted into Cambodia, as Communist forces simply retreated before the allied advance. But Hanoi did not remain powerless in the new situation. When Lon Nol demanded Communist evacuation of the border provinces, Hanoi decided that Cambodian neutrality was of no further benefit and began to train Cambodian guerrillas in an attempt to stir up civil war and overthrow the Phnom Penh regime. To provide leadership and firm guidance over the movement, several hundred Cambodian Communists who had resided in North Vietnam since the Geneva Conference were returned to Cambodia to direct the struggle.For good or ill, Cambodia had become a pawn in the crisis in Southeast Asia.

The Cambodian invasion had an equally noteworthy impact in the United States. While the Nixon administration predictably defended its action as a means of cleaning out the sanctuaries, reducing the likelihood of a new Communist offensive, and thus permitting a further reduction in U.S. force levels in Vietnam, opponents of the war argued that the invasion had simply widened the war and made it more difficult to resolve. Protests against the war on college campuses escalated to new heights.

Whether or not the invasion of Cambodia impeded a new Communist offensive and accelerated the rate of withdrawal of U.S. forces from South Vietnam is a matter of dispute. What is clear is that conflict in South

Vietnam continued at a low level during succeeding months while U.S. force levels in Vietnam gradually declined. On the other hand, the insurgent movement in Cambodia grew steadily, and peace was nowhere in sight. Hanoi was still hoping to achieve a breakthrough on the battlefield in South Vietnam to stimulate antiwar sentiment in the United States and force the administration to the conference table. This may well have been what party strategists had in mind when they planned a new military offensive to be launched over the Easter holidays in 1972. The attack was carefully timed to take place when U.S. force levels would dip below 100,000 for the first time since 1965. Not coincidentally, it would also occur duriong the opening stages of the 1972 presidential election campaign in the United States. The Easter Offensive—like its predecessor in 1968—thus had both military and psychological dimensions.

There were some significant differences in approach from Tet, however. Unlike in 1968, the Easter Offensive would take place almost entirely in rural areas. Cities would be attacked only if the probability of success was high. Second, in contrast to 1968, when few PAVN units were committed to the battle, North Vietnamese troops would play a major role in the fighting in an attempt to deal a severe and perhaps fatal blow to the ARVN. If the ultimate objective of the Easter Offensive was to destroy Saigon, it did not succeed, but it came close. Heavy Communist attacks in the northern provinces led to the virtual disintegration of some of the newer and less experienced ARVN divisions in the area. Only the tenacity of the tougher ARVN 1st Division and U.S. aerial bombing managed to prevent panic and an outright defeat. One Communist commander contended that only logistical weaknesses prevented a spectacular victory. As it was, Communist territorial gains were limitedand casualties were high. But the ARVN's ability to survive alone—the keystone of the Nixon Vietnamization programs—was put once again into serious question.

The Easter Offensive did not lead immediately to a major breakthrough in the peace talks. But during the next few months, the U.S. position began to show signs of a new flexibility. The major sticking points in the negotiations had always been Hanoi's refusal to accept Thieu, who had been reelected virtually without opposition in 1971, as head of a post-settlement government (Hanoi offered to accept members of the government but not Thieu himself) and the U.S. refusal to negotiate a settlement and a departure of U.S. forces without a corresponding removal from the South of the 200,000 North Vietnamese forces (a presence Hanoi had never admitted). Now Henry Kissinger suggested to the DRV negotiator Le Duc Tho that if Hanoi accepted Thieu, a settlement need not require the withdrawal of PAVN units from the South. Hanoi did not immediately respond, but in September Tho indicated that a compromise along such lines might be feasible. For the next several weeks, both sides worked feverishly to hammer out an agreement. Tentative agreement was reached in November, and Kissinger announced, prematurely as it turned out, that "peace was at hand." When Saigon (which had not been consulted) resisted, the U.S. insisted on renegotiating several points. Hanoi, now suspicious, refused, and Nixon ordered a resumption of the bombing of the North over the Christmas holidays in order to bring the North Vietnamese to terms. Final agreement was reached in early January and the treaty, with Thieu's reluctant acquiescence, was signed on the twenty-third. It called for a cease-fire in place and the removal of remaining U.S. fighting forces. The division of territory under the control of the NLF and the government was to be decided in negotiations between the two sides. The Thieu government remained in power but a new "administrative structure" (U.S. negotiators had refused to describe it as a "coalition government") was to be established within three months to prepare for elections and a new government in South Vietnam. This so-called National Council of Reconciliation and Concord was based on a tripartite formula, with representatives from the Provisional Revolutionary Government (PRG—formed by the Communists as an alternative to the RVN after the Tet Offensive), the Thieu regime, and neutral forces.

FROM PARIS TO SAIGON

Like the Geneva Agreement two decades previously, the Paris Agreement did not end the Vietnam War. It simply served to facilitate the removal of U.S. troops and to return the conflict to the two rival forces in Hanoi and Saigon. That in itself was no mean accomplishment. With the Cold War rivalry over Vietnam removed, the likelihood that the conflict there could lead to a major great power confrontation was sharply reduced. But the internal competition between the two sides continued and indeed intensified. In the months following the cease-fire, negotiations on a future political structure and a military settlement quickly broke down amid mutual recriminations. It would be idle at this point to attempt to single out the guilty party, as the breakdown was the product of a generation of accumulated mistrust and hostility. The Thieu government did not carry through on its commitments and harassed Communist forces. On the other hand, the Communists clearly used the cease-fire to improve their military position in the South. At first, they had hoped that the overthrow of the Thieu regime could be achieved without a return to armed struggle. But Thieu's refusal to carry out the agreement and his efforts to reduce the amount of territory under PRG control through armed action soon changed minds in Hanoi. In 1974, party leaders approved a major strengthening of their military capabilities in the South and, in the autumn, adopted a proposal to launch a major offensive in the South early in

1975, with the hope of completing a takeover of the entire country the following year. There was some hesitation caused by concern about the possible U.S. response. Richard Nixon had promised Thieu that the United States would respond vigorously if Hanoi broke the agreement. In order to test the U.S. reaction, Hanois' campaign would open with partial offensives along the Cambodian border and in the Central Highlands. If the U.S. response was weak and the attacks were successful, then a majpr offensive would open in the highlands and in the northern provinces and last until the onset of the rainy season in May.

In any event, the success of the campaign exceed Hanoi's highest hopes. The first stages, in Tay Ninh province, resulted in the seizure of the provincial capital. When Thieu elected not to attempt to retake it and Washington (where Gerald Ford had replaced Richard Nixon as president the previous August) did not respond, the second stage was launched in mid-March in the Central Highlands with a major offensive against Ban Me Thuot, the largest city in the area. The government in Saigon was taken by surprise, and the ARVN forces in the area fled in panic. Other heavy attacks by PAVN forces in the north threatened major population centers and induced President Thieu to abandon virtually all the northern provinces to the Communists in the hope of stabilizing the RVN position further south. In the panic that ensured, the entire North was lost, including the major urban centers of Huê and Da Nang and much of Saigon's armed forces.

Flushed with success, Hanoi decided to press for total victory before the end of the dry season. In Washington, the Ford administration tried to push a $1 billion military aid program through Congress, but gave no sign of reintroducing U.S. forces into the war. Communist forces poured south from the Central Highlands, and along the coast and by mid-April were approaching the outskirts of Saigon. Others were advancing from Tay Ninh toward Tan Son Nhut Airport. For a brief period, hard-pressed ARVN troops held up the Communist onslaught at Xuan Loc, but the effort to stabilize the front failed. In its last days, the Saigon regime attempted desperately to contact Hanoi to seek a compromise settlement, but party leaders were now convinced that total victory was within their grasp and remained silent, even after Thieu had resigned and Duong Van Minh, who, it had long been rumored, was more acceptable to the Communists, had taken over the presidency. By the last week of April, Communist forces were poised on the edge of the city while Saigon's resistance crumbled and helicopters evacuated Americans from rooftops to aircraft carriers waiting offshore. On the thirtieth, North Vietnamese units streamed into the city along the main thoroughfares, encountering little resistance. In Saigon, the party's followers surfaced with flags, leaflets, and microphones to provide enthusiasm along the route. After the three decades of bitter struggle, the long Vietnamese confliuct had come to an end.

The victory of the Communists in Vietnam has been ascribed to various causes. The strategic and organizational genius of the Communists, the weakness and factionalism of their rivals, the military and political misjudgments of the French and the Americans—all these played a significant role in the final outcome. It is fruitless to seek a single explanation for the tragedy of Vietnam. But it is important to recognize that, above all, the results of the war were a consequence of the political, social, and cultural realities within Vietnam. The United States did not militarily lose the war. Certainly the Paris Agreement in 1973 was not the product of U.S. defeats on the battlefield. To the contrary, U.S. military superiority had significantly blunted Communist momentum in the late 1960s, the Tet Offensive notwithstanding. The U.S. failure, above all, was in not being able to overcome the disparity between the political capacities of the Communists and those of its own ally in Saigon. To the end, the deeper meaning in the war was that, without outside intervention, the Communists would have triumphed with ease over their noncommunist rivals.

Could a different strategy, or a higher level of commitment of Washington, have altered the final result? Life does not permit us to relive history. Perhaps a more vigorous U.S. effort to transform South Vietnamese society would have resulted in the emergence of a stronger sense of local commitment to a separate, noncommunist Vietnam. Such a strategy, however, would have aroused charges of neocolonialism and might well have provoked widespread resentment of the United States in the South. Possibly a more aggressive military strategy would have ultimately broken the Communists' will to resist. Certainly the United States possessed the power to destroy North Vietnam. Such a policy, however, risked nuclear confrontation with Moscow or all-out war with China. Moreover, there is serious doubt that U.S. public opinion would have supported such a brutal resolution of what was viewed by most as a problem of only limited importance. The military solution might have worked, but the potential costs were dangerously high.

The fact is that there was no easy U.S. solution for what was, in the last analysis, a Vietnamese problem. In the end, the only unused options for the United States—escalated involvement, a high risk of war with the Soviet Union—were those that, for one reason or another, the American people were probably unwilling to adopt. Recognition of this fact came gradually and painfully and culminated in the Paris Agreement in 1973 and the U.S. disengagement that followed it. The rapid Communist victory two years later served to confirm the estimate.

NOTES

1. For an analysis of the founding of SEATO, see Leszek Buszynski, *SEATO: The Failure of an Alliance Strategy* (Singapore: Singapore University Press, 1983).

2. Bao Dai, *Dragon d'Annam* (Paris: Plon, 1981).

3. For the letter, see Kahin and Lewis, *The U.S. and Vietnam*, appendix item no. 4.

5

Politics and Government

One of the primary objectives of U.S. policymakers during a generation of involvement in Vietnam was to establish an independent state based on the Western democratic model. This objective had first been advanced in the late 1940s by the Truman administration, when it attempted to persuade the French to introduce democratic institutions and promise ultimate independence to the Vietnamese in return for U.S. military assistance against the Vietminh. It was reasserted following the Geneva Conference in 1954, when the Eisenhower administration provided advisers to assist the new government of Ngo Dinh Diem in drafting a constitution for a democratic republic, and continued into the middle and late 1960s, when Washington pressured the military regime led by Generals Nguyen Van Thieu and Nguyen Cao Ky to establish a legal basis for their rule. In 1967, a new constitution was promulgated, and national elections elevated Nguyen Van Thieu to the presidency. In the end, however, the experiment failed. Neither Ngo Dinh Diem nor any of his successors were able to establish a basis of legitimacy for Saigon's governmental authority beyond the sheer application of naked force. While the ultimate defeat of the South Vietnamese government by its counterpart in the North undoubtedly had many causes, the failure to win a popular mandate from the Vietnamese people—millions of whom did not identify with that government or considered it illegitimate—was clearly a major factor in its demise.

The failure of the Saigon regime to plant the seeds of democracy in Vietnamese soil is sometimes attributed to Washington's insistence on emphasizing the goal of anticommunism over that of establishing democratic values, and on placing a higher value on military concerns than on the objectives of political and social development. That charge has some validity, for throughout the late 1950s and 1960s many key U.S. officials were indeed skeptical that a truly pluralistic political system could be installed in South Vietnam at a time when the young nation was still struggling to surmount the challenge posed by the Communist regime based in the North. That conviction had proponents within the academic community as well, as modernization theorists argued that the road from traditional polities to pluralist democracy passed through an era characterized by "mobilization regimes" under strong charismatic leadership.[1]

Still, the charge that the United States bears full responsibility for the failure of the democratic experiment in South Vietnam is certainly an oversimplification. That failure was the product, above all, of deep-seated historical and cultural factors within Vietnamese society, factors that, to one degree or another, were shared by all other societies within the region. It is instructive to note that of the new nations that emerged from colonial rule in Southeast Asia after World War II, virtually all of them initially adopted some form of representative political system based on Western models. Yet within a decade, hardly any remained working democracies. All the rest abandoned democratic institutions and turned to a more paternalistic form of government run by either military or civilian elites. A generation later, democratic institutions are beginning to reappear. Still, many indigenous political leaders and academics continue to insist that Western concepts of political democracy are inappropriate for Southeast Asian societies. Clearly, the hopes of many observers at the end of the Pacific War that independence would lead to the rise of democratic societies in the region were misplaced, at least for the time being. In that context, the failure of the democratic experiment in South Vietnam is hardly surprising, and cannot be ascribed solely to decisions taken in Washington.

In retrospect, it is clear that both Western and Asian proponents of the liberal democratic model were overoptimistic about the ability or the desire of the leaders of newly independent societies in Asia to install systems of government that in the West had taken generations, or even centuries, to evolve. These new states faced severe class divisions and intimidating economic problems that would be sufficient to strain even societies with long experience with democratic practices; equally important, many of the human values and behavioral patterns that underlay political culture in the West were unfamiliar to the indigenous populations in Southeast Asia and frequently ran directly counter to political and social traditions inherited from the past. It is little wonder that in Vietnam, as in most other states in the region, the democratic experiment was quickly aborted. The United States tacitly recognized the trend in 1959 when, in a document entitled "Current Policy in the Far East," the National Security Council declared that:

> To the extent possible as consistent with our continuing aim of encouraging democratic growth, especially respect for basic human rights, encourage strong responsible executive-type governments which are best suited to the

current requirements of various countries taking into account their traditions, circumstances, and capabilities.[2]

KEY CHARACTERISTICS OF VIETNAMESE
POLITICAL TRADITION

To understand the underlying reasons for the failure of Western
democratic institutions to take root in modern Vietnam, then, it is necessary to begin our exploration not in wartime Washington or Saigon, but in
the institutions and values of the traditional era and how they have been
affected by Vietnam's entrance into the modern world.

It has often been observed that the political institutions of traditional
Vietnam were shaped, above all, by centuries of constant contact with
neighboring China. Confucian institutions were probably first introduced
into Vietnam shortly after the establishment of the state of Nam Viet,
when the Chinese-born ruler Trieu Da accepted tributary status to the
powerful Han Empire to the north in the third century B.C. Confucian concepts and practices, introduced into the country by Chinese administrators after the Han conquest in 111 B.C., undoubtedly exerted a heavy impact on the Sino-Vietnamese elite that eventually emerged under the aegis
of imperial authority. Whether Confucian concepts and attitudes had
much impact on the common people is another matter. In his
groundbreaking study of early Vietnamese society, historian Keith W.
Taylor quotes an exasperated Chinese official on how difficult it was to
teach the Vietnamese people the rudiments of proper behavior. Although
we have "taught the people to plow, established schools for instruction in
the classics, and made everyone follow proper marriage ceremonies with
designated matchmakers," he lamented, in actuality those who were exposed to such instruction gained only "a rude knowledge of letters." As
for the effort to persuade the Vietnamese to follow Chinese customs, one
official remarked, "men and women go naked without shame. In short, it
can be said that these people are on the same level as bugs."[3]

Such frustrations may have characterized the first stage of the encounter between Vietnamese society and Chinese political traditions. Still,
centuries of Chinese rule eventually had a perceptible impact on the Vietnamese political culture. This became clear after independence was restored in the tenth century, when the new Vietnamese state of Dai Viet
found Confucian doctrine useful as a means of legitimizing the monarchy
and strengthening the central power of the state. The process, however,
was a gradual one. During the first centuries of independence, Confucian
institutions were compelled to compete with rival ideologies such as Buddhism and various indigenous cults as the central force underlying the political system. Vietnamese rulers still practiced a number of rituals that

dated back to the period prior to the era of Chinese domination. During the Ly and the Tran dynasties, Buddhist monks often played an influential role as advisers at court, and aristocratic families, not officials trained in the Confucian classics, continued to dominate senior positions within the bureaucracy.

Gradually, however, Confucian ideology and practice dominated the political scene, as strong monarchs viewed it as a means of improving bureaucratic efficiency and buttressing their position as the preeminent force within Vietnamese society. The process accelerated during the brief interregnum of Chinese rule during the early fifteenth century. Ming administrators attempted to "Confucianize" the political system and established dozens of public schools throughout the country to indoctrinate prospective indigenous administrators in the Confucian classics.

After Le Loi restored Vietnamese independence in the 1420s, the trend toward the Confucian model continued. Under the dynamic rule of Emperor Le Thanh Tong (1460–1497), Confucianism became the official doctrine of the state, and a new legal system, labeled the Hong Duc (Great Virtue, so named for the emperor's reign title) Code, was promulgated to regularize laws, government regulations, and social practices on the Chinese pattern.

The adoption of Confucianism as the state ideology undoubtedly brought a number of concrete benefits to Vietnamese society. Within the context of Asian political thought and practice, Confucianism can be described as a relatively advanced stage in the process of secularization and rationalization that has taken place in recent centuries throughout the globe. Unlike the Indianized political systems applied elsewhere in Southeast Asia, Confucian Vietnam established a clear distinction between the realms of religion and politics. Where Indian political thought fused the sacred and profane into a single emperor-divinity, Confucianism denied the divine quality of the monarch. Like monarchs in early modern Europe, Confucian rulers were assumed to be mortals who ruled by divine right. By reason of their talent and virtue, they had received a "mandate of heaven" (*thien menh,* in Chinese *t'ien ming*) to govern ordinary human beings.

There was, of course, a magical or religious quality to the Confucian ruler that helped him to establish and maintain a charismatic form of authority over his subjects. But he was expected to adhere to established rules of behavior (*Dao*; in Chinese, *Tao,* or the Way) that were, in effect, a set of common laws that took priority over the king's will. And there was in Confucian tradition—stemming from the thought of the fourth century B.C. thinker Mencius—an implicit right of revolution in cases where the ruler failed to live up to his obligations to society.

In the composition of its ruling elite as well, the Confucian political tradition represented a step beyond those systems used elsewhere in the region. In most Southeast Asian societies, the ruling class was composed almost exclusively of members of the hereditary aristocracy. Vietnamese practice, however, called for the selection of officials through a complex process of civil service examinations to test candidates on their knowledge of the Confucian classics, a system that was first put into use during the T'ang dynasty in China.

After the restoration of Vietnamese independence in the tenth century, the state of Dai Viet adopted the practice, and established a Confucian academy, known today as the Temple of Literature (Van Mieu) to train candidates for the bureaucracy. At first, however, the court restricted candidates for the higher ranks of the bureaucracy to members of noble families. But after the rise of the Le dynasty in the fifteenth century, a more formalized system based on the Chinese meritocratic model was adopted, and the system was opened up to the majority of the male population.

The system was by no means without flaws. As in China, favoritism and nepotism often played a role in the selection of officials; sons of poor parents were much less likely to receive training in Confucian academies throughout the country. But it undoubtedly represented a major advance in the process of creating a bureaucracy based on the concept of rule by talent. The result was seen not only in greater bureaucratic efficiency, but also in a heightened sense of class fluidity and upward mobility that was absent in societies with more rigid class distinctions. In turn, the Vietnamese bureaucracy developed a tradition of professionalism and expertise that, in a manner probably unintended by Le Thanh Tong and his successors, tended to limit the arbitary power of the ruler over his subjects. While emperors and even dynasties came and went, the bureaucracy remained in place.

Through such practices and beliefs, Confucianism thus encouraged the development of a rational and efficient administrative hierarchy that extended its tentacles throughout all levels of society. It promoted the transformation of a social order dominated by a powerful and arrogant hereditary aristocracy into one based at least partly on merit; it provided a system of social ethics based, at least in theory, on hard work, service to the community, personal rectitude, and benevolence. In sum, Confucianism well served the needs of an agrarian society in which such qualities were a prerequisite for social order and economic prosperity.

The beauty of Confucian theory, of course, was not always reflected in practice. Surrounded by eunuchs and sycophants, shielded from personal contact with his subjects by elaborate Confucian rituals that stressed his intermediary relationship between the forces of heaven and the material world below, the emperor was frequently isolated at court, whereas the bureaucracy was often rigid and unresponsive to the needs of society unless prodded by a humane and energetic ruler. Like their counterparts the world over, Vietnamese officials all too often displayed a tendency toward arrogance and self-seeking, and even Confucian scholars, the keepers of the moral law, often ignored the ethical teachings of the Confucian classics and lapsed into ritualism and a pedantic concern for style rather than content.

This tendency was particularly marked during the later years of the Le dynasty. A series of weak monarchs led to the dominance of the political system by powerful princely families at court and eventually to a general breakdown in the effectiveness of Confucian institutions in Vietnamese society. The ineffectiveness of the court encouraged corruption within the bureaucracy and, in rural areas, the increasing concentration of land in the hands of wealthy families. By the eighteenth century, signs of the incipient disintegration of the political and social bonds of the traditional culture became distressingly evident.

The brief reign of the Tay Son emperor Quang Trung, followed by the rise of the Nguyen dynasty at the beginning of the nineteenth century, restored a measure of internal unity to the state. Under the vigorous rule of the founding emperor Gia Long and his strong-willed successor Minh Mang, the Nguyen court attempted to return to the alleged purity of classical Confucian institutions and values. The central administration of the state was designed along Chinese lines, with a Grand Council, a Grand Secretariat, and the "six boards" equivalent to government ministries in the West. The examination system rigidly mirrored the Chinese model, with three levels of evaluation culminating in the doctoral examination held at the imperial palace in Huê. There were some differences between the Chinese and the Vietnamese systems, but they were relatively minor and mostly in deference to the fact that the latter was a smaller and less complex society.

WIND FROM THE WEST

Ironically, the very measures taken by Nguyen rulers to strengthen the power of the monarchy by means of a return to Confucian orthodoxy may have been a major contributing factor in the inability of the court to respond effectively to the challenge posed by the French. To many nineteenth century Vietnamese, as to their counterparts in late Ch'ing China, a return to Confucian precepts precluded an acceptance of exotic new ideas from the West.

It was not that the court sought to isolate itself completely from the outside world. Although Emperor Gia Long had declared a policy of "closed country" (*be quan tua cang*) as a means of fending off the destabilizing effects of contacts with the outside world, in practice he was willing to tolerate a limited amount of trade and missionary activity on the part of European visitors. His successor Minh Mang, although widely considered a Confucian purist with a deep suspicion of foreign ideas, also recognized the necessity of maintaining trade relations with foreign countries. When one xenophobic adviser, Vu Duc Khoe, proposed a policy of total isolation from the West, Minh Mang rejected the idea, responding that Vietnam badly needed to maintain foreign trade relations in order to obtain needed goods and learn Western methods of navigation and shipbuilding. But although Minh Mang recognized the need to borrow in selective areas from the West, he felt that such changes could be carried out without disturbing the fundamental structure of Vietnamese society. Explaining China's defeat at the hands of the British in the Opium War of 1839–1842, for example, he argued that Peking's humiliation was its own fault, since Manchu officials had permitted the foreigners to settle in China and spread their poisonous ideas. Vietnam, on the other hand, had followed a more efficacious path, carrying on commercial relations with foreign visitors and then sending them on their way.

The problem, then, was not that Vietnamese monarchs like Gia Long and Minh Mang closed their eyes to the foreign threat. The real problem, as Alexander B. Woodside has noted, was that they did not realize "the enormity of the gulf" that separated the Vietnamese from Western countries in their mastery of military technology. In this complacency, which can be attributed in part to their Confucian worldview, they were hardly alone.[4]

The complacency of the Nguyen court was shaken somewhat by the French seizure of Cochin China in the late 1850s and early 1860s. It also provoked some thoughtful advisers to urge Emperor Tu Duc to make peace with the French in order to buy sufficient time to reform Vietnamese political and social institutions and modernize the Vietnamese army and navy. Among the most prominent was the Confucian scholar Nguyen Truong To. Deprived of the opportunity to enter the civil service after a brief visit to France because of his Catholic faith, To accepted employment with the French colonial government in Cochin China. In the late 1860s, however, he resigned and offered his services to the imperial court, where he proposed a policy of conciliation abroad and reform at home. The emperor took the first piece of advice, but not the second. In the margin of one of To's proposals for domestic reform, Tu Duc scribbled the note: "Nguyen Truong To is too sure of himself. Reforms need time. Why should we hurry so, when the old ways have always sufficed in managing the affairs of the empire?"[5]

After the French conquest, the toadying of many court officials toward the new rulers, combined with the cavalier treatment of the traditional monarchy by the colonial regime (during the early years of colonial rule, the French replaced emperors on the throne virtually at will), accelerated the demise of the traditional system and undermined public confidence in the validity of Confucian ideology as a foundation for future Vietnamese society. By the end of the first quarter of the twentieth century public confidence was almost moribund.

In general, this process was encouraged by the French. For proponents of the view that France had a *mission civilisatrice* in Indochina, one of the primary assumptions was that the Confucian political system was outmoded and had to be replaced by representative institutions from the West. In actuality, however, French policy was inconsistent in carrying out political change. The imperial court was permitted to retain its authority in Annam, while in Tonkin colonial officials were often slow to replace traditional practices with Western ones. Even in the colony of Cochin China, the French appeared reluctant to move expeditously toward the creation of a political system reflecting Western models. As a result, the pressure to introduce representative democratic institutions came more from within Vietnamese society, among intellectuals familiar from travel or study with European civilization, than it did from the colonial regime itself. By the first decade of the twentieth century, progressive members of the traditional scholar-gentry class had already begun to call for the abandonment of old ways and the transformation of Vietnamese political institutions and practices along Western lines.

It was two Confucian scholar-patriots, Phan Boi Chau and Phan Chu Trinh, who most aggressively urged the adoption of Western political institutions. The former had advocated the creation of a future democratic society in a number of pamphlets that he wrote in Japan, and in 1912 he had responded to the formation of the first Chinese republic by proposing to adopt a similar political system in Vietnam. But Chau, whose views might have been influenced by conversations with the Chinese reformist intellectual Liang Ch'i-ch'ao in Japan, appeared somewhat skeptical that the Vietnamese people were ready for democracy. In one of his letters to Phan Chu Trinh, he had remarked that although in principle he liked the idea of democracy, in his view the Vietnamese people were still too inexperienced to put it into effect. Let's save the country first, he proposed, and worry about ideology later.[6]

Phan Chu Trinh's response to his friend's remark is unknown, but a review of his writings reveals that he placed a different slant on the problems of his country. In his public letter to Governor-general Paul Beau, he made it clear that, in his view, political and social reforms should take place prior to the restoration of Vietnamese independence in order to educate the Vietnamese people about the challenges of democracy they faced before they regained control over their own destiny. Trinh's commitment to the concept of a pluralistic society seems to have been genuine and not simply a ploy to create a strong nation and a united people capable of resisting foreign conquest. Still, like many reformist intellectuals in late Manchu China, he was not averse to promoting his views by using the social Darwinist argument that democracy is the handmaiden of national wealth and power. On one occasion he pointed out that it was the determination of Japanese leaders to make use of Western values and institutions that had enabled their country to defend itself against the encroachments of Western power. This, he felt, was a model for Vietnam to follow. "The currents of the world are powerful," he noted. "Those who respond to them will have a safe journey into the future. Those who do not will be flattened like grass."[7]

Like such Confucian reformists as K'ang Yu-wei, Liang Ch'i-ch'ao, and Yen Fu in late Manchu China—whose works they had indeed carefully read—scholar-patriots like Phan Boi Chau and Phan Chu Trinh were among the first Vietnamese to popularize political ideas from the West among their own compatriots. But like their Chinese counterparts, the depth of their understanding of Western democratic practices and ideals is open to serious question. It was the next generation, raised in the shadow of the colonial regime, often educated in French schools, and engaged in occupations created by the Western presence, which would absorb the full force of Western influence and bring about a transvaluation of values within elite circles in Vietnamese society.

In the diversity of its intellectual currents, the decade immediately following World War I in Indochina resembles that of the early republican era in China, when a number of sometimes contrasting ideas about human nature and the role of the individual in society circulated among the educated elite. The common problem for virtually all Vietnamese intellectuals of the day was how to meet the challenge posed by the imposition of French power and Western culture. But there were wide disagreements over the proper solution to adopt. Some sought the answer in immediate independence and radical political change. Others, like the Francophile Bui Quang Chieu and his colleagues in the Constitutionalist party, advocated greater Vietnamese autonomy from French rule, but feared social disorder more than French domination and advocated a continuing French presence through the formation of a confederationist arrangement similar to that of the British Commonwealth. Others still, like the conservative intellectual Pham Quynh, were profoundly distrustful of the democratic traditions of the West and hoped to fashion a synthesis between the paternalistic elements of traditional Vietnamese civilization and the dynamic individualist culture of the West.

Events in Europe fueled the debate. As in China, some Vietnamese were repelled by the specter of fratricidal war in Europe and aspired to an idyllic vision of humanistic Confucian civilization as a safe haven from the blatant materialism and fractious nationalism of the modern age. In a speech given in Saigon shortly before his death, Phan Chu Trinh took issue with this view, pointing out that the Confucian concept of a harmonious community governed by the benign operation of the heavenly Way had long ago disappeared from Vietnam. Trinh agreed that Europe suffered from serious problems, but he argued that thoughtful people in the West were in the process of devising a new morality that would place the needs of the global community over the demands of narrow nationalism. Not many Vietnamese could share his optimism.[8]

As historian Huê-Tam Ho Tai pointed out in her recent book entitled *Radicalism and the Origins of the Vietnamese Revolution,* one of the dilemmas for intellectuals of this era was that they saw the inadequacies of the present but lacked a clear vision of the future. The 1920s, she argued, represented an experimental and individualistic phase of the Vietnamese revolution, when ardent young patriots sought freedom for themselves and a sense of identity and purpose for their collective community in an uncertain world. In her view, the problem was that many members of the generation of the 1920s were "too drunk with words and ideas for systematic thinking." It would take the emergence of the Indochinese Communist party under the leadership of Nguyen Ai Quoc, she concluded, to provide a concrete strategy and a clear sense of direction to the Vietnamese revolution.[9]

MESSAGE FROM MOSCOW

It is one of the ironies of our day that the philosophy of Karl Marx, which the German philosopher devised for application in the advanced capitalist societies of the West, has had its primary appeal as a vehicle for rapid social change in the developing societies in Africa, Asia, and Latin America. The attractiveness of Marxism to Third World intellectuals and political leaders, however, is quite understandable. For societies suffering from the collapse of traditional institutions and values, Marxism offered a persuasive alternative to Western capitalist democracy as an appropriate tool in the nation-building effort. It not only offered a clear vision of a future egalitarian society free from the exploitative characteristics of modern industrial capitalism, it also provided, in the form of Leninist revolutionary strategy, a clear path to get there.

This was certainly the case in Vietnam. Whereas Western liberal democracy emphasized the individual as the foundation of the political culture, Marxism stressed the subordination of individual human beings to the overall needs of the community, a view quite compatible with the Confucian mindset. Where liberal democracy was gradualist in orientation and stressed the decentralization of power, Marxism provided a dynamic and action-oriented approach to problems of social change and stressed the importance of popular mobilization, centralized leadership, and a single coherent ideology—all features attractive to radical intellectuals who had lost their faith in the Confucian worldview but still harbored subconscious assumptions about the relationship between the individual and society inherited from the traditional era. In effect, Marxism served not only as a developmental ideology, but also as a form of political religion, providing an explanation of history, a doctrine of good and evil, and the promise of a future paradise on earth.

Marxist ideas made their appearance in Vietnam in the years immediately following World War I. At first, vigorous censorship by the colonial regime prevented information about the explosive doctrine from being disseminated among restive Vietnamese intellectuals seeking a solution to the intimidating challenges of social change. Despite such efforts, by the late 1920s Marxism had become a familiar item on the Vietnamese intellectual scene and, to many, a persuasive alternative to the Western democratic model. With the formation of Ho Chi Minh's Revolutionary Youth League in 1925 and its metamorphosis into the ICP five years later, an organization devoted to the realization of the Marxist utopia in Vietnam had come into being.

For the next several decades, the doctrines of liberal democracy and Marxism competed to fill the vacuum left by the gradual demise of the traditional Confucian order. Vietnamese Marxists have interpreted the competition as a struggle between two classes—the bourgeoisie and the proletariat—for the leadership of the Vietnamese revolution. This interpretation is by no means wholly invalid, but it is clearly an oversimplification that does little credit to the complexity of the issue. Although the strongest support for liberal democratic and capitalist ideas undoubtedly came from the emerging commercial and manufacturing bourgeoisie, the majority of early Marxists did not come from the Vietnamese proletariat, but from what is often called the urban petit bourgeois intelligentsia. To this mixed class of students, teachers, journalists, lower-level officials, clerks, and disappointed job seekers (many of whom came from traditional elite families), Marxism was preferable to liberal democracy as a vehicle for national liberation and a model for a future Vietnamese society.

It was only after Marxism had taken firm roots within the ranks of the radical intelligentsia that, through the efforts of Ho Chi Minh and other leading members of the movement, it began to spread to the working class and the more impoverished elements among the peasantry. Ho Chi Minh was especially sensitive to the need to seek the support of Vietnamese peasants, a decision that did not always win favor in Moscow. Beginning in 1928, directives from the Comintern stressed the importance of "proletarianizing" the party (that is, building the party's base among the small urban working class) and downplayed the importance of the peasantry in waging social revolution in Asia. But when Comintern strategy shifted back to a broader united front approach in 1935 (at a time when Ho Chi Minh was living in Moscow), party cadres once again appealed for support in rural areas. When Ho Chi Minh returned to South China in 1940, he discovered that a number of leading party members already appreciated the importance of the countryside in the Vietnamese revolution. It was a realization that was crucial to eventual success.[10]

With the formation of the Vietminh Front in the spring of 1941, the basic components of the party's revolutionary strategy were firmly established. The program of the front was founded on two key planks—the quest for national independence and the call for social justice. The antiimperialist message was designed to appeal to patriotic groups and individuals throughout the country, especially to urban intellectuals and anticolonial members of the landed gentry. The message of social justice focused above all on the importance of land reform as a means of rectifying the inequities of the traditional system of land ownership, and was aimed at poor peasants in the countryside. For the time being, the antiimperialist struggle would take precedence over the antifeudal one; thus, measures to reform the landowning system would be moderate in order to avoid alienating patriotic elements among the bourgeoisie and the landlord class.

The creative tension between the issues of nationalism and land reform is a familiar one in the history of Asian revolution. Historians and social scientists have disputed among themselves over the relative importance of these two factors in the appeal of the communist movement in twentieth century China. A similar debate has arisen among Vietnam specialists over the comparative importance of nationalism and social revolution as a factor in the ability of the Viet Cong to mobilize popular support in South Vietnam during the 1950s and 1960s. Few would deny, however, that during the war against the French, the two factors were of approximate if not equal importance in the emergence of the Vietminh Front as a powerful political force in Indochina. Confirming Ho Chi Minh's judgment that nationalism must initially take precedence over social revolution, the front won broad popular support for its leading role in the struggle against the French, while its message of socio-economic reform was a crucial factor in its ability to mobilize peasants from rural villages to serve in the revolutionary cause. In the end, the Vietminh Front had earned the allegiance of a broad spectrum of the population—rich and poor, rural and urban—as the legitimate representative of Vietnamese national aspirations.

Ho Chi Minh Mausoleum. (Photo property of the author.)

After the beginning of the Franco-Vietminh conflict in December 1946, the French attempted to create a political force that could provide the Vietnamese people with an alternative to Ho Chi Minh and the Vietminh Front. But Bao Dai's Associated State of Vietnam (ASV), formally launched in 1949, gained little credibility among the Vietnamese people, even among anticommunist elements who recognized the Vietminh Front as a front for the ICP. Part of the problem for the new government was that it was obviously identified with the French colonial regime. But another obstacle was the character of Bao Dai himself. The new chief of state was widely criticized for his lack of leadership, and many observers inside and outside the country felt that he did not possess the qualities necessary to provide a convincing alternative to the dedicated and charismatic Ho Chi Minh. Bao Dai himself appeared to lack confidence in the breadth of his popular appeal and the democratic instincts of his people, refusing to hold general elections as a means of providing an aura of legitimacy to his government.

EXPERIMENT IN DEMOCRACY: THE REPUBLIC OF VIETNAM

At the Geneva Conference in 1954, Vietnam was divided into two separate regroupment zones, and the Bao Dai government became the temporary administrative authority south of the seventeenth parallel. The political declaration at Geneva had called for the holding of national elections two years after the signing of the agreement to bring about the reunification of the country. But Ngo Dinh Diem, who had been appointed prime minister by Chief of State Bao Dai in June, refused to hold consultations with representatives of the DRV and commenced to build his own independent government in the South.

The Eisenhower administration, although somewhat uncomfortable at the blunt manner by which Ngo Dinh Diem had rejected the political provisions of the Geneva Agreement, was pleased at his strong anticommunist credentials, and decided to support him in setting up a separate government in Saigon. General J. Lawton Collins, the senior U.S. representative in South Vietnam, strongly encouraged Diem to initiate political reforms designed to create a new system based on the Western democratic model. Diem agreed, but in his own way. Against U.S. advice, in October 1955 he carried out a popular referendum asking the population to choose between himself and Chief of State Bao Dai. The latter, now living in Paris, decided not to contest the referendum and Diem received 98 percent of the vote. The following year a constituent assembly was elected that, with U.S. assistance, drafted a new constitution for an independent republic. The new charter, promulgated in 1957, was based on a combination of the presidential and parliamentary models, with a strong chief executive presiding over a unicameral national assembly. In 1957 Ngo Dinh Diem was elected president of the new Republic of Vietnam.

In fact, Diem's allegiance to democratic procedures was only lip service, since he clearly preferred a more paternalistic approach to governance. At heart, Diem was a traditionalist, more comfortable in the hierarchical world of Confucian enlightened despotism than in the rough-and-tumble arena of democratic politics. In private conversations with some of his more intimate American acquaintances, Diem remarked that he did not believe in the multiparty system and had no intention of forming one of his own. It soon became clear that he had little tolerance for opposition either, and vigorously suppressed all those who opposed him.

Curiously, however, Diem was willing to appropriate modern techniques when they appeared useful. At the urging of his brother Nhu, he eventually made use of such Leninist ideas as the vanguard party (known in South Vietnam as the Personalist Labor party, or Can Lao) and the united front (in South Vietnam, Diem formed a broad progovernmental national front known as the National Revolutionary Movement). The latter was constructed from a base composed of functional mass organizations similar to those used in Marxist-Leninist systems. Knitting the whole together was a syncretic ideology called Personalism, a concept borrowed from modern Catholic thought that combined the Western concepts of individual dignity and freedom with an equal emphasis on the needs of the community.

Diem's effort to unify the South Vietnamese people under his leaderhsip to fight against the menace of social revolution came to a sudden end with his overthrow in November 1963. The reasons for his fall have inspired debate ever since. Some have blamed the message, arguing that Diem's mélange of Confucian, Catholic, and libertarian ideas was doomed from the start. Others point to the weakness of the messenger, noting that Diem had serious shortcomings as a political leader and certainly lacked the charismatic appeal of such contemporaries as Sukarno of Indonesia, Nehru of India, or Vietnam's own Ho Chi Minh. Finally, some maintain that if Diem had been allowed to apply his ideas without U.S. interference, he might have eventually triumphed over his ideological rival in Hanoi.

In retrospect, it seems doubtful that Diem's autocratic tendencies, however lamentable from a democratic point of view, were the heart of the problem. A number of Asian governments elsewhere in the region, from South Korea to Singapore, have been able to combine traditional authoritarian practices with a veneer of democratic institutions into a relatively effective instrument for governing. Why was Diem unable to do the same?

Defenders of Ngo Dinh Diem might point out that, unlike most other political leaders in the region, his regime was challenged by a powerful and well disciplined revolutionary movement actively supported from beyond the frontiers of the RVN. But there is clearly more to it than that, for Diem's problems began long before Hanoi began to play an active role in bringing about his overthrow, and it is clear that Hanoi's supporters in South Vietnam benefitted enormously from his own mistakes. The fact is, Diem was seriously lacking in political acumen. Unlike his more successful contemporaries elsewhere in Asia, Diem did not understand the importance of knitting together a broad alliance of classes and groups that shared his vision of a future Vietnam. In a country predominantly Buddhist (although nominally so), he needlessly alienated millions by his favoritism toward Catholics. A northerner by birth and upbringing, he displayed obvious contempt for the more volatile and easy-going southerners. In a society characterized by a serious inequality of land distribution, he totally failed to understand the need for a comprehensive land reform program. His constituency, like that of his predecessor Bao Dai, consisted primarily of affluent elements in the cities and the landed gentry in rural areas. Like Generalissimo Chiang Kai-shek in China, Diem hearkened back to an era that no longer existed and failed to heed the demands for change that were rising from among his own people.[11]

For years, U.S. policy had been predicated on the assumption that if an effective leader could only be found, victory could be achieved in South Vietnam. With Diem's removal in November 1963, some officials in the Kennedy administration were optimistic that a viable state built on democratic institutions could now be created in Saigon. But the leaders of the coup quickly floundered, confirming the fears expressed by skeptics who in past years had warned that there was no alternative to Ngo Dinh Diem in preventing a Communist takeover in South Vietnam. Nearly two years of ineffective military and civilian governments amply demonstrated the vacuum of political leadership in Saigon.

The rise of the military regime of Nguyen Cao Ky and Nguyen Van Thieu in the summer of 1965 provided a slender basis for optimism that the period of musical chairs that had followed the fall of Diem was at an end. In 1966, the Johnson administration began to pressure the new leadership in Saigon to replace the existing system of military rule, carried on behind the facade of an Armed Forces Council and a directorate (the latter body was composed of ten generals and nineteen handpicked civilians) with a more legitimate source of authority. Washington was still convinced that strong leadership was necessary in Saigon, but felt that at least the appearance of a popular mandate would make U.S. policy more palatable to public opinion at home and abroad, and the regime more acceptable to the South Vietnamese people.

The generals in Saigon were amenable, and in September 1966 a 117-member Constituent Assembly was elected to draw up a new charter. The final draft, issued in March 1967, called for a presidential system with a strong executive and a two-house legislature. The Directorate and the Armed Forces Council accepted the document without change, and it was promulgated as the new constitution of the republic in April. The document was clearly designed to provide the RVN with the centralized authority considered necessary to cope with the challenges of nation-building and internal conflict. The president, who was to be elected by popular vote for a four-year term and was eligible for a single reelection, had substantial authority to promulgate laws, initiate legislation, serve as the supreme commander of the armed forces, determine national policy, and preside over the Council of Ministers. He was also empowered to declare a national state of emergency, although such a decree had to be approved by the National Assembly within twelve days. In time of war, he could appoint province chiefs, subject to approval by a two-thirds vote of a lower house to be called the National Assembly. Although the president was in effect both head of government and chief of state, the constitution provided for a prime minister, who was appointed by and could be removed by the president, to assist him in executive duties. The Assembly could also force the resignation of the prime minister by a two-thirds vote.

The legislative branch consisted of the National Assembly and the Senate, both to be elected by universal suffrage and direct ballot. Deputies in the lower house were to be elected for a four-year term from separate constituencies; senators served for six years and were elected at large by list under a plurality system. The National Assembly voted on legislation, ratified treaties, and determined the declaration of war and the opening of peace talks. It could override a presidential veto by an absolute majority vote, and its members had the traditional legal protections against arbitrary arrest.

Other interesting aspects of the system were an independent judiciary, with a supreme court (empowered to decide on appeals from lower courts and on the constitutionality of all laws and decrees), a bill of rights, and an inspectorate (an organization with a long tradition in imperial China and Vietnam) to oversee the operations of the administrative branch. Political parties were of course permitted, but an article of the constitution declared that "the Republic of Vietnam opposes communism in any form" and prohibited all publicity for communism.[12]

In form, then, South Vietnam in 1967 became a democratic society. National elections held in September resulted in the election of Nguyen Van Thieu as president and Nguyen Cao Ky as vice-president. A new legislature was elected in September and October. During the following eight years, the regime generally managed to give at least the appearance of staying within the bounds of legality, although in several respects the system did not work effectively. Political parties were permitted to operate, so long as they espoused moderate social programs, supported the war effort, and posed no threat to the supremacy of the Thieu regime. Those who advocated neutralism or a compromise settlement of the war, however, were frequently harassed and sometimes arrested. Such practices are hardly unusual in developing societies. Two signs were ominous for the survival of the government: the inability of the Thieu regime to establish a popular base of support and the failure of the system to produce political parties that could compete effectively to voice popular social aspirations on a national scale. The ousted Diem regime had at least attempted (albeit with limited success) to articulate a general philosophy of development (that murky synthesis of Confucian and progressive Catholic thought known as Personalism) and create a popular base of support through the formation of mass organizations and the progovernment National Revolutionary Movement. Yet President Thieu was surprisingly slow to follow the pattern familiar elsewhere in the Third World of setting up a national popular front to support government policies.

Significantly, however, the noncommunist opposition was equally disorganized. Most of the parties operating in the National Assembly were mere cliques and factions, based on regional or religious interests, rather than nationally organized political parties. The legislature appeared to be a mere congeries of diverse interests, and members found it difficult either to coalesce behind the government or in support of an organized opposition. In effect, President Thieu was operating in a political vacuum. Despite widespread discontent with many of his policies, he was reelected in 1971 with virtually no opposition and then attempted with only mediocre success to reorganize the party system on a national basis and set up a progovernment democratic party.

In sum, under Nguyen Van Thieu as under his predecessors, the RVN was democratic in form but not in content, authoritarian in practice but lacking in a popular mandate. Although some of the blame for these shortcomings can be ascribed to overall social conditions and the pressure of war, the failure of the system to evolve over a period of two decades suggests that the origins of the problem were more deep-seated. One reason is that Nguyen Van Thieu, like Ngo Dinh Diem and Bao Dai before him, utterly failed to make Western political techniques relevant to the Vietnamese environment. Unlike the Communists, who after years of careful experimentation had worked out a strategy for revolution and nation-building that blended the theoretical and practical tenets of Marxism-Leninism with the political and cultural realities of Vietnamese society, the political elites in Saigon approached the problem in a perfunctory and disjointed fashion. Western institutions were applied—sometimes, admittedly, at U.S. insistence—with little thought to their relevance in a Vietnamese context, while traditional styles of governance were utilized with no thought to the changes that had taken place in Vietnamese society under colonial rule. Washington did not help by its inconsistent efforts to force Saigon to implement the American political model. It is difficult to avoid the conclusion that political institutions designed for an advanced industrial society characterized by deep-rooted libertarian traditions were simply inappropriate for an agrarian society beset with serious economic and social problems and a populace more accustomed to a paternalistic and communitarian form of political leadership.

Saigon's efforts to build a popular mandate for its authority were equally flawed and similarly ineffective. Throughout most of the life of the republic, the bulk of the population felt little sense of commitment to the government in Saigon, which all too frequently appeared insensitive to the needs and aspirations of its subjects. The fault was not entirely Thieu's. At times he was undoubtedly hindered by resistance from influential forces within the population and expressed through the legislature. At other times he had to cope with interference from Washington. At the root of the problem, however, was the fact that the Thieu regime, like its predecessors, represented an affluent segment of the population—comprised of urban professionals, the mercantile middle class, and the rural landed gentry—that in the course of recent decades had grown increasingly isolated from the problems and concerns of the majority of the population. It was a problem that afflicted many governments in other parts of the region, but none faced the challenge of a highly disciplined and experienced Communist movement dedicated to harnessing the latent energies of the urban and rural poor to the revolutionary cause.[13]

In sum, it was probably unrealistic to expect that South Vietnam, under such conditions, could put into operation a political system patterned after the United States and other Western democracies. What was needed was an approach that could more effectively apply modern political techniques, such as mass mobilization and social action, to attack the burgeoning problems of Vietnamese society. Although the Western democratic experience may by no means have been wholly irrelevant to such conditions, the bulk of the solution would have to come from within. It was the tragedy of the Saigon experiment that South Vietnamese political elites, from Bao Dai and Ngo Dinh Diem to Nguyen Cao Ky and Nguyen Van Thieu, were unable to come up with their own answer to the problem.

THE DEMOCRATIC REPUBLIC OF VIETNAM

While politicians in Saigon were enjoying only limited success in building a stable society based on Western political traditions in South Vietnam, Ho Chi Minh and his colleagues proceeded to install their own version of the Marxist-Leninist alternative in the North. In his own remarks and writings on the subject of governance issued prior to the August Revolution, Ho had often implied that his party would initially adopt a moderate approach based on the support of a broad cross section of the Vietnamese people, prior to moving to the classic stage of the dictatorship of the proletariat. On assuming the presidency of the new provisional government of Vietnam in September 1945, he strengthened that impression. In a speech to an audience of thousands at Ba Dinh Square in Hanoi on September 2, he quoted from both the U.S. Declaration of Independence and the French Declaration of the Rights of Man and declared that "all the peoples have a right to live, to be happy and free."[14]

During succeeding months, Ho's provisional government put in place a set of institutions that on paper did not differ substantially from those of Western liberal democracies. The leaders of the new government adopted such central tenets of Western political practice as elections by secret ballot, separation of powers, supremacy of the legislative branch (a unicameral body called the National Assembly, or Quoc Hoi), a multiparty system, and a constitution with a bill of rights. They also gave the impression cf harboring an inclination, at least on the surface, to share power with their noncommunist rivals. Indeed, as we have seen, in November the ICP declared itself abolished to demonstrate its willingness to sacrifice for the cause of national independence.

Adopting a Western-style political concept such as the balance of power between executive, legislative, and judicial branches, of course, is not contrary to Leninist practice. Although Lenin, like Marx, had scorned Western liberal assemblies as "talking shops," he had found it useful to adopt the forms of liberal democracy in creating the political institutions for the new Soviet state, even though their usage by the Bolsheviks was destined to be markedly different. Behind the facade of democratic institutions, the Communist party played a dominant role in the Leninist political system, and the Bolsheviks did not permit the existence of even the semblance of rival political organizations.

To Ho Chi Minh, however, the Leninist concept of the proletarian dictatorship clashed with the realities of the situation in Vietnam. In the first place, Ho had long been persuaded, in a manner similar to Mao Tse-tung and his mentor Li Ta-chao, that Vietnam was a "proletarian nation," in which vast sectors of the population, including the peasantry and a segment of the patriotic gentry and the bourgeoisie, had been oppressed by imperialism and its local running dogs, the feudalist reactionaries. The party could therefore spread its net more widely than in Soviet Russia to encompass a broader segment of the population. On a more practical plane, Ho was undoubtedly convinced that, at least for the time being, the ICP was too weak to govern on its own and had to disguise its leading role in order to win popular support against the French. It was undoubtedly for this reason that the party was disbanded, although it continued to operate in secret. In accordance with these beliefs, the first constitution of the DRV, promulgated by the National Assembly in November 1946, made no mention of the party. According to the preamble, the new republic would be founded on the following principles:

> The union of all the people without distinction of race, clan, creed, wealth or sex; the guaranteeing of democratic liberties; the establishment of a true people's government. Permeated by the spirit of unity symbolized in the struggle of the entire nation and manifested in an enlarged and enlightened democratic regime, Vietnam now goes forward confidently in consonance with the progressive movements of the world and the peaceful aspirations of mankind.[15]

Behind the scenes, the party maintained a firm control over the reins of power throughout the course of the war against the French, although on paper it was only one of several cooperating parties within a coalition based on the common objective of achieving national independence. It was a masterful application of the concept of the united front, of which Lenin would undoubtedly have approved.

The Geneva Conference of 1954, which returned the Communists to power in North Vietnam, relieved them of any further necessity of disguising their political dominance. Returning to Hanoi in October, the party now consolidated its power throughout the North and inaugurated a "people's democratic dictatorship" following the model applied five years earlier by the communist regime in China. Two small puppet parties formed a few years earlier to flesh out the anti-imperialist alliance, the Democratic party and the Radical Socialist party, were permitted to continue in operation, but the dominant role of the ICP, now renamed the Vietnam Workers' Party (*Dang Lao Dong Viet Nam*), was no longer disguised. Top party figures now occupied most key positions in the government, including such posts as president (Ho Chi Minh), prime minister (Pham Van Dong), minister of defense (Vo Nguyen Giap), and minister of foreign affairs (Nguyen Duy Trinh).

The decision to shift to a more orthodox approach was actually initiated as early as 1951, at the time of the convening of the Second Party Congress, and was apparently related to the growing influence of China on DRV policy. The process accelerated in the months following the party congress, and Vietminh Radio formally announced that henceforth the Vietnamese Revolution was going to proceed along the lines of the Chinese model. It was probably also at Peking's urging that the party had decided to resurface openly and proclaim its dedication to Marxist-Leninist principles. It is not unlikely that some members of the party—including Ho Chi Minh himself—had some reservations about the wholesale adoption of Chinese techniques, which were more defined by class conflict than had heretofore been the case in Vietnam. But it may have been viewed as a necessary by-product of an increase in Chinese military assistance.[16]

As it turned out, if some VWP party members harbored doubts over the wisdom of following the Chinese road to socialism, they were justified, for Chinese methods, applied in the area of party-building, class struggle, and land reform, created serious problems for the DRV during the mid-1950s. The most publicized examples were the land reform program and the regime's treatment of intellectuals (both examples will be dealt with in later chapters). The fallout from such problems created considerable unease within the party, and at the Tenth Plenum in the fall of 1956, General Secretary Truong Chinh, a leading spokesman for agrarian reform and a supporter of the Chinese model, was dismissed from his post, and President Ho Chi Minh publicly conceded that errors had been committed by the party leadership in taking the first steps toward socialist transformation.[17]

The 1959 Constitution

While party leaders were grappling with the problems associated with the use of Maoist methods in the DRV, the regime was also in the process of creating a new constitution to reflect the changing conditions in North Vietnam. A committee to draft the new charter was set up in 1956 and it was ratified by a unanimous vote of the National Assembly in December 1959. The document retained many of the political institutions called for by the original constitution approved in 1946, but it made a number of innovations appropriate to the new situation. In recognition of the need for strong central authority and the somewhat unique role of the party's founder and leader, Ho Chi Minh, the 1959 constitution created a strong presidency. Article 66 gave the president the power "when necessary" to attend and preside over meetings of the cabinet of ministers. Thus, although the system provided for both a president and a prime minister, the former was in effect both chief of state and its leading executive. The president also chaired the new National Defense Council, which included among its members the prime minister, the minister of defense, the minister of public security, and several key military officers.

The new charter retained the unicameral National Assembly first set up after the August Revolution. Its members (including eighteen seats for delegates elected in 1946 to represent the population of the South) were to be chosen by universal suffrage on the basis of one deputy for every 10,000 voters in urban areas and one per 30,000 in the countryside. In theory, the National Assembly was the supreme political body in the state. In practice, its powers were limited to serving as a rubber-stamp ratifier of decisions already taken by the executive branch. Its directing body, the Standing Committee, possessed considerable authority, however. It directed the work of the Assembly and was also empowered to oversee the operations of the prime minister and the Government Council, the DRV equivalent of a cabinet. The new constitution also established a People's Procurate, which oversaw the execution of government and party directives and broadened and strengthened the role of the judicial system and the Supreme Court.

Below the central government, the regime put in place a new administrative structure at all levels down to the basic unit, the rural village. During the Franco-Vietminh conflict, the regime had dispensed with a formal structure of local government. Regional territorial divisions above the level of province had been created to facilitate military operations against the French, with local authority placed in the hands of so-called Committees of Resistance and Administration (CRAs), composed of civilian and military cadres attached to the local chapter of the Vietminh Front. After the return of the government to Hanoi in October 1954, the large regional territorial divisions were abolished, leaving only two levels between the rural village and the central government—the province (*tinh*) and the district (*huyen*). At each level, the CRAs were replaced by elected executive and legislative bodies patterned after the structure at the top. At the village level, local people's councils (*hoi dong nhan dan*) were elected to serve as the supreme legislative body at that level; they in turn would elect from among their members an administrative committee (*uy ban hanh chinh*) to handle executive decisions between sessions of the people's council.

The DRV was a unitary state, and all state laws were operable in every territorial unit throughout the country. To guarantee local conformity with central regulations, all decisions reached by local administrative committees and people's councils could be vetoed by the higher echelons. The only departure from administrative uniformity was in the case of the autonomous zones established in ethnic minority areas in the mountains north and northwest of the Red River delta. In these zones, only members of the local ethnic community were permitted to serve as government officials, and the regime also made a number of concessions in terms of social and economic policies to the "backward" character of the local population.[18]

The 1959 constitution was promulgated at a time when the role of the VWP as the vanguard organization leading the Vietnamese revolution to socialism had been reestablished and when the influence of the Chinese approach was still firmly in evidence throughout the country. But the treatment of the role of the party in the 1959 constitution made it clear that Vietnamese leaders realized that conditions in Vietnam required special treatment. Although the preamble mentioned the "clear-sighted leadership" of the VWP, it made no mention of a dictatorship of the proletariat, stating simply that the DRV was "a people's democratic state based on the alliance between the workers and peasants and led by the working class."[19]

The Role of the Party

Since its formation in 1930, the Indochinese Communist party (and its later reincarnations) has viewed itself as the leading force in the Vietnamese revolution. At times, as was the case during the 1930s and in North Vietnam after 1954, this vanguard role has been openly proclaimed. At others, as during the Franco-Vietminh conflict and in the South after the Geneva Conference, it was carefully disguised in order to maximize support for the revolutionary movement among the population. But, as in all Marxist-Leninist societies, the role of the party in guiding Vietnamese society through various stages to the final realization of communism was a key tenet that could under no circumstances be discarded.

This does not mean that the party was the sole political organization in the DRV. As in China and Eastern Europe, the regime continued to permit the existence of small noncommunist parties as a testimony to the multiclass "people's" character of the Vietnamese revolution. But power in Hanoi clearly resided in the VWP and its core leadership. The party was not only the representative of the leading social class, the proletariat; even more important, it was the guardian of the purity of Marxist-Leninist doctrine, the guiding ideology of the state, the vehicle of social and political change, and the central force of the revolution.

A key component in the party's ability to retain its dominant political role within the state lay in its capacity to maintain inner cohesion and centralization of purpose and authority. The means of achieving such unity resided in the Leninist concept of democratic centralism, according to which the party makes decisions through a free discussion among the membership while enforcing absolute obedience throughout all echelons of the party once a final decision is made. As described in a party directive cited by Douglas Pike, decisions were made at "committee meetings by majority vote and individual Party members must then obey. The minority obeys the decision of the majority. The lower echelons obey the decisions of the upper echelons. All elements obey the Central Committee ... one shout and a thousand echoes."[20]

In effect, the Leninist principle of democratic centralism attempts to create a well-disciplined and cohesive party highly responsive to policy direction from the leadership. Party discipline is rigorously enforced; party members, and the apparatus as a whole, can retreat quickly into clandestinity when the necessity arises. Party organization is designed to maximize centralized authority and efficiency. In theory, the supreme body of all communist parties is the national congress, with its members selected by party organizations at all echelons.

In the DRV, congresses were scheduled to take place every five years, but in practice they were convened on an ad hoc basis to ratify decisions of vital importance already reached by the Politburo and the Central Committee. The Central Committee of the DRV (*Uy Ban Chap Hanh Trung Uong*) is a smaller executive organization elected by the National Congress from among its members to initiate and execute party policy during the long intervals between congresses. In early years, when the party was small and found it difficult to operate because of French repression, the Central Committee was often composed of fewer than ten members and was the de facto decision-making body within the party. As the party grew larger, however, the Central Committee itself grew progressively larger and more unwieldy, and in 1951 a smaller Politburo (*Bo Chinh Tri*) on the Soviet model was created to enable senior party leaders to handle day-to-day issues between plenary sessions of the Central Committee.

During the life of the DRV, the Politburo, composed of an average of about ten members, reportedly met about once per week.

The direction of the party, then, was in the hands of a small number of top leaders concentrated in the Politburo. Until after the end of the Vietnam War, the composition of that leadership was remarkably stable. Indeed, over the years, few communist parties were as successful in maintaining unity under conditions of high tension as the Vietnamese. The first generation of party leadership, most of them a product of the post-World War I nationalist movement, was almost entirely wiped out by French repression during the 1930s. Ho Chi Minh was one of the few to survive. In the years immediately preceding World War II, however, a number of younger party members, including Truong Chinh, Pham Van Dong, Vo Nguyen Giap, Le Duan, Nguyen Chi Thanh, Le Duc Tho, and Pham Hung, rose rapidly within the ranks of the organization and helped Ho Chi Minh to create the Vietminh Front and plan revolutionary strategy for the postwar era. With a few key additions in the postwar years, this inner group retained control over the party until Ho's death in September 1969. Under Ho's successor Le Duan, it led the party to final victory in the South in 1975 and formulated policy in the postwar era until the death of Le Duan and the retirement of several other veteran leaders in the 1980s.

One of the striking facts about the leadership of the party in the DRV was how few of the pre-World War II generation of leaders were ever purged or fell into disgrace. Truong Chinh, who had become general secretary in 1941 after the death of Nguyen Van Cu, was removed from his post in 1956 as a result of mistakes committed during the land reform program. Yet he retained his position in the Politburo and was eventually elected to the influential governmental post of chairman of the Standing Committee of the National Assembly. After Truong Chinh's dismissal, the position of general secretary was temporarily filled by President Ho Chi Minh himself, but in 1960 a rising new star, Le Duan, was elected to the position at the Third Party Congress, probably because of his experience as a senior party leader in the South. During the remainder of the war, there were virtually no changes in the composition of the party leadership at the Politburo level.

This is not to say that there was no controversy among senior party members over domestic or foreign policy or the strategy to be followed in the South. Indeed, internal party sources make it clear that virtually every major decision reached during a generation of conflict against the French and the United States was accompanied by vigorous debate and sometimes by serious disagreements within the Central Committee and the Politburo. During the Vietnam War, it was widely rumored that there were recognizable pro-Peking and pro-Moscow factions within the party leadership. Recent evidence suggests that although some elements within the party and the government bureaucracy tended from time to time to lean toward China or the Soviet Union on specific policy issues, there were no clear-cut factions within the Politburo taking sides in the Sino-Soviet dispute. The Hanoi regime often found it convenient to favor Moscow or Peking according to the needs of the moment, but for most if not all party leaders, dedication to the cause of Vietnamese unification and survival took precedence over loyalty to China or the U.S.S.R.

To the degree that factions did exist, then, they probably reflected differences over revolutionary strategy, the pace of socialist transformation in the DRV, or the degree of priority to be assigned to domestic concerns versus the revolutionary struggle in the South. A number of party and government officials, for example, were dismissed from their positions during the mid-1960s because of their alleged support for Khrushchev's policy of peaceful coexistence at a time when the regime, at Le Duan's urging, had decided to escalate the level of armed struggle in South Vietnam. Internal purges, however, did not take place within the Politburo. Although policy differences and animosities did exist (among knowledgeable Vietnamese, for example, it was common knowledge that Le Duan and Vo Nguyen Giap were often at odds on war strategy), in general the inner sanctum of veteran party leaders was able to maintain a solid front against external challenges until the end of the Vietnam War. Sources in Hanoi identify this ability as a testimony to the concept of collective leadership promoted by Ho Chi Minh himself throughout his lifetime. Among political scientists abroad, it has often been described as the "consensus model," as opposed to the "factional model" proposed earlier.[21]

The party's dominant role in Vietnamese society was out of proportion to its size. With a membership of a little more than 1,000 at the opening of World War II, the ICP boasted about 5,000 members at the time of its seizure of power in the August Revolution. During the Franco-Vietminh conflict it grew rapidly, and by the Second National Congress in 1951 it numbered a reported 500,000 members. Growth brought problems, however, as a number of unqualified and opportunistic elements reportedly entered the organization during its years of rapid expansion. With the assistance of Chinese cadres brought in to transform the organization along Maoist lines, members viewed as unreliable or lacking in revolutionary consciousness were removed from the party.

In 1956, recruiting slowly resumed. Recruitment was undertaken primarily through youth organizations directed by the party, such as the Party Labor Youth Group and the Young Pioneers. During the mid-1950s, when recruitment virtually ceased during the rectification campaign, few youths entered the party, and by the Third Congress in 1960 only about 10 percent of party members were under the age of 26. Vigorous efforts were made to lower the average age of party members, and by the late 1960s more than three-quarters of all members were under the age of 30.

Similar efforts were made to increase the number of women and workers in the party. The percentage of female party members increased from slightly more than 9 percent in 1960 to about 20 percent five years later. Similar increases took place in the percentage of workers and poor peasants in the party, although workers were still a clear minority, and the upper levels of the organization were dominated by members of middle-class origin. As we have seen, during the early years most recruits were intellectuals from petit bourgeois or landed gentry families. Active recruitment of workers during the 1930s, and of peasants after the formation of the Vietminh Front in 1941, gradually changed the class balance of the organization. However, the recruitment of workers was persistently hindered by the small size of the working class in Vietnam, as well as by the fact that, during both the Franco-Vietminh conflict and the later revolutionary struggle in South Vietnam, most workers lived in urban areas occupied by the enemy. As the Third Party Congress convened in 1960, the party was still primarily rural or petit bourgeois in origin, with workers only accounting for an estimated 5 percent of total party membership. The lack of worker representation was particularly noticeable at top levels, where urban intellectuals have been dominant since the early years of the organization.

The Mass Associations

Because of the small size of the VWP in relation to the population as a whole, the relationship between the party and the masses was a crucial one and a determining factor in the party's ability to mobilize popular support for its goals. In North Vietnam, the key link between party and the people was the so-called mass association. Mass associations are organizations grouping individuals by sex, religion, or occupational function, what in a Western society might be termed interest groups or pressure groups. The concept of the mass association goes back to Lenin, who viewed the formation of such organizations as a means of mobilizing various elements of the population to help a communist party to achieve its goals. The first such organizations appeared in Vietnam at the time of the formation of the ICP in 1930. Comintern directives had instructed the Revolutionary Youth League to organize support groups among workers, peasants, youth, and so on, and formal organizations to that effect were created at the emergence of the party in 1930. But the development of the mass association as a key element in party strategy really dates from 1941, when party leaders decided to form what were called national salvation associations (*cuu quoc hoi*) among workers, peasants, students, women,

Ho Chi Minh at Third Party Congress in 1960. (Courtesy *Veitnam Pictoral.*)

and even intellectuals and artists, to provide a recruiting base for the Vietminh Front. The associations were arranged on a vertical basis, with
branches at the local level linked to higher echelons up to a central organization. At all levels, the associations were linked to the front organization
dominated behind the scenes by the party.

During the Franco-Vietminh conflict and the later war in the South,
the mass associations played a significant role in winning mass support
for the revolutionary movement. Thousands of Vietnamese were involved in the Vietminh Front and its successors in the North (the Fatherland Front) and the South (the NLF) through the mass associations without being active members of the party or, in many cases, even being aware
of the party's guiding role within the movement. Organizations representing functional interests, as well as religious groups representing Buddhists, Catholics, and even the sects, gave the party the capacity to recruit
actively at the riceroots level of Vietnamese society. In times of peace, the
mass associations provided the party with a means of mobilizing the
masses in support of its political and social goals and a means of permitting the various elements in the populace to express their aspirations
within the system. In Maoist parlance, the mass associations were a key
component in the concept of the "mass line" (from the masses, to the masses), by which the party represented the interests of the population and
mobilized it in support of party policies.[22]

The Armed Forces

Because of the violent and protracted character of the Vietnamese revolution, the military consistently played a crucial role on both sides of the conflict. The Vietnamese National Army (VNA), formed by the French during the conflict with the Vietminh, was a significant actor in politics during the Bao Dai regime. After the division of the country at Geneva in 1954, the ARVN became a major force in Saigon politics. Senior military officers were directly responsible for the overthrow of the Diem regime in 1963, and from that time until the end of the war in 1975, military figures such as Nguyen Van Thieu, Nguyen Cao Ky, Nguyen Khanh, and Duong Van Minh dominated the South Vietnamese political scene, sometimes under the veneer of a civilian elected government. In the RVN, where a cohesive political movement based on resistance to communism never really materialized, after the fall of Ngo Dinh Diem in 1963 the armed forces served as virtually the only organized and certainly the dominant force in Saigon politics.

On the surface, the military did not have equivalent influence within the DRV. Since the formation of the first armed propaganda brigades in December 1944, the Communists had followed the familiar Maoist maxim that the party controls the gun. Within the party, as within the government itself, the armed forces were firmly subordinated to civilian authority. Throughout a generation of struggle, first against the French and later against the United States, the armed forces of the DRV appeared totally loyal to the party leadership, which exercised its authority through the Central Military Conference, a body placed under the direction of the party Central Committee. Government direction over the military was carried out through the National Defense Council, chaired by the president.

This does not mean that the military lacked influence within the party. With the adoption of the strategy of people's war after the outbreak of the Franco-Vietminh conflict in December 1946, party leaders were perfectly aware that armed struggle would be a key element in their drive for victory, and throughout the remainder of the war military needs were consistently given high priority. A number of the top figures in the party were career military officers, and presumably represented the interests of the armed forces at party meetings. The most prominent undoubtedly was Vo Nguyen Giap, the commander of the first armed propaganda units upon their formation in 1944 and later minister of defense of the DRV. Later, General Giap's influence within the Politburo waned and he was replaced as the party's chief military strategist by General Nguyen Chi Thanh, commander of Communist forces in the South from 1964 until his death in 1967. Other career military officers within the party leadership were the minority generals Chu Van Tan and Le Quang Ba as well as Van Tien Dung, commander of the final offensive against the Saigon government in 1975 and later minister of defense of the Socialist Republic of Vietnam (SRV).

On the one hand, although prominent military figures undoubtedly played a major role in decision making (and several served in the top councils of the party), there is no evidence that there was a coherent military faction within the Central Committee or the Politburo. Nor is there evidence that military officers ever imposed their will on civilian leaders, as had briefly been the case in China after the Great Proletarian Cultural Revolution. Throughout the war, the party's tradition of civilian leadership remained unshaken, and final decisions relating to military strategy were apparently made by civilian figures such as Ho Chi Minh and Le Duan. Indeed, there is persuasive evidence that Le Duan was the chief strategist for the struggle in South Vietnam from the time of his elevation to party first secretary in 1960.

On the other hand, it is clear that the role of the military in North Vietnamese society was much stronger than in most other countries in the region. During the Vietnam War, the DRV became one of the most militarized societies in Asia. Military conscription took most young males of draft age. Vietnamese women, and those males who for whatever reason were not in the armed forces, were mobilized to serve in the artillery, in bomb-defusing units or, in the countryside, to join self-defense militia units to defend their villages against saboteurs or possible attacks by the enemy in the South. At the same time, military units stationed in the North were assigned duties in economic construction, such as planting and harvesting, or repairing bomb damage to bridges and roads. As the slogans of the day confirmed, North Vietnam was a totally mobilized society—"All for the front lines" and "every citizen a soldier."

UNIFICATION

The entrance of North Vietnamese forces into the city of Saigon in the spring of 1975 brought to a close a generation of civil war and introduced the sweet smell of victory to Hanoi. For Communist leaders, however, success brought new challenges. How quickly should the South be integrated with the North? Should an additional period of separate existence be contemplated, as the program of the NLF had promised and as a means of reassuring southerners that their own aspirations for freedom and regional autonomy would not be crushed under the heels of hard-bitten cadres sent down from the North? Or should political assimilation be brought about rapidly on the assumption that a prolonged separation between the two zones would only exacerbate the delicate problems that the future united Vietnam would inevitably encounter?

For a brief period after the fall of Saigon, party leaders appeared to hesitate over such questions. By the midsummer of 1975, however, Hanoi decided to move expeditiously toward unification. In November, a joint meeting of northern and southern leaders held in Saigon (now renamed Ho Chi Minh City) reached agreement to bring about political and administrative unification during the following year. Elections for a joint National Assembly composed of 492 members from both North and South, slightly less than half of whose deputies represented the population in the southern provinces, were held in April 1976. The People's Revolutionary party (PRP), which had served as the southern branch of theVWP during the war, was abolished and its members integrated into a new nationwide Vietnamese Communist party (VCP), which replaced the VWP at its Fourth National Congress, held in December 1976. The NLF was also dissolved, and its local organizations in the South were absorbed into the Fatherland Front, which had replaced the Vietminh Front as the nationwide front organization in the country in 1955. Finally, in early July 1976, the unified Socialist Republic of Vietnam was established with its capital in Hanoi.

The decision to advance expeditiously toward reunification, a decision that clearly departed from Hanoi's announced intentions during the war, was laden with risks. It could undermine the fragile situation in the South, where many viewed the new revolutionary regime with a wary eye. Moreover, southern members of the liberation movement, who had anticipated playing an active role during a period of regional autonomy after the end of the war, would undoubtedly be outraged at the flagrant disregard of the program adopted by the NLF and the rapid absorption of the southern provinces into the DRV. It could also have serious ramifications abroad, where leaders of many nations in Asia and elsewhere would interpret such a move as confirmation of their worst fears about Hanoi's expansionistic designs throughout the region. Why then had party leaders decided to take such a risk?

In fact, they probably felt that they had little choice. The violence of the Vietnam War had seriously depleted the stock of experienced and dedicated cadres in the South. Replacements would have to be brought down from the North to handle the complex problems of postwar reconstruction and the consolidation of revolutionary authority. The economy, now in a perilous state throughout both zones because of war damage, the flight of farmers to the cities, and the drying up of foreign aid, would have to be nurtured gradually back to health. In the view of many senior party leaders in Hanoi, this could more easily be realized if administrative unity had already been achieved. Finally, a prolonged period of continued separation could encourage potential dissident elements in the South to enhance their own efforts to oppose the eventual transformation of southern provinces into an integral part of a future socialist Vietnam. In sum, the longer the delay in unification, the more potential obstacles could be expected to arise to hinder the realization of the long-term political, social, and economic objectives of the regime. As a final rationalization, Le Duan and his colleagues must have convinced themselves that the sudden end to the war and the flight abroad of thousands of supporters of the Saigon regime in the baggage of the Americans had reduced the potential for active resistance and would ease the transition period to a new socialist era in South Vietnam.

In the months following the end of the war, South Vietnam was steadily integrated with the North. With the aid of northern cadres and units of the PAVN, a new revolutionary administration was established at all levels in the South. A comprehensive survey of the population was carried out, and those considered potentially hostile to the regime (such as military officers, government officials, high-level employees of foreign firms, and so on), were instructed to report to newly established reeducation camps for indoctrination. Some were retained for only a few weeks and then permitted to return to society. Others were dispatched to work camps for extended periods of incarceration. There was no visible evidence of the "bloodbath" feared and predicted by Hanoi's enemies, but according to foreign estimates, several hundred thousand prisoners remained in the camps a number of years after the end of the war. There also were reports that thousands had died of maltreatment or execution by the authorities, an estimate that was vigorously denied by authorities.[23]

There was relatively little open resistance in the South to the new administration. A few hostile elements fled to the hills and attempted to continue the struggle. Some members of the NLF resented the takeover of the administration by northerners and complained that their services to the revolution had not been recognized. In general, however, the population appeared to acquiesce in the new situation, if not with enthusiasm, then with curiosity or resignation. One obvious factor in the regime's ability to bring about compliance with its policies was a suffocating security system that spread from state security services in Hanoi to sector committees in urban neighborhoods and rural villages that kept a sharp eye out for any indication of hostility to the revolution. Despite such efforts to bring about an ideological conversion among the population of the South, many foreign visitors reported that the population in Saigon appeared to adjust rapidly to the presence of northern cadres in the streets and sometimes even to ignore them. Hanoi would find that it would not be easy to change the profligate and corrupt ways of its new charge.[24]

Indeed, the problems of peace soon began to pose new obstacles to the party's plans. Attempts to impose government control over minority areas in the Central Highlands reportedly caused discontent among mountain peoples and led to the re-creation of FULRO, a dissident movement that had caused the Saigon regime difficulties in the 1960s. Opposition activities also erupted among Buddhists and Catholics and in areas inhabited primarily by members of the Hoa Hao and Cao Dai sects; there were even rumors of the creation of a national resistance front of diverse antiregime groups somewhere in the Mekong delta. Although such groups did not pose a serious threat to the survival of the revolutionary order in South Vietnam, they were a disquieting sign of growing opposition to Hanoi's policies.

One of the factors provoking resentment to the new administration within the southern population was the behavior of representatives of the new revolutionary regime. For a generation, the party had been the driving, pulsing heart of the struggle for national independence and reunification. The willingness of its members to dedicate their lives to the cause had been a crucial factor in its success. By the late 1960s, however, there were visible signs of strain in the almost legendary inner strength and self-discipline of the organization. Weariness at the seemingly endless war affected northerners and southerners alike. Press reports of arrogance, laziness, and corruption among party members in the DRV had become increasingly frequent. Internal documents show that similar problems were plaguing cadres in the South. In 1974, the party called for a new rectification campaign to cleanse the organization of its internal impurities.

Victory only added to the problem. In order to cope with the dearth of reliable cadres in the southern provinces, party leaders felt compelled to introduce northerners into the new revolutionary administration. Many had been accustomed to the personal privations and the puritanical lifestyle in the DRV and were seduced by the relatively affluent and hedonistic conditions in the South. Others, accustomed to the "guerrilla mentality" of life in the bush, found it difficult to develop bureaucratic skills and an effective manner of dealing with the masses. Articles in the official press cited cases of flagrant official corruption, arrogance, incompetence, and favoritism. The problem reached crisis proportions in 1978, when stringent new economic policies nationalized businesses, confiscated property, and led thousands of Vietnamese, many of them of Chinese descent, to attempt to flee the country. Some charged that local officials were accepting bribes of up to $3,000 to $4,000 to grant exit permits and arrange for transport by junk or freighter to other countries in Southeast Asia. It was even claimed that senior leaders were officially involved in the traffic and were deliberately attempting to fleece the affluent *Hoa* population of their savings before permitting them to leave the country. Hanoi vehemently denied the latter charge, but conceded that many officials had accepted bribes from those desiring to leave Vietnam.

By the late 1970s, party leaders had become convinced that a thorough cleansing of the party membership was required to purge the organization of its impure elements. Le Duc Tho, chairman of the party's Organization Department, charged that many party members were guilty of serious errors such as corruption, favoritism, or oppression of the masses. During succeeding months, the party began to issue new membership cards. Only those who received cards would continue to be members. There were rumors that up to two-thirds of current members, now numbering well over 1.5 million, might be purged. At the Fifth Congress of the VCP held in April 1982, however, it was announced that only 86,000 members had been expelled. In the meantime, a recruitment program to bring new blood into the organization was initiated. According to one report, 90 percent of the 370,000 new members were under 30 years of age; 70 percent had served in the armed forces. Clearly, the leadership had encountered difficulties in weeding out impure elements and was hoping that the younger generation, who had formed the foot soldiers of the revolution in its early stages, would now help to build a new socialist Vietnam. Yet there was still a serious imbalance between the role of the party in the North and the South. While an estimated 3 percent of all Vietnamese were members of the VCP in the late 1980s, the figure was less than 1 percent in the southern provinces and over 6 percent in North Vietnam.[25]

Troubles within the ranks of the party did not leave the senior levels unscathed. For a generation, the party leadership had maintained its internal unity in the face of the intimidating problems of insurgency and war. But with the restoration of peace, latent disagreements over key issues in foreign and domestic policy emerged. At the Fourth Party Congress in December 1976, several members of the party, including the veteran Politburo member Hoang Van Hoan, were deprived of their posts. At the time, reports circulated that Hoan, a member of the party since its founding and a one-time ambassador to the PRC, may have stepped down because of age. But it later became clear that the move was related to growing tensions in Sino-Vietnamese relations. In the summer of 1979, while traveling to East Berlin ostensibly for medical reasons, Hoang Van Hoan defected to China. On arrival in Peking, he charged that VCP General Secretary Le Duan had established a party dictatorship and was ruthlessly suppressing all forms of dissent within the organization.

A second major problem facing the party was the advanced age of its veteran leadership. Here the impressive stability that had characterized the wartime period now turned into a disadvantage. Virtually all Politburo members were in their late sixties or older, and by 1981 the average

age of the twelve most senior members of the organization was over 70. Top party officials had been aware of the need to introduce younger figures into responsible positions but, as in China and the U.S.S.R., generational change at the senior level was always complicated by the fears of veteran leaders that younger colleagues lacked the toughness and conviction to carry out the sacred duties of the revolution. At the Fifth Party Congress in 1982, several party veterans, including Vo Nguyen Giap and Foreign Minister Nguyen Duy Trinh, were dropped from the Politburo and replaced by younger men. But key figures such as General Secretary Le Duan, Le Duc Tho, Pham Van Dong, and Truong Chinh retained their posts, a clear signal that senior officials felt that continuity at the top was vital in such difficult times.

In the meantime, a new constitution for the SRV was ratified by the National Assembly in December 1980. The new charter, which was designed to carry Vietnamese society into a period of socialist industrialization in coming decades, introduced a number of changes into the administrative structure of the state. A new collective body called the Council of State (similar to the Presidium in the U.S.S.R.) replaced the position of the president as chief of state. The office of the presidency had been a problem in Hanoi since the death of Ho Chi Minh in 1969. Ho had been succeeded in the office by his vice president, the aging labor organizer Ton Duc Thang. But because of Thang's age and relatively limited influence in party ranks, the position had declined to one of mere ceremonial importance. Thang died in March 1980 and was briefly replaced by Nguyen Huu Tho, the one-time chairman of the NLF in South Vietnam. With Ho Chi Minh gone and no comparable figure having arisen in his place, the position of ceremonial president was viewed as an anomaly.

The 1980 constitution empowered the new Council of State to "decide on important matters concerning the building of Socialism and National Defense" and to "supervise the implementation of the laws, decrees, and resolutions" of the SRV. The size of the council was to be determined by the National Assembly. In the early summer of 1981, it was announced that party veteran Truong Chinh had been named chairman of the Council of State and thus the de facto head of state. By its choice the SRV indicated that it did not intend to follow the practice in the U.S.S.R., where party chief Leonid Brezhnev was simultaneously chairman of the Presidium. Instead it would continue the policy of collective leadership to avoid the concentration in one person's hands of power over both the party and the state, a tradition that had first been established during the life of Ho Chi Minh.

Still, the new constitution betrayed the determination of veteran leaders to maintain the party's traditional position of total dominance over the affairs of the Vietnamese people. The concept of the proletarian dictatorship and the leading role of the VCP in leading the Vietnamese people to socialism was for the first time "solemnly acknowledged." The party, declared Article 4 of the new charter, was "the only force leading the state and society, and the main factor determining all successes of the Vietnamese revolution."[26]

During the first decade after the fall of Saigon, then, the party continued to be guided by the first generation of leaders who had entered the organization in the early years of its existence and, under the leadership of the party's founder Ho Chi Minh, had led the movement to victory in the war against the French and then the United States. The effects of that continuity in leadership had serious ramifications that rippled through Vietnamese society. Although the members of the wartime generation were undoubtedly motivated by strong patriotic convictions, they were also Leninists, and thus true believers in the validity of the Leninist approach to building a socialist society. That attitude had been in evidence after the fall of Saigon in 1975, when the party opted to move rapidly toward integrating the southern provinces into the socialist North. It was demonstrated again at the Fourth Party Congress in December 1976, when a decision was reached to move rapidly to complete the dismantling of the capitalist sector in the South and bring about the creation of a fully socialist society throughout the country.

The first cracks in the facade appeared at the end of the 1970s, when economic problems forced the party leadership to announce a number of reforms to stimlulate increased productivity in the national economy. Incentives were provided to farmers to increase food production; other measures led to a decentralization of the planning process and the emergence of a small private industrial and commercial sector. The reforms were interpreted by some observers as a victory for pragmatic over ideologically conservative elements within the Politburo, but as time passed it became evident that many senior leaders were reluctant to abandon plans to bring about a rapid transformation of the South into a fully socialist society. General Secretary Le Duan, now in poor health, reportedly brought about a compromise in an effort to maintain a fragile balance between reformists and conservatives within the party leadership. The continuing influence of the latter, however, was demonstrated at the Fifth Congress, when the party's senior representative in the southern provinces, Nguyen Van Linh, was dropped from the Politburo, allegedly because of his overly permissive attitude toward private economic activities in Ho Chi Minh City.[27]

During the first half of the 1980s, then, the party leadership attempted to avoid a bruising internal struggle by maintaining a delicate balance between the demands of ideology and pragmatism. But economic stagnation persisted, and grumbling from within the ranks and among the population at large that the "old men at the top" seemed unable to keep abreast of changing needs intensified. In 1981, the noted Vietnamese historian Nguyen Khac Vien voiced the frustrations of many Vietnamese when he charged in a public letter that the Fatherland Front—the system's vaunted link between the party and the masses—had become nothing but a facade. The party, he complained, intervened in all aspects of national affairs and seemed oblivious to the needs of the Vietnamese people.[28]

By the spring of 1986, there were widespread rumors that major changes in the leadership would take place at the party's Sixth National Congress, scheduled (after a number of postponements) to be convened at the end of the year. Le Duan himself was reportedly ill, and many hoped that his retirement would clear the way for further changes in policy and personnel. But his sudden death during the Tenth Plenum in the early summer of 1986 did not have any immediate effect on either issue, suggesting that the crux of the problem was not Le Duan, but fundamental policy differences within the leadership. A few days after Le Duan's death, Chief of State Truong Chinh, the second-ranking member of the Politburo, was elected the new general secretary. Some observers speculated that the appointment of Truong Chinh, now almost eighty years of age, was an indication that conservatives had defeated reformist elements within the party leadership. During the next several months, however, the old party veteran began himself to move toward the center, conceding— however cautiously—the regime's past shortcomings and the need for wide-ranging reforms in the near future.[29]

Despite his advanced age, Truong Chinh apparently wished to seek reelection as general secretary at the upcoming party congress and, according to sources in Moscow, reportedly had the support of the new leadership under Mikhail Gorbachëv in the Soviet Union. But resistance to his candidacy, sparked in part by the circulation of a draft political report to the upcoming congress that placed more attention on the past achievements of the regime than on its shortcomings, was strong among reformist elements within the VCP. As the date for convening the congress approached, a bitter struggle took place within the Politburo over the selection of a new leadership and, by extension, over the future direction of the Vietnamese revolution.[30]

RENOVATION

The Sixth National Congress of the VCP, held in mid-December 1986, is generally considered to mark a watershed in the history of the party and of modern Vietnam. It formally inaugurated a program of *doi moi* (renovation) to extend the reforms that had first been launched in the 1970s to bring about an end to the period of stagnation and introduce a new era of rapid economic growth. In the political arena, it called for a heightened effort to enable the party to "serve the people" while increasing the role of the masses in the political and economic decision-making process. And it heralded several personnel changes in the party leadership to put those reforms into effect. Most notable was the election of a relative unknown, the one-time chief of party operations in the South, Nguyen Van Linh, as the new general secretary. Several senior party officials were dropped from the Politburo and replaced by younger men.[31]

A retrospective view, however, suggests that the changes announced at the congress were less extensive than they appeared at the time and that the battle for control over the levers of power in the party had not yet come to an end. One clear indication of this fact came from the nature of the personnel changes announced at the congress. In the first place, although Nguyen Van Linh had a deserved reputation as a reformist because of his performance as the senior party representative in the South in the early 1980s, he was nonetheless a member of the veteran leadership that had led the struggle for national liberation since the war against the French and presumably shared many of its assumptions. Moreover, although six members of the wartime generation were dropped from the Politburo at the congress, three—party stalwarts Truong Chinh, Le Duc Tho, and Pham Van Dong—were retained as advisers in a newly created Council of Elders. And though they were no longer voting members of the party's highest decision-making body, by all indications they would continue to take an active part in policy debates, as their counterparts did in a similar position in China. There also were indications that Le Duc Tho, reputedly the most influential figure in the party after Le Duan during the postwar era, apparently continued to exercise a significant degree of influence through the appointment of several of his protégés to the Politburo.

For the moment, the impact of such personnel changes was unclear. Perhaps the most visible immediate legacy of the Sixth Congress was in the area of political reform, where the party set itself the task of strengthening its links with the masses, overcoming the tendency toward bureaucratism and commandism and encouraging critics and the population at large to exercise their creative freedoms. Whether Vietnamese leaders were influenced in this respect by recent events in Moscow, where Mikhail Gorbachëv had just launched his own campaign for *glasnost*, is uncertain. In declaring its determination to cleanse itself of its shortcomings and impurities, of course, the party was on familiar ground. But in stressing the need to reduce the party's dominant role over all aspects of society and to "guarantee the genuine democratic rights of the people" to criticize the performance of the regime it was moving into virtually uncharted territory.[32]

Party leaders attempted to reduce their risks by framing the projected reforms within familiar and acceptable limits. In institutionalizing the slogan "leadership by the Party, mastery by the people, and management by the State," the congress made it clear that, as emphasized in the 1980 constitution, the VCP would play the leading role in guiding the nation toward socialism. Its decisions would continue to be reached by the Leninist process of democratic centralism, and the dictatorship of the proletariat would remain in place throughout the transitional period to the final stage of communism.[33]

Still, during his first few months as general secretary, Nguyen Van Linh made a number of public gestures to encourage a new attitude of openness in Vietnamese society. In an anonymous column (but published over his initials) in the party newspaper *Nhan Dan*, he encouraged his readers to speak out against the shortcomings of the government and the party. Intellectuals in particular were singled out as the conscience of the Vietnamese people. In a speech before the Association of Writers and Artists in October 1987, he conceded that the regime had not always been fair-minded and democratic in its treatment of intellectuals and encouraged them to speak out against injustice, even at the risk of persecution. The government soon followed up his words with actions, announcing early in 1988 that all remaining political prisoners would be released by the end of the year.[34]

The party also made a serious effort to increase popular participation in the governing process and strengthen its own links with the masses. In elections for the National Assembly held in April 1987, the number of candidates, many of them not party members, increased significantly, and debates within the chamber were conducted in a freer and more open manner than in past years. Caucuses of delegates from individual districts and provinces were convened to discuss issues of common concern to their constituents. The role of the non-governmental mass organizations under the umbrella of the Fatherland Front was also strengthened to permit them to play a more active role in the political process. To tighten the links between the party and the people, major decisions under consideration by the party leadership were circulated to party units at the local level and to members of mass organizations for public scrutiny and comment. This was one of the most significant reforms introduced in the period following the Sixth Congress, since it enabled delegates from individual districts and provinces to seek out a coherent position to adopt on measures proposed by the party or the regime.

But the party attempted to establish clear limits to the boundaries of the new freedoms. The Sixth Congress had emphasized that the regime would continue to suppress enemies of the state and the socialist system. While the regime had adopted a more conciliatory attitude toward Catho-

lics and the overseas Chinese, it did not hesitate to crack down on elements considered hostile to the revolution. In a celebrated trial held in
July 1988, five prominent writers were convicted of political crimes and
sentenced to long terms in prison. Some interpreted the move as a signal
to intellectuals not to carry their criticisms of the party and the socialist
system too far. Show trials of dissident members of Buddhist and Catholic
religious organizations were also staged to signal the regime's determination not to let the situation get out of hand.[35]

The regime's continuing reluctance to leap into the unknown was reflected in the continuing influence of convinced Leninists, such as party
veterans Pham Hung, Do Muoi, and Vo Chi Cong, within the Politburo. In
early 1988, Nguyen Van Linh publicly identified himself as a reformist
and complained about the existence of a conservative faction within the
leadership that was opposed to change. In a comment to a Hungarian
journalist in April, however, he voiced his optimism that the momentum
within the leadership was shifting toward the advocates of reform. At
first, his optimism appeared to be justified. When Prime Minister Pham
Hung, who had replaced Pham Van Dong in the office the previous
spring, died in March, he was temporarily replaced by Deputy Prime
Minister Vo Van Kiet, a prominent and outspoken supporter of economic
liberalism. But at the National Assembly session in July, Kiet was in turn
replaced by Do Muoi, a veteran party member with a reputation for ideological conservatism. According to reports, for the first time in the history
of the regime there was a contest for the election, and Kiet received strong
minority support from members of the Assembly.[36]

By the end of 1988, there were stronger signs that the reform movement had lost momentum from the heady days immediately following the
Sixth Party Congress. Even Nguyen Van Linh, dubbed "Hanoi's little
Gorbachëv" by journalists, appeared to have shifted to a more cautious
position. The trend was most visible in the realm of political reform. Comments by official sources indicated a growing level of concern that political unrest could undercut favorable trends in the economy. Undoubtedly
recent events taking place in China, Eastern Europe, and the U.S.S.R. were
a factor in Hanoi's heightened determination to keep the demand for
democratic reforms under control. In March 1989, Nguyen Van Linh
spoke to senior journalists and appealed to them to place an emphasis on
positive as well as "negative phenomena." That same month, in an address to the Sixth Plenum of the Central Committee, he quoted a famous
metaphor by the Chinese leader Teng Hsiao-p'ing, while reaching a quite
different conclusion from his Chinese counterpart. We must uphold our
vigilance, he warned, against negative influences from abroad. "Once the
door is open, not only will the pure and healthy air pour in but dust, flies
and mosquitoes will also follow ... Recently, no sooner after [sic] did we

start opening our door and sending our cadres abroad, than we committed several regrettable mistakes."[37]

Hanoi's reluctance to adopt political reforms that could undermine the authority of the party was undoubtedly confirmed by the T'ien An Men demonstrations in Peking in May and June, as well as the stunning events in Eastern Europe later in the year. In a speech to the Central Committee in August, Nguyen Van Linh reaffirmed the importance of democratic centralism and the dictatorship of the proletariat in the SRV, making it clear that the regime had no intention of following the path of other communist systems in permitting the formation of opposition parties. The speech was particularly harsh in tone, accusing the United States of "very insidious tricks" to undermine communist states in Eastern Europe. He warned his audience that democracy "does not mean that one is free to say what one wants to say, write what one wants to write, do what one wants to do, no matter what the consequences."[38]

The debate within the senior councils of the party over political reform continued, however, and at the Eighth Plenum held in late March 1990 it led to the dismissal from the Politburo of Tran Xuan Bach, a vocal supporter of political liberalization. Official sources insisted that his demotion was not a consequence of the fact that he had recommended a move toward political pluralism, but that he had ignored party discipline by speaking publicly about his views after the decision had been reached. Still, the message was clear. Democratization, Vietnamese-style, was still to be in the form of participation, not choice.[39]

The regime followed up its dismissal of Tran Xuan Bach by cracking down on reformist elements in the South. The object of the attack was the Club of Former Resistance Fighters, an organization established in 1986 by prominent members of the southern revolutionary movement, including the one-time commander of Viet Cong forces in the South, General Tran Van Tra. By the end of the decade, the organization had recruited an estimated 4,000 members. Leaders were vocally critical of the rising level of official corruption and advocated more openness and an independent National Assembly, but insisted that they were loyal to the constitution and committed to the ultimate goal of building a socialist society. In late March, several outspoken club members were forced out of office and replaced by more pliant individuals who could be expected to follow official policy.

At the end of the year, the regime published two draft documents for public comment that set forth the regime's plans for the coming decade. In the political arena, the documents reiterated the importance of political stability as a prerequisite to economic growth. Socialist democracy, they contended, is the Vietnamese way. Every individual must have a right to select his representatives and to take part in the construction of society and the defense of the homeland. The party and the government would solicit the opinions of the people prior to making policy, and the basic freedoms of speech and press were guaranteed. But the state would resist all tendencies toward what was variously called "formal democracy," "extreme democracy," or "bourgeois democracy." The Vietnamese Communist party was the leading force in society, and would lead the people to socialism. But it is also the "sincere servant" of the people, and regularly undergoes inspection by the people.[40]

Criticism of the new program was quick to appear. Bui Tin, deputy editor of *Nhan Dan*, and the noted Vietnamese historian Nguyen Khac Vien, were especially harsh in their judgments. According to Western press reports, the latter labeled the party leadership "totally impotent" and "incapable of following the changing times." Pointing to the official emphasis on the need for political stability, he remarked, "Unless a set of broad-based rules for democracy are drawn up and implemented, the country will never be able to stand alone and compete with its neighboring countries."[41]

Such criticisms, however, did not deter party leaders from their determined course. In his report to the Seventh Party Congress in June 1991, Nguyen Van Linh continued his attack on advocates of political pluralism. While acknowledging the "crisis of socialism" throughout the world, he reiterated that the party would not agree to share power in the SRV, and contended that socialism was "the only right direction" for the country to follow. At the close of the conference it was announced that Linh, long rumored to be in poor health, had been replaced as general secretary of the party by Do Muoi, another of the dwindling core of veterans of the wartime leadership and reputed to be an advocate of ideological orthodoxy in internal matters.

Do Muoi had earned his reputation for ideological conservatism partly on the basis of his performance as the senior party official responsible for carrying out the rapid socialist transformation of the South in the late 1970s. But in his early months as general secretary, he went out of his way to portray himself as an advocate of reform, simultaneously launching a renewed effort to cleanse the party, now numbering slightly over 2 million members, of its corrupt and incompetent elements. As an indication that the party leadership was still attempting to maintain the fragile balance between conservatives and reformists in senior positions within party and government, the reformist Vo Van Kiet was named to replace Do Muoi as prime minister.

The party's now-familiar penchant for cautious change was graphically displayed in the revised state constitution, promulgated in 1992. For years there had been rumors in Hanoi that the 1980 Constitution would be revised to bring it abreast of the changes that had taken place in the SRV since the Sixth Party Congress in 1986. In the summer of 1991 a committee to propose revisions was established under the chairmanship of Vo Chi Cong, an elder statesman of the party and chief of state since the resignation of Truong Chinh in 1987. The final version of the revised charter was passed by the National Assembly early the following year and put formally into effect in April 1992.

The guiding principle of the new state law was rooted firmly in the concept of "economic reform and political stability" that had guided the deliberations of the regime since the Sixth Party Congress and then been adumbrated in the draft strategy presented for public debate in December 1990. Unlike the 1980 constitution, which had described the SRV as a proletarian dictatorship, however, the revised version labeled it "a State of the people, from the people and for the people," thus borrowing the phrase "state of all the people" that had been applied by the Soviet Union in its own constitution passed in 1977. As in the U.S.S.R., "the people" were divided into three classes—the working class, the peasantry, and the intelligentsia—thus signaling that an exploiting class no longer existed in Vietnamese society. The role of the party, however, remained essentially the same. As in the case of its predecessor, the revised constitution described the party as "the force leading the State and society." All party organizations were to operate "within the framework of the Constitution and the law," but the concept of democratic centralism was to be applied as the operating principle for all party and state organizations.

There were a number of changes of more potential significance in regard to the role and responsibility of the National Assembly. The new assembly, now reduced in size to 395 deputies, was given more authority to debate and implement laws as well as to pass those submitted to it by the executive branch, although the wording of the relevant articles was too ambiguous to indicate clearly how this new authority was to be carried out. The new charter also replaced the collective Council of State that had been created by the 1980 constitution with a president, who was to be elected by the National Assembly from among its own members and to serve as head of state to represent the SRV in its formal dealings with foreign countries and to chair the National Defence and the Security Council. Elected to the position was the veteran military commander Le Duc Anh.[42]

It is too soon to judge how much effect the new constitution will have on political behavior in Vietnam. Party leaders are clearly trying to maintain a precarious balance between a policy of tolerance towards responsible criticism and the vigorous suppression of any activity that represents a threat to the rule of the party and its ultimate goal of building a socialist society. The balance is often not an easy one to maintain, and a number of critics have recently been harassed or arrested for being too outspoken in their criticism. One example is the prominent mathematician Phan Dinh Dieu. For two years, the regime took no action in response to Dieu's charges that the VCP had grown too detached from the masses and had thus outlived its usefulness. In 1991 he had circulated a petition containing the charge that the party "had a very great success when it remained a party of patriotism. It failed when it became Communist." But in late 1993, after some especially blunt comments, he was unceremoniously removed as vice chairman of the National Center for Scientific Research.[43]

Another source of political opposition to the regime comes from within the Buddhist movement. For years, many Buddhist monks and lay activists connected with the Unified Buddhist Church, an independent organization of Vietnamese Buddhists, have charged that the government has systematically sought to undermine the organization by restricting its activities, arresting and torturing its members, and establishing a rival state-run organization, the Vietnamese Buddhist Church, to dilute its influence. In May 1993, General Secretary Do Muoi made a ceremonial visit to a Buddhist pagoda to symbolize the regime's desire to mend relations, but a number of highly publicized protest demonstrations, sparked in part by the suicide of a Buddhist under mysterious circumstances in Huê, inflamed tensions between the government and the Buddhist community once again.[44]

THE FATE OF POLITICAL REFORM

Today, nearly two decades after the end of the long Indochina War, Vietnam remains, in political terms, a communist society. In an era when communist systems have collapsed all over the world, most notably in Eastern Europe and the U.S.S.R., the Vietnamese Communist party remains one of the few ruling Marxist-Leninist parties in the world today. Although the party has suffered through the tribulations of a difficult period marked by popular alienation and economic crisis, there are no visible threats to its dominant position within the SRV.

To what factors can the party ascribe its impressive longevity? Certainly one explanation lies in the paternalistic character of the Vietnamese political culture, a characteristic that it shares with many other societies in the region. At a time when autocratic governments have begun to crumble in much of the rest of the world, the tradition of centralized government has survived almost intact throughout most of Southeast and East Asia. Only in the past few years have events in Taiwan, South Korea, and the Philippines suggested that an evolution toward more pluralistic political systems might be taking place, notably (in the case of the first two) as a by-product of growing economic prosperity.[45]

Vietnam certainly is no exception to the general rule. Deeply impregnated with Confucian precepts originally introduced from China, the Vietnamese political culture traditionally idealized benevolent despotism and a hierarchical view of social relationships. Individualism, far from being prized as a desirable characteristic, was decried as an indication of selfish behavior destructive of social order, filial piety, and the needs of the community. The heroic figures of Vietnamese history, from the Trung sisters to Tran Hung Dao, Le Loi, and the Tay Son leader Nguyen Huê, were either strong rulers or patriotic figures who sacrificed their lives for the cause of the Vietnamese national independence. And although the French introduced Western political concepts such as individual liberty and representative democracy to Vietnamese society after their conquest of Indochina in the nineteenth century, such ideas clearly had less emotive power to their Vietnamese subjects than that of the national destiny. Even a libertarian thinker such as Phan Chu Trinh found it advisable to identity democratic freedoms with the cause of national self-realization. The placement of the words in Ho Chi Minh's famous phrase "nothing is more important than independence and freedom" is surely no accident.[46]

An additional factor that may have contributed to the survival of the Communist regime in Vietnam is the party's historically central role in the creation of an independent and unified Vietnam. Like the communist party in China, Vietnamese communism emerged as a popular movement with deep roots among the Vietnamese people and was not imposed from without, as had been the case in a number of Eastern European countries. Its causes—national liberation and social justice—were the people's causes. Over the years, the party was singularly adept at maintaining the vitality of these links with the mass of the population, through the various functional organizations and the incessant use of popular themes linking itself with the great traditions of past heroic ages. Above all, it utilized the personality and reputation of Ho Chi Minh—the beloved "Uncle Ho"—to cement the party's reputation as the legitimate representative of Vietnamese national tradition as well as the leading force in the Vietnamese revolution. It was no mean feat.

After the end of the Vietnam War, the party was able to bank on its formidable reputation, using it as a technique to persuade the Vietnamese people—or at least those living north of the seventeenth parallel—that it was the only organization truly capable of leading the nation to a bright and independent future. And clearly, up to a point, it has succeeded. Even today, many Vietnamese who are vocally critical of the regime's recent performance nevertheless concede that there is no alternative to party rule on the horizon.

Such trust, however, must be constantly reaffirmed, for human memories are short, and belief in the party's capacity to lead has been badly eroded by its recent performance. This is especially the case among the young, for whom the heroic deeds of the past are now nothing but dry lessons taught in history books. To the millions of Vietnamese too young to remember the war, even Ho Chi Minh is just another figure from the past.

An additional challenge for the regime is the fact that the people in the southern provinces—almost one-half the entire population of the country—did not fully share in the revolutionary experience of their compatriots in the North, and some have reason to view the current government as an illegitimate one imposed on them by force of arms. Up until the present, latent discontent in the South, lacking any realistic alternatives, has not erupted into open resistance to the ruling authority. But the history of the Vietnamese revolution provides ample evidence that, given the provocation, popular discontent is only a step from outright revolt.

Vietnam's current leadership can thus not blithely assume that the party's half-century of service to the cause of independence and national unity will exempt it from the obligation to perform effectively as the new century dawns. And it is here that the warnings of the nation's intellectuals are coming through loud and clear. Ideological rigidity, internal corruption, and the monopoly of power have badly corroded the party's ability to perform in the national interest, and it is time for other voices, and other ideas, to play a role in the future of the country.

Can Vietnam manage to make the difficult transition from a proletarian dictatorship to a more pluralistic political system without running the risk of political instability and perhaps civil war? The party's current leadership, citing recent experiences of other communist systems, appears to believe that it cannot, and many thoughtful Vietnamese, however reluctantly, appear to share that assessment. But one of the lessons of the contemporary world is that economic development inevitably brings with it popular pressures for greater individual freedom of expression and political choice. Here indeed is the ultimate paradox, for greater material prosperity, whether or not sustained, is likely to lead to increased contacts with the outside world and inexorably to a rise in popular demands for greater political freedom. Although the current generation of Vietnamese leaders may not have to face that dilemma, the next one undoubtedly will.

NOTES

1. For example, see the article by David Apter entitled "Political Religion in the New Nations," in Clifford Geertz (ed.), *Old Societies and New States: the Quest for Modernity in Asia and Africa* (New York: Free Press, 1963). For a comment by Secretary of State John Foster Dulles that strong executive leadership should have priority over the ultimate goal of political pluralism, see Secretary of State to Em-

bassy in Vietnam, October 6, 1955, in *Foreign Relations of the United States* (1955–57), vol. 1: p. 559.

2. This document is contained in *United States–Vietnam Relations, 1941–1967* (Washington, D.C.: Government Printing Office, 1971), Book 10, III, pp. 1196–1210.

3. Keith W. Taylor, *The Birth of Vietnam* (Berkeley: University of California Press, 1983), pp. 75–76.

4. For a discussion, see Alexander B. Woodside, *Vietnam and the Chinese Model* (Cambridge: Harvard University Press, 1971), pp. 290–292.

5. See Thai Van Kiem, "Nguyen Truong To: patriote et reformiste, poete et homme d'action," in the *Bulletin de la Societe des Etudes Indochinoises*, vol. 47, no. 3 (1972), p. 497. For Nguyen Truong To's ideas for reform, also see Van Tan, "Nguyen Truong To va nhung de nghi cai cach cua ong" (Nguyen Truong To and his reformist ideas), in NCLS (Historical Research), no. 23 (February 1961).

6. Dang Thai Mai, *Van Tho Phan Boi Chau* (Essays and Poems of Phan Boi Chau) (Hanoi: Van Hoa, 1960), pp. 156–157.

7. Phan Chu Trinh, "Quan tri chu nghia va dan tri chu nghia" (Monarchism and Democracy), in NCLS, no. 67 (October 1964).

8. Phan Chu Trinh, "Dao duc va luan ly Dong Tay" (The morality and ethics of East and West), in NCLS, no. 66 (September 1964), pp. 22–31.

9. Huê-Tam Ho Tai, *Radicalism and the Origins of the Vietnamese Revolution* (Cambridge: Harvard University Press, 1992).

10. The decision to adopt a rural strategy in Vietnam was thus not—as is sometimes mistakenly believed—undertaken in imitation of Mao Tse-tung's "people's war" approach in neighboring China. Ho Chi Minh had begun to emphasize the importance of the peasantry in the Asian revolution as early as 1923, and although he undoubtedly made creative use of the experience of the CCP in its struggle against Japan and the government of Chiang Kai-shek, his ideas on strategy were based primarily on conditions inside Indochina. For a discussion of the role of the Comintern in the early development of the ICP, see Huynh Kim Khanh's *Vietnamese Communism, 1925–1945* (Ithaca: Cornell University Press, 1981), and William J. Duiker, *The Communist Road to Power in Vietnam* (Boulder: Westview Press, 1981).

11. Perceptive U.S. officials were well aware of these shortcomings, but were unable to come up with an alternative. There is still no definitive biography of Diem or his era. For a biting treatment, now somewhat out of date but still useful, see Robert Scigliano, *South Vietnam: Nation Under Stress* (Boston: Houghton Mifflin, 1963).

12. For a detailed analysis of the 1967 charter of the RVN, see Robert Devereux, "South Vietnam's New Constitutional Structure," in *Asian Survey* (August 1968).

13. The difficulties encountered by the Saigon regime in building an effective political system in the South are chronicled in Allan Goodman's *Politics in War: The Bases of Political Community in South Vietnam* (Cambridge: Harvard University Press, 1973).

14. For indications of his ideas on the future Vietnamese political system, see his early pamphlet entitled *Duong Kach Menh* (The Revolutionary Path) and the po-

litical program adopted under his direction at the founding of the first Vietnamese Communist Party in February 1930. For the quote, see Bernard B. Fall, *Ho Chi Minh on Revolution: Selected Writings, 1920–1966* (New York: Signet, 1967), p. 141.

15. Bernard Fall, *The Vietminh Regime* (Ithaca: Cornell University Southeast Asia Program, 1956), Appendix 1. For a discussion of the concept of the "proletarian nation," see Maurice Meisner, *Li Ta-chao and the Origins of Modern Communism* (Cambridge: Harvard University Press, 1967). This view had been concretely expressed in Ho's early pamphlet, *The Revolutionary Path.*

16. For an excellent discussion of this issue, see George Boudarel's article entitled "l'idéocratie importé au Viet Nam avec le Maoisme," in his *La Bureaucratie au Vietnam* (Paris: l'Harmattan, 1983), pp. 31–107. According to unconfirmed sources, Joseph Stalin had added his own recommendation to Ho Chi Minh to bring his government more in line with accepted Marxist-Leninist practice, and it seems probable that a number of leading figures in the VWP agreed with the 1951 decision to adopt a more sectarian approach. Unfortunately, sources in Hanoi are still reticent about this period.

17. For a recent account of the Chinese role in the suppression of intellectual dissent in the DRV, see Georges Boudarel, *Cent Fleurs Ecloses dans la Nuit du Vietnam: Communisme et dissidence* (Paris: Jacques Bertoin, 1991). The failure of the land reform program is chronicled in Edwin Moise, *Land Reform in China and North Vietnam* (Chapel Hill: University of North Carolina Press, 1983).

18. The classic study of DRV political institutions is still Bernard B. Fall's *The Vietminh Regime*, cited in note 15 above and originally published in French as *Le Vietminh: La République Democratique du Vietnam, 1945–1960* (Paris: Armand Colin, 1960).

19. By comparison, the 1954 constitution in China assigned the "leading role" in governing to the CCP. The term "people's democratic state" appears to have been appropriated from the "people's democracies" established in Eastern Europe after World War II and refers to a state ruled by a communist party but still in an early transitional stage to socialism.

20. Douglas Pike, *History of Vietnamese Communism: 1925–1976* (Stanford: Hoover Institution Press, 1978), p. 136, citing Lao Dong Party Directive 31 CT/TW, June 4, 1957, p. 7.

21. For a discussion of the debate within the social science community over the nature of inner-party relationships, see Gareth Porter, *Vietnam: The Politics of Bureaucratic Centralism* (Ithaca: Cornell University Press, 1993), pp. 115–116. The dismissal of pro-Soviet elements from the VWP took place primarily in 1964, and was a consequence of Moscow's refusal to grant its approval to Hanoi's decision to escalate the level of military struggle in the South. For a comment, see Georges Boudarel, *Cent Fleurs Ecloses*, pp. 257–258.

22. For an inside account of the formation of the NLF and its subordinate mass associations in South Vietnam, see Truong Nhu Tang, *A Vietcong Memoir: An Inside Account of the Vietnam War and its Aftermath* (San Diego: Harcourt Brace Jovanovich, 1985).

23. The most publicized charge of the existence of a bloodbath was that leveled by Karl Jackson and Jacueline Desbarats, both of whom during this time were

at the University of California at Berkeley. For a brief report of their findings, see the article entitled "Peacetime Bloodbath Takes its Toll on Vietnam, Too," in the *Los Angeles Times,* May 1, 1985. Also see *Asiaweek,* June 7, 1985.

24. There are a number of journalistic accounts of the first few months of revolutionary administration in South Vietnam. See, for example, Tiziano Terzani, *Giai Phong! The Fall and Liberation of Saigon* (New York: Ballantine Books, 1976). Two accounts written by exiles hostile to the regime are Nguyen Long (with Harry Kendall), *After Saigon Fell: Daily Life under the Vietnamese Communists* (Berkeley: Institute of East Asian Studies, 1985), and Nguyen Van Canh, *Vietnam under Communism, 1975–1982* (Stanford: Hoover Institution Press, 1983). For an account of the disillusionment of one prominent member of the NLF with the new situation, see Truong Nhu Tang's *Viet Cong Memoir.*

25. See Gareth Porter, *Vietnam: The Politics of Bureaucratic Centralism,* pp. 69–70.

26. The chairman of the drafting committee for the new constitution had been Truong Chinh, long reputed to be one of the most ideological doctrinaire members of the party leadership. For an English-language version of the 1980 Constitution, see William J. Duiker, *Vietnam Since the Fall of Saigon,* second revised edition (Athens: Ohio University Monographs in International Studies, 1989), Appendix. Also see William J. Duiker, "The Constitutional System of the Socialist Republic of Vietnam," in Lawrence W. Beer (ed.), *Constitutional Systems in Late Twentieth Century Asia* (Seattle: University of Washington Press, 1992), pp. 331–359.

27. Evidence that a precarious balance between reformist and conservative elements was maintained at the Fifth Congress is suggested by the elevation of Nguyen Co Thach (an economic pragmatist) and To Huu (an ideologue) to Politburo status (the former as an alternate). For an analysis, see the *Far Eastern Economic Review,* April 2, 1992. (Hereafter cited as FEER.)

28. Nguyen Khac Vien's open letter to the party leadership is translated into French in Georges Boudarel (ed.), *La Bureaucratie au Vietnam,* pp. 115–119.

29. For a discussion, see Lewis Stern, "The Scramble Toward Revitalization," in *Asian Survey,* vol. XXVII, no. 4 (April 1987), p. 490.

30. Rumors over the nature of the succession dispute, of course, were rampant, with most reports pitting conservatives backing Truong Chinh against reformist elements supporting the candidacy of Vo Nguyen Giap. The eventual appointee, Nguyen Van Linh, was viewed as a compromise candidate acceptable to both sides. For a discussion, see the article by Murray Hiebert in FEER, January 31, 1991.

31. For an analysis of the congress by foreign observers, see Lewis Stern, *op. cit.,* Carlyle A. Thayer, "Vietnam's Sixth Party Congress: An Overview," in *Contemporary Southeast Asia* (June 1987), and William J. Duiker, "Vietnam Moves Toward Pragmatism," in *Current History* (April 1987).

32. In public, official sources in Hanoi deny that events in Moscow had had a significant impact on the decisions reached at the Sixth Congress and contend that they were a reflection of conditions inside Vietnam. In private, some concede that the launching of *perestroika* in the Soviet Union had indeed been a factor in encouraging reformist elements in the SRV.

33. *6th National Congress of the Communist Party of Vietnam: Documents* (Hanoi: Foreign Languages Press, 1986), pp. 131, 141.

34. According to news reports, many of the prisoners were released in a bid to bring about better relations with the United States. See the article in the *New York Times*, July 18, 1988. In a playful mood, Nguyen Van Linh once remarked that the initials N.V.L. under the *Nhan Dan* editorials meant "speak and act" (*noi va lam*). Later, when Linh appeared to back away from his promises, cynics suggested that they really meant "speak and cheat" (*noi va lua*).

35. For reports, see the *New York Times*, July 5, 1988, and *Indochina Chronology* (January–March 1988), p. 8.

36. For a report on the debate at the session, see *Foreign Broadcast Information Service, East and Southeast Asia* (hereafter FBIS-EAS), 88-121, June 23, 1988.

37. Teng, in admitting that undesirable elements could take advantage of political reforms to undermine the socialist system, had remarked that the party could use a flyswatter to get rid of them. See Nguyen Van Linh's speech at the closing session of the Sixth Plenum, in FBIS-EAS 89-061, March 31, 1989, p. 68.

38. *New York Times*, September 20, 1989. Also see FBIS-EAS 89-166, August 29, 1989. Apparently the speech was circulated to members of the Politburo for comments prior to the meeting, and only Foreign Minister Nguyen Co Thach objected.

39. FEER, April 12, 1990, p. 13.

40. The Draft Program and Strategy for the 1990s were printed in *Nhan Dan*, December 1 and 3, 1990.

41. Nguyen Khac Vien's comments were reported in the *International Herald Tribune*, March 6, 1991. In the past, Vien had been permitted to voice his criticisms without hindrance from the regime. According to one report, however, his latest outburst caused consternation and led to rumors that he might be arrested. See *Indochina Chronology*, April–June 1991, p. 33.

42. For the above changes, see the *Socialist Republic of Vietnam: Constitution 1992* (Hanoi: Foreign Languages Publishing House, 1992).

43. For an account of his activities that was written prior to his removal from office, see the editorial in FEER, February 11, 1993, p. 66.

44. For an overview, see the article on Do Muoi's temple visit in FEER, May 13, 1993.

45. According to political scientist Lucian Pye, one of the shared characteristics of Asian cultures is their tendency to idealize benevolent and paternalistic leadership. See Lucian W. Pye, *Asian Power and Politics: The Cultural Dimensions of Authority* (Cambridge: Belknap Press of Harvard University Press, 1985), pp. vii–viii.

46. The parallel with the Chinese case is obvious. For a recent discussion of the effect of the authoritarian tradition in contemporary Vietnamese politics, see Gareth Porter, *Vietnam: The Politics of Bureaucratic Centralism*, 1993), esp. p. xiv.

6

The Economy

Like most of its neighbors, Vietnam has been a predominantly agrarian society since its emergence from prehistory more than twenty centuries ago. And for the Vietnamese, agriculture, almost by definition, implies the cultivation of wet rice. Indeed, recent archeological evidence suggests that the Vietnamese may have been one of the first peoples in Asia to master the art of growing rice. As time passed, farmers in the fertile delta of the Red River learned to control the passage of the waters to flood their fields, and by the time of the Chinese conquest in the late second century B.C., the Vietnamese had already become advanced practitioners of irrigated agriculture.

The hydraulic character of Vietnamese civilization has had a profound impact on Vietnamese history. It has sharpened the self-image of the Vietnamese people as rice farmers living in lowland river valleys or along the seacoast of the South China Sea, scorning neighboring populations living in the mountains as barbarians lacking in the rudiments of proper culture. It has shaped the value system of its inhabitants and led them to emphasize the importance of farming in the overall scheme of human activities and to denigrate commerce and manufacturing as subordinate or even vulgar occupations. If the contentions of some scholars are valid, the hydraulic character of Vietnamese civilization even helped to shape the political culture itself, giving rise to a professionally competent but rigid and potentially oppressive bureaucratic system characterized by centralized controls and headed by a despotic monarchy.[1]

Whatever the truth of such speculation, there is no doubt that traditional Vietnam was a classical example of a water-based agrarian society similar in many basic respects to such famous riparian civilizations as China, India, Mesopotamia, and the ancient kingdom of the pharaohs in the Nile River valley. From time immemorial, the wealth—indeed, the very survival—of Vietnamese society was based on agriculture, and well into the twentieth century, the vast majority of the population was engaged for its livelihood in tilling the soil.

This is not to say that the premodern Vietnamese were entirely lacking in manufacturing and commercial skills. Archeological evidence shows that the early Vietnamese were familiar with the arts of woodwork, metalworking, lacquerware, ceramics, and silk weaving and had engaged in regular commercial contacts with their neighbors since the time of the Lac Viet. Under Chinese rule, and especially after the restoration of independence in the tenth century B.C., trade and manufacturing continued to develop. Handicrafts attained a degree of sophistication comparable to that in China and other advanced societies in East Asia. Vietnamese embroidery, ceramics and porcelain, and metalwork were renowned throughout the region. The capital of Thang Long (present-day Hanoi) emerged under the state of Dai Viet as a major commercial and manufacturing center, while the river port of Hoi An (first under Cham, and later under Vietnamese rule) became an important center for trade with other countries in the region and eventually a base for European traders in the sixteenth and seventeenth centuries. Cottage industries began to spring up in villages throughout the lowland areas, and markets developed along the major highways. Salt and iron were exchanged with mountains peoples for forestry products, and ships built in Vietnamese ports plied the South China Sea.[2]

Such developments, however, did not significantly alter the fundamentally agricultural character of Vietnamese society. Unlike neighboring Champa and the archipelagic states to the south, Vietnam did not become a major participant in the commercial network that connected the various states of Southeast Asia and linked them with the major civilizations of India and China beyond the horizon. Nor was it often visited by the Islamic merchants, who visited the region beginning in the twelfth and thirteenth centuries and eventually created a trading network stretching from the Spice Islands in the Indonesian archipelago to the shores of East Africa and the Red Sea. Throughout the precolonial period, manufacturing and commerce were always subordinate in importance to agriculture in Vietnam. As in northern China, merchants were scorned by Confucian elites as corrupt and low-class, and eventually much of the commercial activity in Vietnam was handled by foreign residents, mainly Chinese from the southern coastal provinces of Kuangtung and Fukien, who immigrated in increasing numbers after the fall of the Ming dynasty in the seventeenth century.

CAPITALISM AND COLONIALISM

The arrival of European merchant ships in the sixteenth and seventeenth centuries introduced Vietnam to the spreading world market, but did not immediately have much effect on the nature of Vietnamese soci-

ety. Several European countries set up small trading stations at the capital
of Thang Long and at Faifo (as foreign merchants sometimes called Hoi
An) on the central coast, but Vietnam had few of the tropical products that
had lured adventurers to the islands further south and many merchants
were alienated by the arrogance and corruption of Vietnamese officials as
well as the lack of interest in commercial activities on the part of the imperial court. By the early seventeenth century, most of the European trading
stations were closed, as Western merchants drifted off to seek greater
profits elsewhere.[3]

In the nineteenth century, however, fundamental changes began to
take place in the pattern of European economic activity throughout Asia.
The increasing tempo of the industrial revolution caused Western nations
increasingly to view eastern Asia as a source for industrial raw materials
and a possible consumer market for manufactured goods. The French conquest of Vietnam was directly related to this process. At first, French advocates of colonial expansion in Southeast Asia viewed Vietnam more as a
stepping-stone to the mythical Chinese market than as an area endowed
with economic wealth of its own. Once the conquest was completed, however, colonial interests were not slow to discern that although Vietnam
lacked the economic resources of some other societies in the region, it was
by no means totally bereft of commercial potential. The primary source of
profit was the export of rubber and rice. Rubber, introduced from Brazil
and cultivated on plantations in the *terre rouge* region along the Cambodian frontier, became a major source of export earnings in the early twentieth century. Rice production was stimulated by the opening of the new
lands in the coastal provinces of the lower Mekong delta. Marshlands in
the Plain of Reeds were drained and an irrigation network was constructed, making it possible for the first time to cultivate thousands of
acres of previously unusable land. By the early years of the twentieth century, rice exports had begun to increase and by the late 1920s exceeded
300,000 metric tons annually.

The effects of colonial rule in urban areas were no less lasting. Stimulated by the import of European capital, a commercial and manufacturing
sector began to emerge in several cities during the early twentieth century.
For the most part, the first stages of growth took place primarily in light
industries such as sugar refining, food processing, the assembly of bicy-
cles and small appliances, textiles, and pharmaceuticals. There was also a
relatively unspectacular but steady growth in the output of coal mines
along the rocky coast east and northeast of the port city of Haiphong.
Transport and communications were vastly improved with the construction of the best road and rail network in Southeast Asia.

Defenders of French colonialism pointed to these developments as
evidence that French rule had brought tangible benefits to the peoples of

Indochina. Vietnam had been introduced to the expanding international economic market, and the first seeds of a new capitalist order had been planted. A commercial bourgeoisie and a small but growing industrial proletariat also appeared. But critics retorted that the advantages of these changes for the local population were minimal. Denying the alleged benefits of the *mission civilisatrice,* they pointed out that French policy did not really promote the growth of trade and industry in Vietnam. To the contrary: The aim of the colonial regime was to discourage the local production of goods that might compete with French manufactured goods exported, at low import duties, to the colonies. Such commercial activities as did take place tended to be dominated by Europeans, Indian money lenders, or the ubiquitous overseas Chinese. Even the manufacture of *nuoc mam,* the popular local fermented fish sauce, was monopolized by Chinese interests. According to some estimates, non-Vietnamese dominated up to 90 percent of all trade and manufacturing in the commercial hub of Saigon-Cholon.

Whether French agricultural policies were of overall benefit to the local farming population is also a matter of dispute. The draining of the marshlands in the Mekong delta, the development of a cash crop economy, and the expansion of rice exports were all cited by defenders of the colonial regime as proof that France was fulfilling its obligation to build a modern agricultural sector in Indochina. But others contended that such superficial indications of progress were seriously misleading. The commercialization of agriculture and the draining of the marshes, though undoubtedly helping to expand the amount of land under cultivation, did not raise the rural standard of living. Rapid population growth, combined with rising exports, tended to wipe out gains in rice production, and per capita food consumption may even have declined during the colonial period. Nor did colonial policy lead to the growth of a new class of private landholding farmers. Commercialization led to further land concentration and, in the Mekong delta (where new lands were opened to the highest bidder), to the development of a class of wealthy landlords, many of whom lived not on their farmlands but in Saigon. Land-hungry peasants flocking to the area from more crowded parts of the country were forced to work as tenants or even as landless laborers. Others sought employment in the crowded and unsanitary factories or on the rubber plantations along the Cambodian border, where they worked long hours under abysmal working conditions for paltry wages.[4]

Any balance sheet on the colonial experience in Indochina is bound to reflect the prejudices of the writer. Advocates of modernization theory are likely to view developments during the colonial era as a painful but necessary first stage of the industrialization process. Dependency theorists will retort that colonial policy resulted above all in locking the Vietnamese economy into an inferior relationship with the advanced capitalist nations of the West. In Vietnam, as in many other cases, the truth is somewhere in between. The introduction of Western capitalist technology and practices into Vietnam, as well as the construction of an advanced system of transport and communications throughout the country, undoubtedly represented an important first step in the emergence of a modern balanced economy. Its potential significance for the future transformation of Vietnamese society should not be dismissed out of hand. The human costs, however, were needlessly high. Although the early stages of industrialization are difficult for any country, the situation in Vietnam was especially tragic since the poor suffered for so little, whereas upon independence the country as a whole, despite the inflated claims of the defenders of colonialism, started off in a position too weakened to compete successfully in the international marketplace. The end result of the French colonial experience in Vietnam was not the creation of a society on the verge of rapid economic development, but a classic example of a dual economy, with a small and predominantly foreign commercial sector in the cities surrounded by a mass of untrained and often poverty-stricken peasants in the villages.

THE ECONOMY OF SOUTH VIETNAM

The Geneva Conference of 1954 split Vietnam into two separate zones, each with a distinct economic structure reflecting the competing ideologies in the Cold War. In the North, the DRV began gradually to build a socialist economy; in the South, the regime of Ngo Dinh Diem adopted a modified capitalist model. But the differences between the two zones were defined by economic factors as well. In the South, the new regime in Saigon possessed fertile farmlands, a climate conducive to the cultivation of tropical export products, and a relatively well-trained industrial and commercial elite. The primary challenges for the new government were the lack of a resource and industrial base and the inequality of landholdings in the Mekong delta. Most of the nation's mineral resources—gold, iron, tin, and zinc—were located north of the demilitarized zone. Although the South possessed in Saigon the most vibrant commercial center in the country, its contribution to the national economy during the colonial era had been primarily in the form of agricultural production.

The Diem regime had merely indifferent success in responding to these challenges. Because of its limited resource base, industrial development in the RVN took place primarily in the production of consumer goods. With assistance from the United States and a number of other Western countries, industrial zones were established on the outskirts of

Saigon, in some of the larger cities of the delta, and along the central coast. Sugar refineries, cement works, and plants for the manufacture of textiles, pharmaceuticals, processed foods, and paper products began to appear. At best, however, the country's small manufacturing sector did not meet the needs of the expanding population. Despite efforts by the U.S. government to encourage foreign investment, capital inputs from Western countries were limited, while another potential source of foreign currency— that of tourism—was hindered by growing evidence of political instability in the countryside. As a result, South Vietnam became increasingly dependent upon imports. With exports limited, the balance of payments was highly unfavorable, and the economy was sustained only by rising assistance from the United States.

If South Vietnam had only limited potential for industrial development, the agricultural picture, at least on paper, was more optimistic. With the rich rice lands in the Mekong delta and the rubber plantations along the Cambodian border, more than one-sixth of the total land area of the South was under cultivation. The major problems were low productivity and inequality of land distribution. Under U.S. pressure, the Diem regime inaugurated a land reform program in 1956 that called for the breakup of large landholdings in the delta and the purchase of farmlands at low interest rates by the previous tenants. But implementation was hampered by landlord resistance and loopholes in the law, and after several years of operation only about 10 percent of the eligible tenant families had received any land under the program. In the late 1960s, behind the shield of the massive U.S. military presence, the regime tried again. Nguyen Van Thieu's "land to the tiller" program, financed in good measure by the United States, realized substantial progress in achieving a greater degree of equality in landholdings. Under the program, tenants received title to their lands without charge, while the government provided financial compensation to the previous owners. The program was sufficiently successful that, after the fall of Saigon in 1975, party leaders in Hanoi discovered to their surprise that most of the exploited sharecroppers of the Mekong delta during the Diem era had become prosperous farmers. By then, however, it was too late for the Saigon regime to reap the benefits.[5]

Efforts by the RVN to expand rice production and the export of rice and other agricultural products ran into similar problems. Plagued by low productivity and the disruption caused by the civil insurgency, rice production failed to achieve a satisfactory rate of growth commensurate with the population increase. After 1965, South Vietnam ceased to be a net exporter of rice and for the remainder of the war was compelled to import food. Rubber, the South's other major source of export earnings, encountered similar problems, and as the borderlands became the scene of contention between ARVN and insurgent forces, rubber production declined from 78,000 metric tons in 1961 to only 20,000 metric tons in 1972.

By the late 1960s, the South Vietnamese economy had become almost totally dependent upon U.S. assistance. Imports of consumer goods, encouraged by Washington to prevent galloping inflation in the RVN, were financed in large part by the U.S. Commercial Import Program. Several hundred thousand Vietnamese worked for U.S. agencies in South Vietnam or otherwise serviced the needs of the large foreign community. Food imports from the United States made up for chronic shortages of production in the countryside. An affluent urban middle class thrived amid a swelling urban population of poor workers, beggars, and refugees flooding into refugee camps in the suburbs.

BUILDING SOCIALISM IN THE NORTH

Ho Chi Minh and his colleagues, returning to Hanoi in triumph in the autumn of 1954, faced economic problems that were equally as intimidating. The urban sector, still relatively primitive under French colonial rule, had been badly neglected during the Franco-Vietminh conflict. Much of the nation's technological elite had left Hanoi to serve in the revolutionary armed forces or had emigrated to the South after the Geneva Conference to live under the noncommunist regime in Saigon. In the countryside, agricultural production was hindered by the low level of mechanization and the lack of artificial fertilizer. The per capita production of rice in North Vietnam was one of the lowest in Asia.

In the longer term, of course, the regime's solutions to these problems were the abolition of private property and the building of a communist society. For the immediate future, however, the primary concern of party leaders was to consolidate support for the regime among the mass of the population and put the economy on a reasonably stable footing. Radical policies, such as the nationalization of industry and the collectivization of agriculture, could alienate many Vietnamese who had supported the Vietminh movement in its struggle for independence. For that reason, the economic policies adopted in the years immediately following the Geneva Conference were essentially moderate. Although major utilities, banks, and some of the largest business enterprises were placed under state control, trade and manufacturing were left in private hands, and the middle class was assured that its profits would be guaranteed and its talents utilized by the new order. In order to extend government control over the economy and to make preparations for a future advance to public ownership, the regime did take steps to regulate wages, prices, and the allocation of goods and private entrepreneurs were encouraged to transform their businesses into so-called joint private-state enterprises—an innovation borrowed from China where private firms agreed to accept a measure of government involvement in decisionmaking and ownership in return for state subsidies and easy access to raw materials.

So long as the agricultural sector remained primitive, however, no program to develop the manufacturing sector could hope to succeed. The excess labor in the rural villages—well over 80 percent of the entire population of North Vietnam lived on the farms—would have to be resettled from the countryside into the cities in order to relieve the population pressure in the villages and provide manual labor for the growing industrial sector. To party leaders, the ultimate solution to that problem was collectivization. In the Marxist view, collective ownership in rural areas would permit a more effective use of the land through the consolidation of small farm plots and the introduction of widespread mechanization. In order to win the support of land-hungry peasants, for whom socialist ownership had no inherent attraction, the regime decided to precede collectivization with land reform. Arable lands belonging to wealthy landlords were confiscated and distributed to the poor and landless peasants. Middle and rich peasants (the latter loosely defined as farmers who owned more land than they could cultivate with their own labor) were not generally affected. The objective of the program was political as well as economic. If the economic purpose of land reform was to encourage peasants to increase grain production, the political objective was to destroy the power of conservative elements at the village level and to create a new village leadership made up of formerly poor and landless peasants who would be grateful to the party and loyally carry out its policies.

In some respects, the land reform program was a success. More than 2 million acres (800,000 hectares) of land were distributed; more than 2 million farm families, well over half the total number in the DRV, received at least some land under the program. The historic domination of the landed gentry was broken, and a new village leadership composed of poor and middle peasants emerged. But although the strategic objectives of the program were realized, the tactics applied left a bitter legacy. In some areas, land reform cadres—influenced in many cases by Chinese advisers—had been too zealous in carrying out the program, provoking resistance among reluctant villagers. In other instances, farmers took advantage of the program to avenge themselves by accusing their enemies of counterrevolutionary activities. In some instances, revolutionary cadres drawn from poor peasant backgrounds attacked the families of Vietminh veterans who had just been released from military service after the restoration of peace. It was hardly the politics of inclusion that Ho Chi Minh had earlier promised.

On the one hand, undoubtedly, government directives were sometimes at fault for not instructing local cadres how to carry out the program. On the other hand, it is likely that the harsh tone of the program was deliberate, for key members of the party's senior leadership had become convinced adherents to the violent class-based approach that had been recently applied in China. Each village was expected to classify a percentage of local residents as reactionary landlords and to divide up their land, even in cases where there were few landlords and no excess land in the village.

Inundated with criticism, in 1956 the party formally conceded that errors had been made in the implementation of the program and that many innocent Vietnamese had been wrongly classified as enemies of the people and thereby deprived of their land. Party General Secretary Truong Chinh and several other senior officials who were responsible for carrying out the program were removed from office, although Truong Chinh retained his membership in the Politburo.

In 1958, party leaders decided to begin the process of collectivization. The decision could not have been an easy one. Since the days of Lenin, Marxist doctrine had held that socialization of the countryside could not take place until mechanization was sufficiently advanced to demonstrate to suspicious peasants the potential benefits of collective farming. Under Lenin's policy of "mechanization before collectivization," the transformation to socialist ownership in the countryside was to be delayed until the urban economy had reached a relatively high level of industrialization. In the U.S.S.R., for example, the collectivization program was not launched until after the establishment of machine tractor stations in rural districts after 1928.

China was the first to abandon this premise. In 1955, facing the frustrating reality that industrialization could not be achieved on the foundation of a backward agricultural sector, CCP Chairman Mao Tse-tung sought to break out of the dilemma by reversing the Leninist process—placing collectivization before mechanization. By Mao's reasoning, Chinese peasants were "poor and blank," lacking the innate bourgeois tendencies of their counterparts in Europe. They would thus be willing to follow the party's lead and move to socialist ownership before mechanization brought with it the promise of increased food production. If Mao and his colleagues were correct, collectivization by itself would lead to production increases, thus releasing capital and labor to stimulate the growth of the industrial sector.[6]

In 1958, the Hanoi regime, perhaps noting the lack of peasant resistance to the Chinese program, decided to embark on a similar path. Following the Chinese example, the program was carefully crafted to achieve maximum voluntary support. The first stage consisted of the establishment of seasonally based labor exchange teams, wherein peasant families shared labor during the harvest season but retained ownership over land

and tools and kept the profits. The second stage, launched on a large scale in 1958, involved the formation of semisocialist cooperatives the size of rural hamlets, in which the peasants pooled their tools and farmland and received a portion of the final harvest in proportion to their labor and the amount of land they contributed to the organization. In theory, membership in the cooperatives was voluntary, and the individual peasant family could withdraw its land, tools, and draft animals from the organization at any time.[7]

The final stage of socialist transformation in the rural areas was the fully socialist collective farm, similar to the *kolkhoz* in the Soviet Union. The collective was larger in size than the cooperative, and those peasants who agreed to join abandoned their title to all land, tools, and farm animals contributed to the organization. Payment was based on the amount of work performed, not on the output or the amount of land contributed by the individual family.

By the early 1960s, the collectivization program was substantially completed, and more than 80 percent of all farm families in lowland districts (areas inhabited by mountain minorities, in general, were exempted from the program) had been enrolled in either semisocialist (the cooperative) or fully socialist collective organizations. As in China, there had been relatively little open resistance to the program on the part of peasants, in part because the government permitted farm families to cultivate food for their own use (or for sale at the local markets) on small private plots consisting of no more than 5 percent of the total land of the collective.

To the disappointment of the regime, however, collective ownership did not significantly increase grain production, in part because mechanization remained low, with less than 7 percent of the land plowed by tractor. Food output increased gradually from pre-Geneva levels but did not achieve planned goals, and with the rate of population increase running at over 3 percent annually, the DRV was plagued with a continuing shortfall in food production throughout the 1960s, forcing the government to import grain from abroad. A campaign to reduce the rate of population increase was launched in 1963, but in the face of resistance from the populace and a lack of will at the leadership level, it remained a dead letter.

The move toward collectivization of the countryside had been accompanied by the transition to long-term planning within the North Vietnamese economy as a whole. In 1955, the National Planning Board had been established to bear responsibility for the preparation of plans for the future transition to a fully socialist, technologically advanced society. In 1958, a Three-Year Plan was inaugurated to accompany the first stages of socialist transformation in the countryside and lay the groundwork for the promulgation of a Five-Year Plan scheduled to begin in 1961. The primary objective of the latter was to complete the socialist transformation of the economy while promoting the rapid development of the industrial and agricultural sector through the shift from small-scale to large-scale production.

In some respects, the Five-Year Plan was a success. By 1965, the public sector had begun to play a dominant role within the national economy. According to official statistics, more than 90 percent of the industrial and agricultural sector was now under state or collective ownership. Only in such areas as transport and domestic trade were private businesses (often those of overseas Chinese) still active. Significant advances were also realized in some areas of industrial production, notably in the output of coal and cement and the production of electricity. Much of this progress had been achieved as the result of assistance from the Soviet Union, China, and other socialist countries. According to one source, between 1955 and the end of the first Five-Year Plan, Hanoi's socialist allies provided more than $1 billion in economic aid. Eighty percent came from the U.S.S.R. Most of the difference came from China, with whose assistance the DRV was able to build fertilizer plants and two power stations and to begin a major steel complex at Thai Nguyen, 40 miles (64 kilometers) north of Hanoi.

Initially, the regime planned to follow the first Five-Year Plan with a second, scheduled to begin in 1966. By then, however, the growing needs of the war in the South had intervened, and until the seizure of Saigon in 1975, economic development took second place to the war effort. With males now being conscripted into the armed services and precious resources being monopolized by the needs of the battlefield, the second Five-Year Plan was scrapped and replaced by annual plans. The launching of full-scale bombing of the North by the United States in 1965 undoubtedly added to the regime's economic difficulties. Intensive bombing raids decimated the small industrial sector as well as the transportation network. To minimize damage, the government ordered the dispersal of industrial plants wherever possible into rural areas.

To alleviate the problem, Hanoi's socialist allies increased their economic assistance to the DRV. According to official figures, between 1965 and the end of the war a decade later, aid from China, the U.S.S.R., and the socialist countries of Eastern Europe totaled over $4 billion. Despite such efforts, however, the overall effects of the war on the northern economy were undoubtedly severe. Agricultural production stagnated as industrial output in key areas declined significantly from the levels achieved at the end of the first Five-Year Plan.[8]

UNIFICATION AND THE ECONOMY

With the end of the Vietnam War in 1975, the Hanoi regime was finally able to turn its attention to the economic front and the arduous process of postwar recovery. The problems were intimidating. Throughout the country, the damage from a generation of conflict would have to be repaired and the economy placed on a peacetime footing. More than 2 million young people serving in the armed forces would have to be demobilized and returned to peacetime occupations. In the South, the legacy of the American era would have to be eradicated. In Saigon and other major cities, an estimated 3 million refugees huddled in camps to escape the ravages of war in the countryside. Many rural districts were virtually depopulated. In the cities, industrial and commercial activity was at a virtual standstill and unemployment was in the millions.

Beyond such immediate economic problems lay an issue of compelling long-term significance. How long should the new Vietnam remain divided into two separate economic systems, one capitalist, the other socialist? As in 1954, the party initially approached the problem with caution. In order to attract the widest possible spectrum of support in the South, the program of the NLF had been cast in moderate terms, stressing basic issues such as land reform, higher salaries, and better working conditions and avoiding all references to the ultimate goal of a communist society.

After the seizure of Saigon, the party leadership initially decided to follow the gradualist approach in order to reassure the local population and to encourage a resumption of productive activities. The new revolutionary authorities directed that all businesses remain in operation and promised that the profits of private operations would be guaranteed. As in 1955 in the North, banks, utilities, and a few major firms were nationalized. The property of wealthy entrepreneurs was confiscated, and a few of the more powerful and wealthy enterpreneurs, many of them ethnic Chinese, were accused of speculation, hoarding of goods, or other crimes against the people. A handful were publicly executed *pour encourager les autres.* During the next three years, a number of private firms were taken over by the government or transformed into joint private-state enterprises.

The government announced that its ultimate objective was to restore the South to its traditional position as breadbasket for the entire country as the North assumed the lead in manufacturing. This goal could not be achieved, however, until the peasants were lured back to the villages. During the last years of the war, vast numbers had fled their villages for the relative security of the cities. By the early 1970s, nearly one-half of the entire population in South Vietnam was living in urban areas, many of them in refugee camps, while nearly one-third of the arable land in the countryside reportedly lay fallow.

The first priority, then, was to persuade the refugees from the countryside to return to their farms. The regime's solution to the problem was to create so-called New Economic Areas (NEAs) in rural areas as a focus for agricultural development. The NEAs were extensive plots of unused land set up in selected regions of the country and scheduled for reclamation and resettlement by the government. Sometimes they were established in previously occupied areas that had been abandoned by their owners. In other cases, they were in piedmont areas adjacent to the Central Highlands that had not been previously used, but were considered appropriate for farming. The excess population in the cities—refugees and the unemployed—were now encouraged to settle voluntarily in such areas. In return, the authorities promised to provide them with tools, seeds, materials for housing, and basic amenities such as electricity, water, schools, and transportation. The original plan called for the eventual resettlement of more than 3 million people in the NEAs. The majority would come from the burgeoning cities in the South, but some were to be resettled from the crowded provinces in Central Vietnam and the Red River delta.

In theory, the program was to be voluntary, and it is probable that the regime attempted to avoid compulsory resettlement wherever possible. But as the program got underway in the summer and fall of 1975, complaints soon appeared in the Saigon press that in some instances citizens were forced to move. Some critics charged that the program was simply a plan to rid the cities of the *Hoa* and other elements considered potentially hostile to the new regime. Official figures claimed that the program had achieved substantial success in relieving overcrowding in the cities, but reports soon began to circulate that it had serious flaws. Refugees claimed that many of the NEAs had been poorly prepared by government cadres and that many settlers were abandoning the areas to return in secret to the cities. The government denied that the program had been a failure (one official report stated that the attrition rate from the NEAs was no more than 3 percent) but conceded that it had not lived up to early expectations.

In areas already under the plow, the government followed a moderate line. Farmers were assured that their lands would not be seized (after some hesitation, Hanoi decided that because of the success of earlier programs launched by the RVN or by revolutionary authorities in liberated areas, a land reform program such as had taken place in the DRV before and after the Geneva Conference would not be necessary in the South) and were encouraged to increase their production of grain for sale on the market. There were few references to the future collectivization of the countryside, although a number of pilot cooperatives were set up in areas considered sympathetic to the revolution. The authorities also took initial steps toward controlling the price and distribution of grain by setting up an agency to purchase for later sale grain from private farmers and by directing retailers to obtain licenses from the government to continue their operations.

In sum, the government attempted to deal with its economic problems at the end of the war with a combination of haste and caution. Problems requiring immediate attention, such as urban unemployment and rural depopulation, were approached with a sense of urgency. But in order to promote the revival of the productive forces in the South, the authorities refrained from taking measures that might frighten the middle class or landholding peasants and thus disrupt the fragile stability of the postwar period. Within a year after the fall of Saigon, official sources were openly stating that although political unification had been quickly realized and the long-term goal was the creation of a socialist economy throughout the entire country, for the time being the government would tolerate a mixed or what it labeled a "multi-sectored" economy, half-socialist and half-capitalist. Indeed, for the foreseeable future, the national economy would be divided into five separate categories: (1) government ownership, (2) collective ownership, (3) joint private-state ownership, (4) private capitalist ownership, and (5) individual ownership. The ultimate goal of building a socialist society had by no means been abandoned, but it was conceded that the new Vietnam faced economic problems so severe they could not be resolved within a period of five to seven years.

The Second Five-Year Plan (1976–1980)

The party leadership's long-term economic objectives began to clarify in December 1976, when the Fourth National Party Congress convened in Hanoi. One of the primary purposes of the congress was to approve a new five-year plan to cover the remainder of the decade. The plan was originally drawn up shortly after the Paris Agreement to undertake economic construction in the North. When victory in the South was realized earlier than anticipated, party leaders at first considered scrapping the plan until the postwar situation became clear. Eventually, however, it was decided to retain the plan and use it to promote the party's economic objectives in both zones of the country.

In the broadest sense, the objectives of the new plan were to promote the transformation of Vietnamese society in terms of what were called the "three revolutions"—production relations, ideology and culture, and science and technology. Official sources made it clear that the primary emphasis would be placed on the latter, the assumption being that the major obstacle to economic development in Vietnam was the backward state of the national economy. Industry and commerce were still burdened by primitive technology and characterized by small-scale and labor-intensive techniques. The creation of large-scale industry and mechanized agriculture would be an issue of the highest priority. Official sources conceded, however, that such improvements could not take place within the scope of a single five-year plan but would require at least thirty years.

Predictably, heavy industry was to receive high priority. The output of coal, iron, machinery, and hydroelectric power was to be substantially increased and the transportation and communications networks improved. Agricultural goals were equally ambitious, calling for an annual increase of nearly 8 percent in food production through a combination of improved irrigation and fertilizer, higher crop yields, increase in cropland, and the planting of subsidiary crops. One interesting aspect of the plan was the proposal to create new agro-industrial centers at the district level as a means of relieving population density and diversifying the productive capacity throughout the country.

Patterned after the *agrogorods* developed in the U.S.S.R. under Nikita Khrushchev, the agro-industrial center concept was reportedly a pet project of Le Duan's that was originally launched during the first Five-Year Plan in 1961, but which had achieved only limited success because of the war. Now the program was to be revived and given maximum support. Centers capable of supporting up to 30,000 to 40,000 people and focusing on both industrial and agricultural development were to be established at the district level throughout the country. It was projected that during the course of the plan, 4 million people would be resettled in such areas, mostly through the improvement of the NEAs. Ultimately, the regime planned to move more than 10 million people into the new centers— mostly from the crowded North into less populated areas of the South.

Another major objective of the plan was to initiate the process of socialist transformation in the South. Although party leaders had been careful to reassure the local population that the system of private property would not be abolished in the near future, a majority had by now become convinced that an indefinite postponement of the socialist revolution in the southern provinces would pose a severe obstacle to the ultimate objective of seizing control over the southern economy. The decision to hasten the process was clearly set forth in the second Five-Year Plan, which declared that the creation of socialist ownership in the southern provinces would be "basically achieved" during the course of the plan.

THE CRISIS ON THE ECONOMIC FRONT

The efforts of the regime to assert state control over the national economy and simultaneously stimulate economic growth soon ran into serious difficulties. Part of the problem came from inadequate financing. Hanoi had hoped for substantial foreign assistance in carrying out its ambitious economic program, not only from its traditional allies, but also from Western countries, international organizations, and even from the United States, which had promised $3 billion in reconstruction assistance as part of the Paris Agreement of 1973.

Such optimism, it turned out, was seriously misplaced. Despite the fact that Hanoi moved closer to Moscow's position in the Sino-Soviet dispute following the end of the Vietnam War, Soviet economic assistance was lower than anticipated, averaging only about $1 billion annually through the end of the decade. Chinese aid was even more disappointing. Irritated at the Vietnamese for a variety of reasons, Peking informed them in the fall of 1975 that because of growing domestic priorities, Chinese economic assistance would continue only at current levels. By the spring of 1978, the program became a casualty of increasing tension between the two countries, and China canceled several of its ongoing projects in Vietnam. The following month, Hanoi accepted Moscow's invitation to join the Soviet-sponsored Council for Mutual Economic Assistance (CMEA). Peking responded by canceling all its remaining projects and withdrawing all its technicians from Vietnam.

Hanoi was moderately successful in obtaining promises of assistance from European countries, notably France and Sweden, in the years immediately following the end of the war. But its expectation of reconstruction aid from the United States was dashed when the Carter administration, citing Vietnam's failure to live up to the terms of the Paris Agreement, refused to honor President Nixon's commitment to provide reconstruction aid to all the Indochinese countries after the end of the war. It did agree, however, to pursue trade talks.

Hanoi's hopes for assistance from private sources were also doomed to disappointment. Despite the promulgation of a new and relatively liberal investment code, the regime was unable to attract substantial foreign capital from Western countries, a problem that was exacerbated after 1979, when the United States and a number of its allies, in response to the Vietnamese invasion of Cambodia, declared an embargo on trade relations with the SRV. One of Hanoi's major sources for optimism was the possibility of substantial oil finds in Vietnamese territorial waters in the South China Sea, and during the mid-1970s a number of Western oil companies leased offshore tracts to undertake exploratory drilling. By the end of the decade, however, optimism was tempered by reality and a number of companies allowed their claims to lapse.

If the lack of foreign assistance was one cause for the regime's continuing economic problems, it was by no means the only one. As official press reports conceded, Vietnam was having considerable difficulty in absorbing foreign aid even when it was provided. The transportation of goods was a particularly serious problem. Shipments from abroad were often held up at dockside for lack of equipment or stevedores. After leaving port, goods were sometimes delayed in reaching their ultimate destination by bottlenecks caused by primitive road and railway systems that had been badly damaged by a generation of war. The national highway that ran the entire length of the country was pockmarked with potholes. At one time, an estimated one-third of all trucks in Vietnam (most of them Soviet trucks of 1950s vintage) were idle because of a lack of spare parts.

Insufficient technological and managerial experience also plagued the state-owned industrial sector. Press reports frequently criticized administrators and cadres for their incompetence or inability to abandon the "guerrilla mentality" and admitted that many cadres were having a difficult time making the transition from a wartime to a peacetime society. In the meantime, individuals with managerial or other useful experience were prohibited from holding responsible positions in commerce or industry because of their class background, their suspected ties to the Americans or the South Vietnamese government during the war, or simply because they were of Chinese descent.

Within the private economy in the South, the regime's uneasy effort to "advance on two legs," one capitalist, one socialist, was not markedly successful. Hoarding of goods and price speculation by private producers and merchants, a familiar technique in Asian business dealings, created a thriving black market and chaos in the availability and distribution of consumer goods. Although the public sector made modest progress in output, unemployment remained high as the program to resettle refugees in the new economic zones stagnated. In rural areas, agricultural production was hindered by bureaucratic ineptitude, unrealistic bureaucratic regulations, and bad weather. To depress food prices, the regime attempted to compel peasants to sell their grain to government purchasing agents at low official prices. Recalcitrant farmers reacted by hoarding, selling on the black market, or feeding their grain to their livestock. A series of climatic disasters (floods and typhoons along the central coast, unseasonably cold weather in the North) consistently kept grain harvests from meeting ambitious annual targets and forced the regime to use its precious hard currency reserves to import grain from abroad, notably from the U.S.S.R.. By the late 1970s, even the importation of food failed to meet national needs, and food rationing was instituted.

THE TRANSFORMATION TO SOCIALISM IN THE SOUTH

Whether or not the deteriorating the economy was instrumental in persuading the regime to speed up its schedule for launching socialism in the southern provinces cannot yet be said with certainty. Speeches by senior party leaders at the Fourth Congress in December 1976 had indicated that the transition to socialist ownership would be completed "in the main" by the end of the 1976–1980 Five-Year Plan. If allusions in the official press to innerparty discord over domestic policy are accurate, the decision to move rapidly to extend government controls over the southern economy must have been a controversial one. Nevertheless, in late 1977 the party leadership decided to begin the process of socialist transformation in the southern provinces early the following year. The first stage involved the abolition of private trade and manufacturing. Most remaining private enterprise, of course, was in the South, but a small private sector, consisting primarily of ethnic Chinese merchants and manufacturers, was still in operation in the larger cities in the North. Once this step had been completed, the second stage of collectivizing the southern countryside could begin.

The regime made its move on March 23, 1978. All major industrial and commercial enterprises remaining in private hands were suddenly placed under state control and their goods confiscated. Only small firms under family ownership were permitted to continue in private hands. In an effort to avoid the disruption and hoarding of goods that had occurred at the time of the 1975 campaign against wealthy speculators in Ho Chi Minh City, the announcement came without advance warning. "Youth squads" were sent out to private businesses during the preceding night to confiscate all goods on the premises and prevent the owners from attempting to evade the provisions in the new regulations. The government promised that compensation would be provided for all goods seized (albeit at prices established by the state) and offered incentives to encourage merchants to establish joint enterprises, join collective organizations, or find alternative sources of employment. At the same time, new regulations limited the amount of money that could be retained for private use. All amounts above the legal limit were required to be placed in savings accounts. Such funds could be withdrawn only by application to the authorities. In May, a new united currency was issued, and the old southern bank notes (the southern *dong*, separate from that in use in the North) were withdrawn from circulation.

The reaction within the business community to the new government regulations was intense and predictably unfavorable. Press reports contended that the first stage had been a success, resulting in the abolition of some 30,000 private firms throughout the South, but discontent led to turmoil in the urban sector of the economy and, by midsummer, to a growing flood of refugees attempting to escape Vietnam to other countries in the region. Critics contended that the decision had been deliberately undertaken as a means to destroy the overseas Chinese community in Vietnam. Likewise, critical attitudes were common among the *Hoa* population in the North, where new regulations discriminating against Chinese nationals had already been in effect since the previous year. The decision to nationalize private enterprises in March 1978 heightened the concern and led to a mass exodus of Chinese refugees back into China.

At first, the regime appeared to be taken aback by the intensity of the reaction to the new regulations and insisted that they had not been issued, as was charged, in order to destroy the economic influence of the overseas Chinese community. Abundant evidence, however, suggests that party leaders, convinced that the *Hoa* could not be effectively assimilated into a new socialist Vietnam, had already decided to adopt severe measures to reduce the power of Chinese business interests in the country. That the regime may not initially have intended to force all Chinese to leave Vietnam is suggested by the fact that, in the beginning, those attempting to flee across the Chinese border were apprehended and returned to Vietnam. Eventually, however, party leaders apparently changed their opinion and began to encourage the departure of those who wished to leave, but prohibited them from taking their savings out of the country.

The move to collectivize the agricultural sector in the South also began in early 1978 and accelerated during succeeding months. A decision to move expeditiously toward the adoption of large-scale collectivization throughout the country had already been reached in 1974, prior to the end of the Vietnam War. The program, known as the New Management System, was confirmed at the Fourth Party Congress in December 1976. It represented an enormous gamble, because widespread dissatisfaction among private landholding peasants in the South could have a catastrophic effect on grain production. In order to minimize the risk, the regime followed the gradualist approach that it had originally borrowed from China and applied during the earlier collectivization campaign in North Vietnam.[9]

The first stage, launched in the winter of 1977–1978, consisted of the formation of low-level work exchange teams, through which farmers established contracts for production goals with government purchasing agencies, but retained ownership over their land and draft animals. In the meantime, pilot cooperatives were set up in areas where the rural population appeared receptive, where there was much wasteland or reclaimed land, and where private landownership was not well established. Only after the work exchange teams had become fully operational would the authorities proceed to the next stage of establishing collectives throughout the countryside.

Throughout the remainder of the decade, the enrollment of southern farmers into collective organizations continued on a gradual but steady basis. In areas where sentiment was relatively favorable, such as the impoverished coastal areas of Quang Ngai province (the notorious "pinkville," so labeled by wary U.S. soldiers during the Vietnam War), few difficulties were encountered. But in the Mekong delta, where private farming had now become well established (according to outside observers, at least two-thirds of all farm families in the southern provinces were classified by the regime as middle or upper-middle peasants), and especially in sect areas traditionally resistant to outside authority, farmers resisted government appeals to join the new organizations. In theory, the decision to join them was to be voluntary, but press reports conceded that in many instances compulsion was used by overzealous cadres. For the most part, resistance to the program was apparently passive rather than violent, and usually took the form of evasion or refusal to heed production quotas rather than open revolt. By the early 1980s, all but 3,000 of an estimated 13,000 production collectives established in the southern provinces had collapsed.[10]

By late 1979, the impact of the government's effort to socialize the South was clear. The flight abroad of refugees had reached significant proportions. Whether to China on foot, or to neighboring countries in Southeast Asia by sea, several hundred thousand residents left Vietnam in 1978 and 1979. According to some estimates, two-thirds of the first wave of refugees were *Hoa,* but the percentage of native Vietnamese increased in the early months of the new decade. In the meantime, the economic crisis deepened, shortages of consumer goods were common throughout the country (according to foreign travelers, goods were more plentiful in the South than in the North), and, despite stringent efforts by the government authorities to stop illegal traffic, black market operations thrived.

The agricultural sector was particularly hard hit. Not all the problems could be ascribed to human causes. Bad weather continued to plague parts of the country, and grain harvests in 1978 and 1979 in central and northern Vietnam fell far short of their targets. Food rationing was instituted to equalize the burden, but did not prevent widespread hunger and malnutrition. Per capita food consumption was reportedly well below subsistence levels, and visitors to the SRV noted the physical evidence of malnutrition on the Vietnamese population, particularly on the children.

In the fall of 1979, in tacit recognition of the seriousness of the crisis, the Central Committee moderated its efforts to force the population in the South into a socialist mold. Farmers were once again authorized to sell their produce at open markets, and a limited degree of private commerce and manufacturing was again tolerated. To persuade farmers to increase food production, the regime instituted a variety of material incentives to whet their interests. The official purchasing price of grain was raised and in 1981 a new program to stimulate agricultural production, known as the "contract system" (*khoan san pham*), was approved, according to which collective lands were distributed to farm families for their private cultivation. Each family was required to provide the state with a quota of grain in the form of rent, but any grain produced on the land beyond the established quota could be consumed or sold on the free market. Although all farm lands legally remained the property of the state, subsidies were provided to those who reclaimed unused lands.

As Adam Fforde had shown, the so-called contract system was actually not introduced at the instigation of the party leadership, but could be more accurately described as the product of experimentation at the local level. The concept of leasing contracted land to farmers had originated during the 1960s, when local officials had adopted it as a means of increasing food production in the collective But in 1969 it had been formally prohibited by state authorities, who feared that it would open the door to a return to capitalist practices in rural areas. Still, farm communities in many parts of North Vietnam had for years tacitly evaded state regulations in order to increase food production, and in the late 1970s they began openly to experiment with the contract system, along with other means, to provide peasants with incentives to increase productivity on collective lands. When it became clear that the awarding of contracts had a salutary effect on food production, the party leadership abandoned its determination to wipe out the practice. By the early 1980s, even without official encouragement, the system had spread throughout the northern provinces.[11]

In the meantime, the regime intensified its efforts to bring about increases in foreign assistance. Hanoi's primary target was Moscow. In the summer of 1981, the Soviet Union announced an increase in its economic and military assistance to the SRV. Thousands of Vietnamese students were sent to train in the U.S.S.R. and Eastern European countries, and thousands of others were assigned to work in factories in Soviet bloc countries to increase their technological abilities. The number of Soviet technicians posted to Vietnam was also increased in an effort to help the country resolve its economic problems. To help Hanoi relieve its balance-of-payments difficulties, a substantial portion of the workers' salaries was withheld to assist the regime in paying off foreign debt.

The regime had thus taken its first halting steps to resolve the economic crisis in the South. But, for some senior leaders, the decisions reached in the fall of 1979 represented a response to necessity rather than a change of heart, and it soon became clear that key members within the party leadership had not abandoned their determination to proceed with socialist transformation as soon as conditions permitted. At the party's Fifth National Congress, held in the early spring of 1982, an uneasy compromise between reform and ideological orthodoxy was patched together. In a new Five-Year Plan announced to cover the first half of the new decade, the congress broke with the traditional Stalinist emphasis on socialist industrialization and placed primary emphasis on increasing food production and the output of consumer goods; the practice of granting profit incentives to increase productivity would continue. But it was clear that conservative elements retained a significant influence within the party leadership, for Nguyen Van Linh, who had earlier been criticized for dragging his feet on eliminating the remnants of capitalist practices in the South, was dismissed from the Politburo. The congress also reiterated the party's intent to complete the process of socialist transformation "in the main" by the middle of the decade.[12]

During the next few years, the economy began to show halting signs of recovery. According to official figures, during the early 1980s industrial production increased at a rate of nearly 10 percent annually and the output of grain grew by nearly 5 percent a year, leading official sources to proclaim that the nation was gradually approaching the level of food self-sufficiency, albeit at a low level of consumption. Still, the economy faced intimidating problems, including a primitive infrastructure, insufficient capital, excessive bureaucratic controls (including government subsidies on the price of key consumer goods), a galloping inflation rate, and a massive foreign debt. There were also signs that the salutary effect of the contract system was beginning to wane, as many peasants backed out of their contracts and began to enter the household economy.[13]

The regime's efforts to improve economic performance were also hindered by lingering ideological differences within the party leadership. In the months following the Fifth Congress, articles in *Nhan Dan* and the official party journal *Tap Chi Cong San,* undoubtedly inspired by conservative members of the Politburo, sternly criticized the senior party and government representatives in Ho Chi Minh City for adopting policies that were excessively tolerant of private economic economic activities and allegedly had "harmful effects on the socialization process in South Vietnam." Eventually the southern leadership was brought to heel, and at its Fifth Plenum in November 1983, the Central Committee agreed to step up the pace of collectivization and called for the "immediate removal" of the local bourgeoisie from commercial activities.[14]

But the slow pace of economic growth, combined with a rising chorus of criticism from reformist elements within the party and government bureaucracy, was beginning to wear down the resistance of the senior leadership. In June 1985, the Central Committee announced what were described as "drastic and extraordinary reforms" aimed at reducing centralized bureaucratic controls by providing local managers of state enterprises with authority to make decisions on prices, wages, and production schedules. State subsidies on food and other consumer items for government employees were abolished as a means of reducing government expenditures and encouraging market forces, and the Vietnamese *dong* was devalued in an attempt to bring it into line with its actual value on the international exchange market. The overall objective was to set up a system of "socialist economic accounting by business methods."[15]

But these halfway measures, reminiscent of the abortive efforts of the Ch'ing and Nguyen courts in nineteenth-century China and Vietnam to restore national wealth and power by an "East for Essence, West for Practical Use" piecemeal approach to social and economic change, had little success. The rule of bureaucrats in Hanoi continued to reign supreme. Economic performance remained sluggish and inflation soared, compelling the regime to reinsitute price controls on some key commodities. Lashed by the whipsaw of rising prices and the abolition of subsidies on key commodities, urban Vietnamese grew especially outspoken in their criticism of veteran party leaders who failed to understand the source of the current economic problems and stubbornly stood in the way of a new generation of leaders more sympathetic to the cause of drastic economic reform. Statements in the official press openly conceded the serious character of the country's economic difficulties and pilloried the rising incidence of official corruption, low morale, and self-serving behavior on the part of the party and the bureaucracy.

Party leaders had hoped to resolve the question of the future direction of the economy before the convening of the Sixth National Congress of the VCP sometime in 1986. But divisions within the leadership continued into midsummer, and when Le Duan died suddenly of illness during a Central Committee plenum held in late June, the problem of selecting a successor was quickly linked to resolution of the economic crisis. The appointment of Truong Chinh, widely regarded as a doctrinaire Leninist on economic matters, was interpreted by many observers inside Vietnam and abroad as a sign that the conservative faction had temporarily prevailed in the struggle to define the future course of the revolution. In fact, however, the new party chief had himself come around somewhat reluctantly to the reformist view, at the same time insisting on the validity of the long-term strategy of bringing about the creation of a fully socialist society.

Truong Chinh's cautious approach was tacitly reflected in the opening speech that he presented to the congress on December 15, 1986. His report admitted that in the past the party leadership had been afflicted with a sense of "hastiness and wishful thinking," and had attempted to bypass the necessary stages of transition by basically completing socialist transformation within the term of each congress. Now, Truong Chinh asserted, it was important to be more realistic:

> It is a permanent and continuous task throughout the period of transition to socialism to step up socialist transformation in appropriate forms and steps, making the production relations tally with the character and level of development of productive forces and always be a driving force for the development of productive forces.

In the future, he said, the transition to socialism must be carried out in a more steady manner by bringing into play the "positive effect" of the multi-sectored economic structure. In short, there must be a continuous effort to decentralize the planning mechanism and to shift to cost-accounting methods, while the process of collectivization in the South must not be carried out in haste. But Truong Chinh made it clear that the overall objective of moving steadily toward the creation of a fully socialist society remained in place. The most important thing, he said, was "to strengthen and develop the socialist economy" in order to enable the state sector to "play the leading role and control the others."[16]

But Truong Chinh's conversion to the need for reformist measures was apparently unconvincing to more radical elements, who threw their support to the election of Nguyen Van Linh to the senior position in the party. As one of the few senior members of the party leadership who had demonstrated a willingness to experiment with capitalist techniques in southern provinces, Linh's return to prominence was a promising indication that for once the regime was serious about discarding its ideological blinders and embarking on a more pragmatic road to economic development.

The first signs were promising. In the months following the close of the congress, the regime took a number of steps to carry through on its pledge to continue the process of decentralizing the planning system and the management of state enterprises. It reduced the number of government ministries and the size of the government bureaucracy, and publicly encouraged a limited degree of private sector activities. It carried through on its earlier pledge to eliminate the system of subsidies in key commodities and to allow market forces to determine prices in the market place. And it devoted increased attention and resources to the promotion of agriculture, consumer goods, and export commodities at the expense of the classic Stalinist focus on heavy industry.

The regime also passed a new investment law to provide more attractive conditions for the investment of foreign capital in the SRV. The new code authorized foreign investors to operate in Vietnam through a wide variety of arrangements, including the creation of joint enterprises and foreign-owned corporations. In an effort to remove the international embargo on trade instituted after the Vietnamese invasion of Cambodia in 1978, the regime held talks with the United States to resolve the issue of American soldiers missing in action from the Vietnam War.[17]

By 1988, however, there were disquieting signs that the reform movement had lost considerable momentum from the heady days immediately following the Sixth Congress. According to official figures, industrial production in 1987 grew at an annual rate of only 6.7 percent, down from 7.3 percent the previous year and significantly below rates achieved earlier in the decade. Inflation remained rampant and unemployment was rising rapidly, as the state-owned industrial sector was able to employ only a small fraction of the labor force, which was being augmented by increasing numbers of young people released from the armed services as the regime gradually removed Vietnamese troops from Cambodia.

The agricultural situation was even worse. With the state purchasing price of rice too low to encourage farmers to expand production, food output in 1987 was only 17.6 million tons, a drop of nearly 1 million tons from the previous year and significantly below the official target. Amid reports of widespread hunger, in the spring of 1988 the regime appealed to potential foreign donors for food assistance, warning that otherwise the country faced the possibility of widespread starvation. To relieve the food shortage, the regime adopted a number of steps to encourage productivity, including abolishing compulsory grain deliveries, authorizing farmers to negotiate contracts with government or collective enterprises to provide food, and announcing that long-term leases would be provided on land contracted from collective farms. It also transferred a number of productive responsibilities from the collective to the individual farm family.[18]

The immediate results of these measures, in the word of one seasoned observer of the Vietnamese economy, were "spectacular." Annual production levels for the calendar year 1989 were up substantially in agricultural goods as well as export commodities. Private trade increased, particularly in the marketing of consumer goods, and the rate of inflation dropped precipitously. Yet a number of intimidating problems were still unresolved. The state-owned industrial sector remained stagnant, with few enterprises showing a profit and many reaching the brink of bankruptcy. Rural credit and fertilizer were scarce, and local bureaucracies, loath to abandon their traditional role in the process, often hindered the productive efforts of individual farmers. Unemployment remained at alarming levels, with the predictable impact on the attitude of young people. On the international front, perhaps most disquieting were the signs of disintegration in the Soviet Union, Hanoi's main supplier of aid as well as the recipient of well over one-half of its total exports.[19]

By the fall of 1990, the results of the program of economic renovation announced at the Sixth Congress presented a mixed picture. Food production was on the rise, permitting the SRV for the first time in decades to export rice. Prices were relatively stable, at least by recent standards, and consumer goods were in greater supply. Roadside stalls in Hanoi and other cities in the North overflowed with a variety of consumer goods for the first time in decades. But the state-owned industrial sector, still the largest sector of the economy, remained stagnant, and with thousands of soldiers being demobilized as occupation forces withdrew from Cambodia, the number of unemployed reached over 3 million. With the international embargo still in effect, foreign investment and assistance remained negligible, and negotiations with Moscow over future assistance to Vietnam indicated not only that Soviet aid levels would drop, but that Moscow would now demand payment in convertible currency rather than in rubles.[20]

Public uncertainty over future policies was another factor in the equation. The Sixth Congress had announced a delay on the road to socialism yet was not specific on how long the transition period would last. After the congress had adjourned, factional struggles between conservatives and radical reformers within the party leadership, combined with bureaucratic resistance to official directives, presented a confusing picture of the regime's ultimate intentions and undoubtedly served to deter future planning on the part of farmers, entrepreneurs, and potential foreign investors alike.[21]

The Sixth Congress had announced that a specific program setting forth the party's plans for the indefinite future would eventually be outlined to give the public a clear picture of the future course of the Vietnamese revolution. But disagreements within the Politburo had prevented the party leadership from reaching a consensus on the issue, and official statements often left the impression that the regime had no overall plan of action to resolve the nation's economic difficulties. The approach of the Seventh Party Congress, scheduled to take place in the spring of 1991, compelled the Politburo to come to grips with the issue, and a draft strategy drawn up at the Tenth Plenum of the Central Committee was finally submitted for public debate in late November of 1990.

A GOAL FOR THE NINETIES: IN SEARCH OF WEALTH AND POWER

The regime's strategic plan for the 1990s consisted of two documents, a "Draft Strategy for the Stabilization and Development of the Economy and Society to the year 2000" (*Du thao chien luoc on dinh va phat trien kinh te-xa hoi cua nuoc ta den nam 2000*) and a "Draft Platform to Build Socialism in the Transitional Period" (*Du thao cuong linh xay dung chu nghia xa hoi trong thoi ky qua do*). The two documents were hailed in many quarters as marking a clear departure with the past and the adoption of a bold new approach to the problems of nation-building.

In retrospect, however, the most noteworthy aspect of the draft plan was how little it departed in its essentials from existing guidelines. Although conceding that the road to socialism in Vietnam would be more arduous and time-consuming than party leaders had originally anticipated, the authors insisted that existing difficulties would be overcome and that the socialist system would ultimately triumph in its historic struggle with capitalism. In the meantime, a transitional period would be necessary before the rapid march to socialism could resume. In effect, the party leadership was reaffirming the decisions reached at the Sixth Party Congress in 1986, but postponing the eventual transformation to a fully socialist society to the indefinite future.

The party's plan for this transitional period was also short on detail. According to the draft documents, the ongoing effort to decentralize the state planning mechanism and introduce a commodities economy would continue, although the market mechanism was still to be directed by the state (*co su quan ly cua nha nuoc*). The economy would remain "multi-sectored" (*kinh te nhieu thanh phan*), with a variety of private and collective as well as state-owned enterprises, but the predominant role was still assigned to the state sector. Private economic activities were assigned predominantly to the area of the production of consumer goods. Where proper conditions existed, the leading role of the state-owned sector was scheduled to be enhanced, although unprofitable enterprises were to be transformed to private or collective ownership in areas not considered essential to the overall plan.

Finally, the existing emphasis on agriculture, consumer goods, and the development of the export market would continue. The overall goal for the transitional period was to double the current per capita standard of living and meet the general needs of the population in such key areas as food, housing, clothing, transportation, education, and health. Once this goal had been realized—hopefully within a period of two or three five-year plans—the rapid march to a fully socialist economy could be resumed.[22]

Initial reactions to the new program from foreign observers tended to be favorable, but criticism from within Vietnam, where skepticism as to the ultimate intentions of the regime was widespread, quickly appeared. At meetings of provincial representatives of the National Assembly held in the months following the December plenum, many delegates reportedly complained that the draft program was excessively optimistic about past achievements and irrelevant to practical needs at the local level. Like the French, who had promised independence to the peoples of Indochina on several occasions without ever giving it to them, the party had failed to carry through on its promises of reform on so many occasions that many Vietnamese now considered such promises difficult to believe.

Despite criticism that the draft reform program was too little too late, the regime refused to be deflected from its chosen course, and in recent years it has steadfastly pursued a strategy designed to bring about the creation of a mixed economy with strong market characteristics, though maintaining the essential primacy of the state-owned sector. Although official declarations stress the long-term character of the present approach, occasional remarks by senior officials indicate that the ultimate goal of building a socialist society has by no means been abandoned. Early reports on the midterm party conference held in January 1994 suggest that the regime's cautious approach to economic reform will continue. And though the political report presented to the delegates indicated that one of the tasks for the future was to bring about "economic restructuring along the line of industrialisation and modernization," there were no indications that key decisions on how to achieve that goal had been reached and the report reaffirmed the previous goal of building "a socialist-oriented market mechanism under state management."[23]

In some respects, the regime's attempt to craft a compromise between central planning and a market-oriented approach has been successful. During the early 1990s, both the industrial and the agricultural sectors began to show signs of a new vitality that in statistical terms has substantially surpassed performance levels achieved during the preceding decade. Spurred by the steady growth of the private sector, industrial production increased by double digits in 1992, leading Singapore's former prime minister Lee Kuan Yew to remark that Vietnam might become the next of the Asian "little tigers." In the meantime, an increase in food production, sparked in part by new regulations that guarantee peasants long-term use rights to their farmland, has enabled the country in recent years to become the third largest (after the United States and Thailand) global exporter of rice.[24]

Surprisingly, such advances have been achieved even while the regime has managed to reduce the level of inflation to an annual average of about 15 percent and realize a trade surplus for the first time since the end of the Vietnam War. It is also worthy of note that such gains occured when the U.S.-led embargo on trade with the SRV was still formally in effect, although a number of advanced capitalist nations, including such local powerhouses as the Republic of China and Singapore, have become active trading partners of the one-time pariah state. The level of foreign investment is also increasing sharply, with the major providers coming from within the region, including South Korea, Japan, the Republic of China, and Singapore. Oil revenues, although not spectacular, are increasing steadily, and the country has become self-sufficient in energy production. Tourism is still in its infancy but shows some promise of becoming a major source of foreign exchange in the near future. Cruise ships operating within the region have begun to schedule stops at Haiphong, Da Nang, and Saigon, and reports by visitors suggested that most are impressed with the tourist potential of the country.

Most promising of all, in early February 1994 the Clinton administration, after a number of transitional steps taken the previous year, announced the end of the U.S embargo. A number of major U.S. firms had al-

Free Market. (Photo property of the author.)

Ad for population control program. (Photo property of the author.)

Japanese ads in downtown Saigon. (Photo property of the author.)

ready positioned themselves to take advantage of the new policy and were quick to seek new opportunities for investment. These developments promise to go a long way toward offsetting the collapse of the Soviet Union and other members of CMEA, who as recently as a decade ago were the SRV's primary trade partners. Vietnam is finally ready to become an active participant in the international marketplace.[25]

These economic gains have had a visible impact on the standard of living of the population, both in rural areas and in the cities. Improving conditions have been apparent in the countryside since the mid-1980s, when the contract system began to take effect, and have led to improved housing and living conditions for Vietnamese farmers. Signs of growing prosperity in urban areas have been somewhat slower to appear, at least in the long-stagnant northern provinces, but have increased in recent years with the appearance of massive amounts of consumer goods—much of it smuggled in from China, Thailand, and Singapore—on the shelves of private shops newly opened in the major cities. The capital of Hanoi now even has its own equivalent of a new generation of "gilded youth," many of them sons and daughters of senior party and government officials, riding on motorbikes, wearing designer clothing (or at least a reasonable fascimile thereof), and listening to taped Western rock music on the ubiquious "ghetto boxes" so commonly seen in other major cities in the region.

But there are ample warning signs to temper expressions of excessive optimism. The steady increase in the population, now estimated at more than 70 million and growing at a rate of well over two percent annually, threatens to outpace the increase in food production. The economic infrastructure, from the transportation and communications networks to skilled labor and sources of energy, is still one of the most primitive in Asia. Government favoritism toward the state-run sector, combined with resistance to economic liberalization from within the bureaucracy, continue to drag on the private economy. For their part, many state firms have ignored regulations directing them to adopt a more market-oriented approach (according to one recent report, for example, only five of thirty-two state firms surveyed were implementing reforms mandated by the government). One sympathetic foreign businessman warned that bureaucratic red tape and official corruption remained serious problems that could pose a serious obstacle to further progress in the economic field.[26]

Vietnam, then, has a long way to go before it can aspire to become the next "little tiger" in Southeast Asia. It lacks some of the resources that provide other nations in the region with ample supplies of foreign exchange. A generation of war left the nation with one of the most primitive transportation and communications infrastructures in the region and the educational base, to be examined in Chapter 7, is in dire need of a massive influx of money and technology. At the top of the political pyramid, the commitment by party leaders to the goal of rapid economic development is still distorted by ideological considerations as well as security concerns left over from revolution and war. But after nearly two decades of doctrinal disputes, bureaucratic infighting, and economic stagnation, there are now promising signs that the nation may be on the verge of achieving the level of economic development already realized by counterparts in the region. If so, it will be no mean achievement.

PERESTROIKA, VIETNAMESE-STYLE

It is undoubtedly no coincidence that the Vietnamese choose to describe their reform program as renovation (in Russian, *obnovlenie*) rather than restructuring (*perestroika*). In the years following the end of the Vietnam War, Hanoi became one of the most orthodox practitioners of the Stalinist approach to nation-building. Even after party leaders decided to embark on the road of reform at the Sixth Congress in December 1986, the new program was not nearly as much a departure from past practice as was the case in China or even the Soviet Union. It is equally clear that, for some members of the senior leadership, the ultimate goal of building of a fully socialist society has by no means been abandoned.

This is not to say that the regime has always followed the Soviet economic pattern of development. During the 1950s, party leaders briefly experimented with the Chinese model, carrying out a comprehensive land reform program, assigning priority attention to the agricultural sector, engaging in the pursuit of collectivization before mechanization, and reportedly even giving some consideration to the adoption of people's communes. But they soon discovered that Mao Tse-tung's "heaven storming" approach had little relevance in Vietnam, where it left a legacy of public alienation and emotional trauma that was clearly detrimental to the party's priority objective of bringing about national liberation and reunification. Eventually, the Vietnamese turned back to the Soviet economic model as a more reliable blueprint for the building of a socialist society. The Stalinist emphasis on central planning, rapid industrialization, and a fully socialist pattern of ownership was highly congenial to veteran Vietnamese leaders, most of whom had little acquaintance with or liking for the capitalist system as it had been practiced in Indochina and were fully convinced of the moral and practical superiority of the socialist system of ownership.

But the weaknesses of the Soviet approach became glaringly evident in the late 1970s, when the decision to move rapidly toward socialist transformation in the South led to widespread popular hostility, evasion, and economic crisis. Party leaders were quick to make superficial adjustments, but reluctant to change their long-term strategy. Although pragmatic elements may have envisioned a strategy resembling Teng Hsiao-p'ing's program of "four modernizations" in China, several members of the party's veteran leadership undoubtedly preferred a much more limited approach that would not necessitate an extensive delay in the process of socialist transformation or a degree of economic liberalization that could pose a serious threat to the predominance of the state-owned sector of the economy. Equally significant, the regime was also unwilling to make the necessary concessions in the realm of foreign policy to bring an end to the international embargo and increase the likelihood of economic assistance from the capitalist nations.

One of the reasons for Hanoi's reluctance to adopt reforms similar to those that had been adopted by the post-Maoist leadership in China was undoubtedly the high level of tension in Sino-Vietnamese relations. During the early 1980s, the Chinese model was anathema in Hanoi, and few would concede that decisions reached in Peking had any relevance in Vietnam. But there were undoubtedly a number of other factors involved. One was the Vietnamese sense of vulnerability in a dangerous world. Although Teng Hsiao-p'ing and his allies apparently felt sufficiently secure within their borders to risk a measure of internal political instability in the interest of bringing about rapid economic modernization, their counterparts in Hanoi—still scarred by their conflict with the United States and made doubly cautious by the dispute with Peking—were clearly determined to look out for the interests of Vietnamese national security, whatever the costs in terms of economic development.

However, the passage of time and the gradual transition to a new generation of leadership has slowly eroded the conviction in Hanoi that socialism is inherently superior to capitalism. Recent moves also indicate that the regime has belatedly recognized that economic interests cannot indefinitely be subordinated to the imperatives of national security. Still, many senior Vietnamese leaders still appear to harbor deep-seated suspicions about the capitalist system and its potentially corrosive impact on Vietnamese society. The recent party conference held in February 1994 repeated Nguyen Van Linh's earlier warning about "hostile forces" seeking to "abolish the party and socialist regime in our country." Clearly, many remain reluctant to open windows to all the dangerous ideas floating about outside.

The Hanoi regime thus continues to face the same cruel dilemma encountered by other Marxist-Leninist societies in deciding how to stimulate rapid economic growth without running the risk of undermining the foundations of socialism and facing a collapse of the dictatorship of the proletariat. The problem is complicated by the historic tensions between conservative bureaucrats in the North and entrepreneurial elements in the South, tensions that were exacerbated by the separate roads followed by the two zones after the Geneva Conference. Recent events in Eastern Europe and China have demonstrated only too graphically that the regime's fears of potential political chaos and national disintegration are well-founded and have made Vietnamese leaders doubly cautious in following the same road.

What, then, of the future? Can Vietnam achieve an abundance of goods and industrial productivity without adopting the central components of the capitalist system? So far, party leaders have managed to realize a modicum of success by adopting an incremental approach that blends a degree of economic laissez-faire into an essentially state-controlled economy. But many observers will question whether such a syncretic approach can long succeed, or whether it will inevitably result in either drastic change or popular revolt.

At the moment, it is still too early to predict with certainty which path Vietnam will follow. Past performance suggests that, in the face of severe challenge, party leaders are willing to make tactical concessions when necessary to avoid disaster but will resist compromising on basic principles. The current generation of leaders will strive, above all, to preserve the dominant role of the party over the Vietnamese revolution. Can such an approach succeed in the postwar period as it succeeded in time of war? Only time will tell.

NOTES

1. I refer, of course, to the concept of "oriental despotism" put forth by Professor Karl Wittfogel in his book of the same name. The concept has been somewhat discredited in recent years, but many scholars will concede that agrarian societies based on the control of water resources have often given birth to centralized and autocratic political systems.

2. For a recent discussion of the role of Hoi An as a major trading port in the region, see *Ancient Town of Hoi An* (Hanoi: The Gioi, 1993).

3. For an interesting survey of early European contacts with Vietnam, with a primary emphasis on the role of the British, see Alastair Lamb, *The Mandarin Road to Old Huê: Narratives of Anglo-Vietnamese Diplomacy from the 17th century to the Eve of the French Conquest* (London: Chatto & Windus, 1970).

4. For an informative discussion of the economic impact of French colonialism in rural Indochina, see Robert L. Sansom, *The Economics of Insurgency in the Mekong Delta of Vietnam* (Cambridge: MIT Press, 1970), esp. pp. 48–56.

5. Gareth Porter says that about 25 percent of farm families in the southern provinces were without land after the fall of Saigon, while a little over 50 percent were classified by the Hanoi regime as middle peasants. See his *Vietnam: The Politics of Bureaucratic Centralism* (Ithaca: Cornell University Press, 1993), p. 60.

6. For an analysis of the collectivization drive in China, see Kenneth R. Walker, "Collectivization in Retrospect: the 'Socialist High Tide' of Autumn 1955–Spring 1956," in *The China Quarterly*, No. 26 (April–June 1966), pp. 1–43.

7. According to Gareth Porter, Truong Chinh wanted to move ahead rapidly to fully socialist collectives, while newly appointed acting first secretary Le Duan (perhaps out of concern for its possible effect on the struggle in the South) wanted to delay the transition until the technology existed to guarantee production increases. The result was a compromise. See *Vietnam: The Politics of Bureaucratic Centralism*, pp. 115–116.

8. For a discussion of the impact of the war on urban areas in North Vietnam, see Nigel Thrift and Dean Forbes, *The Price of War: Urbanization in Vietnam, 1954–1985* (London: Allen & Unwin, 1986).

9. According to Christine Pelzer White, there was some disagreement among leaders at the 1974 conference over the methods to be used in carrying out the collectivization program. Prime Minister Pham Van Dong recommended a gradualist approach, supplemented by large-scale agricultural mechanization and a liberal application of profit incentives along the lines of the Bukharin model in the Soviet Union. First Secretary Le Duan argued that such gestures were not necessary. See her "Alternative approaches to the socialist transformation of agriculture in postwar Vietnam," in David G. Marr and Christian P. White (eds.), *Postwar Vietnam: Dilemmas in Socialist Development* (Ithaca: Cornell University Southeast Asia Program, 1988), pp. 136–40.

10. Vo Nhan Tri, "Party policies and economic performance in the second and third Five-year Plans examined," in Marr and White, pp. 79–80.

11. For a discussion, see Adam Fforde, *The Agrarian Question in North Vietnam, 1974–1979* (Armonk, N.Y.: M.E. Sharpe, 1989). According to the economist Vo Nhan Tri, one of those who had opposed the concept of contracts was Truong Chinh. See his article in Marr and White, p. 84.

12. Gareth Porter asserts that some veteran party leaders worried that, in the absence of a target date, the campaign to collectivize the countryside would drag. See *Vietnam: the Politics of Bureaucratic Centralism*, p. 119. Evidence for the existence of a division between "conservative" and "reformist" elements within the Politburo in the mid-1980s is primarily circumstantial, but virtually all sources agree that Nguyen Van Linh was dropped from the party's senior decision-making body because of his failure to curb private enterprise activities in the South. Most of the party's veteran leadership, such as Truong Chinh, Le Duc Tho, Pham Hung, Do Muoi, and Le Duan himself, were identified with the conservative faction. For discussion of the results of the Fifth Party Congress, see the articles by Nayan Chanda in the FEER, April 16, 1982, and by Nguyen Duc Tam in *Vietnam Courier* (May 1983).

13. The statistics are cited in the Political Report of the Sixth Party Congress, See *6th National Congress of the Communist Party of Vietnam: Documents* (Hanoi: Foreign Languages Publishing House, 1987), p. 11.

14. For references, see William J. Duiker, *Vietnam Since the Fall of Saigon,* second revised edition (Athens: Ohio University Monographs in International Studies, 1989), pp. 75–78.

15. Press Release, Permanent SRV Mission to the United Nations, June 25, 1985.

16. Ibid., p. 66. Italics in the original.

17. An English translation of the new investment code appeared in the *Vietnam Courier*, March 1988, p. 9.

18. See the text of Politburo resolution no. 10-NQTU, dated April 5, 1988, in FBIS (APA), May 6, 1988. In December, the regime announced that contracts for farmland could be extended up to a period of ten to fifteen years. It gave no indication, however, as to what would happen at the end of that period. See David Wurfel, "Doi Moi in Comparative Perspective," in William S. Turley and Mark Selden, *Reinventing Vietnamese Socialism: Doi Moi in Comparative Perspective* (Boulder: Westview Press, 1993), p. 32.

19. For an overview of conditions at the time, see Per Ronnas and Orjan Sjoberg (eds.), *Doi Moi: Economic Reforms and Development Policies in Vietnam* (Tryck: Norstedts Tryckeri, Stockholm, 1989).

20. Cf. the article in the FEER, February 29, 1991, p. 46.

21. See the comments by foreign observers in Ronnas and Sjoberg, *passim.*

22 The Draft Program and Strategy were printed in *Nhan Dan,* December 1 and 3, 1990.

23. See the article by Murray Hiebert entitled "More of the Same" in FEER, February 10, 1994, p. 15.

24. For statistics, see *Indochina Chronology* (July–September 1992), p. 6. On the new regulations stipulating that farm households will be given twenty-year re-

newable leases on their croplands, see Murray Hiebert, "Land of Hope," in FEER, July 29, 1993, p. 52. For some farmers, notably in the southern provinces, any limit on ownership rights was unsatisfactory.

25. Vietnamese sources are quick to point out, however, that until the SRV has received most favored nation status from Washington, its opportunity to develop a mutually fruitful trade relationship with the United States will be limited. See Murray Hiebert and Susumu Awanohara, "Lukewarm Welcome," in FEER, February 17, 1994. For an overview of current prospects in the area of foreign development assistance, see Shada Islam's article "Welcome Back" in the FEER, November 25, 1993, p. 59.

26. See the article by Rodney Tasker in ibid., p. 50.

7

Culture and Society

It has been observed that Vietnam, although physically located in Southeast Asia, is actually a part of the cultural world of East Asia, dominated by Vietnam's great neighbor China. The argument has some merit. Not only was Vietnam for 1,000 years under direct Chinese rule, but even after regaining their independence in the tenth century, the Vietnamese turned to China as a model for their literature, their art, their architecture, many of their religious beliefs, even for their written language. For nearly ten centuries, the Vietnamese almost seemed to style themselves as a carbon copy of China. In the words of one modern Vietnamese historian:

> Our nation has been influenced by China in all regards, with regard to politics, society, ethics, religion and customs. As far as literature is concerned, we studied Chinese characters, practiced Confucianism, and gradually assimilated the thought and art of China. The scholars in our country studied Chinese classics and histories, read Chinese poetry and prose, and also used Chinese characters when reciting and composing. Even in literary works written in Vietnamese, authors could not escape the influence of Chinese literature. Some of the literary forms were distinctly ours, but most were borrowed from China. Even the characters used to write Vietnamese—Nom characters—were made up of elements of Chinese characters.[1]

Few contemporary Vietnamese would deny that historically their country has been strongly influenced by China. Many would contend, however (and in this they are joined by many Vietnam specialists in the West), that the degree of Chinese influence over Vietnamese society has sometimes been exaggerated and that many of the primary components of Vietnamese culture have roots indigenous to Southeast Asia.

The question is an interesting subject for scholarly debate, but it is ultimately a fruitless one. The fact is that Vietnamese culture, like that of many other societies on the periphery of great civilizations, has absorbed a considerable degree of influence from China, at the same time reflecting elements from other nearby civilizations or the local environment. Culturally and historically as well as geographically, Vietnam lies at the cross-roads between the Sinitic world of East Asia and the more Indianized world of mainland Southeast Asia. And just as the civilization of the United States, for example, can be described as the result of the interaction between elements of foreign cultures brought to its shores by immigrants and exposure to the indigenous environment, so Vietnamese culture represents, in broad terms, the product of a similar interaction between Sinitic customs, institutions, and values and those emanating from the native soil of Southeast Asia.

For scholars, this polarity between Chinese and Southeast Asian elements represents one of the more intriguing and persistent themes in Vietnamese history. For Vietnamese politicians and statesmen, the issue has often had more practical implications. The impact can be seen not only in the traditional era, when Confucian bureaucrats and scholars frequently cast their glances to the north for answers to political and social problems, but in the current century as well, when Ho Chi Minh and his colleagues borrowed liberally from the Maoist strategy of people's war and the Chinese approach to building a socialist society. Even in recent years, a period of deep-seated tension in Sino-Vietnamese relations, Vietnamese leaders have turned to China for solutions to problems brought about by rapid social change. This Jekyll-and-Hyde relationship between China and Vietnam is thus one of the most enduring, and complex themes in Vietnamese history, and its course has by no means run to conclusion.

Unfortunately, too little is known about the nature of Vietnamese society prior to the Chinese conquest in the second century B.C. to permit a definitive assessment of the cultural roots of Vietnamese civilization. As we have seen, the limited evidence that is available suggests that in late prehistoric times the Vietnamese were one among several Bronze Age peoples (called by the Chinese the *Yueh*) living in an area that stretched from the Red River delta to the valley of the Yangtze River in China. It seems likely that even at that early date the peoples in the Red River delta shared some cultural traits with their neighbors to the north while they displayed others emanating from the local environment. It seems clear that by the first millennium B.C. a growing sense of local identity had begun to emerge among the peoples within the delta and along its fringes, a relationship allegorically symbolized by the fable of the merger of mountain and water kingdoms as marking the appearance of the first Vietnamese state.

The southward expansion of Chinese civilization and the integration of the state of Au Lac into the Han empire undoubtedly hindered the emergence of a distinctive sense of identity among the peoples of the Red River delta and facilitated the introduction of elements of Chinese civilization into Vietnamese society. Earlier chapters have noted the impact of

Chinese rule in politics and economics. Chinese influence was no less manifest in social institutions, in the realm of religion, and in the creative arts. This process, sometimes described as Sinification, was the result of a deliberate policy of assimilation applied by Chinese administrators acting at the behest of an imperial government that, in the manner of great states everywhere, viewed China as the fulcrum of culture, bringing advanced civilization to the barbarian peoples along the frontier. It is a measure, not only of the brilliance of Chinese culture, but also of its apparent relevance to the lands of the "pacified south," that it had such a long-lasting and profound impact on the peoples of Vietnam.

Chinese influence, however, was strongest within the elite class and at court. In this sense, the integration of Vietnam into the nexus of Chinese civilization resembled the spread of Indian and Muslim influence into other areas of Southeast Asia and that of the civilization of the West during the era of colonialism. Under a Chinese cultural veneer, life at the village level was relatively untouched by the winds blowing from the north. Thus emerged one of the enduring features of Vietnamese civilization: the dichotomony between an elite culture reflecting the multifaceted influence of imperial China and a popular culture at the village level based primarily on indigenous traditions dating back to the preconquest period. In the interpretation of Marxist historians in Hanoi, this dichotomy between court and village reflected the historical tension between feudal elements slavishly imitating foreign culture and the oppressed urban and rural masses, who represented the genuine force of Vietnamese identity and patriotism. The truth is undoubtedly more complex than that—witness the staunch defense of Vietnamese political independence by the Confucian scholar-statesman Nguyen Trai—but there is little doubt that the social habits, religious beliefs, and even the language spoken by the common people were descended more from indigenous roots than were those of the educated elite.[2]

PHILOSOPHY AND RELIGION

In Vietnam, as in most other societies in Southeast Asia, the dichotomy between center and periphery, between court and village, was reflected in philosophy and religion. For centuries, the philosophical and religious beliefs of the Vietnamese people, as of other peoples in the region, had functioned at two levels—the "Great Tradition" religious-philosophical systems such as Confucianism, Buddhism, Hinduism, and Islam and the "Little Tradition," rooted in the belief in the existence of village spirits and spirits in nature, such as wind, water, and mountains. Belief in the existence of nature spirits, of course, was characteristic of all human societies in prehistoric times, and it can safely be assumed that the early

Vietnamese possessed such beliefs themselves. It was probably only during and after the era of Chinese conquest that the Vietnamese became acquainted with the Great Tradition systems of Confucianism and Buddhism. More a social and political philosophy than a religion, Confucianism may have first been introduced by the Nam Viet ruler Trieu Da, then undoubtedly promoted by Chinese administrators and scholars in the wake of the Han conquest of the Red River delta a century later. Buddhism was brought to Vietnam during the early stages of Chinese rule by missionaries traveling between China and India, where Buddhism had originated several hundred years earlier.

As in China, Buddhism and Confucianism coexisted with each other as well as with indigenous traditions of spirit worship in Vietnam. In effect, each belief system fulfilled different social, religious, and emotional needs in Vietnamese society. Whereas faith in the existence of spirits provided an initial element of meaning to the manifold aspects of nature in the universe, Confucianism served above all to provide the state with a political philosophy and a system of ethics to maintain social order and to promote the material welfare of the mass of the population. Through its emphasis on rule by merit, Confucianism helped to create a sense of professionalism in the bureaucracy, the key to efficient and honest government in an authoritarian society. Through its emphasis on filial piety and the subordination of wife to husband, son to father, and younger brother to older brother, it made the family the key unit in society and the eldest male the linchpin of the family. Finally, through its emphasis on hard work and service to the community, Confucianism furnished the positive "work ethic" so necessary to the effective functioning of an agrarian hydraulic society.

If Confucianism served the interests of social order and the state, Buddhism reached out to the individual, to the emotions and spirit. Where the former focused on this world and advocated concrete actions to bring about improvement in this life, the latter was otherworldly in its orientation and taught the rejection of the material environment in favor of quiescence and an effort to escape the evils of everyday human existence. Confucianism provided a vehicle for order in this life; Buddhism provided solace for life's tragedies and a release from the evil of existence through a rejection of desire and (at least for the common people) the belief in an afterlife. In practice, it is probably safe to say that Confucianism became primarily a philosophy for the elite, whereas Buddhism appealed to rich and poor alike. In rural villages it supplemented spirit worship and Taoism (another Chinese import) in providing a persuasive hypothesis about the nature of metaphysical reality.

After the restoration of independence in the tenth century, Buddhism temporarily became a dominant force in Vietnamese society, even at court. Kings took Buddhist monks (commonly known as bonzes) as their advisers, and great monasteries controlling vast tracts of land and thousands of serfs dotted the countryside. Even in the civil service examinations, the *locus classicus* of Confucian doctrine, Buddhist and Taoist texts were included as frequently as those of the great Chinese philosopher. In the long run, however, Buddhism fell victim to its own limitations as a potential ideology of the state. With its emphasis on passivity, individual salvation at the expense of community responsibility, and a renunciation of the material world, Buddhism could not effectively serve as the official religion of a dynamic and centralizing monarchy, and it gradually lost influence to Confucianism. With the rise of the Le dynasty in the fifteenth century, Confucian literati began to attain great influence at court, and Confucian texts served as the primary source material used for the training of government officials. Buddhism retained some influence as the dominant religion among the mass of the population, but it lost its privileged position at court and among the educated. Buddhist monasteries, once the repository of great wealth and influence, were despoliated by the state, and their residents were periodically harassed and persecuted by haughty Confucian mandarins.

On the one hand, the triumph of Confucianism as the official philosophy of the state during the Le dynasty had a positive impact on social institutions and mores in Vietnam. With its emphasis on government by men of talent and virtue, Confucian doctrine undoubtedly helped ambitious monarchs to break down the dominance of the landed nobility and provided opportunities for individual advancement for poor but able young men. No doubt it also had its use in maintaining social order, promoting a sense of commitment to public service and loyalty to the larger community and the state. Confucianism thus served a number of useful purposes as the official philosophy of a densely populated agrarian society.

On the other hand, Confucianism also contributed to an increasing formalism and social rigidity in Vietnamese society. The relatively informal social mores that had once characterized Vietnamese social life and gender relations (frequently disparaged by righteous Confucian officials during the early period of Chinese rule) were replaced by a more hierarchical and inflexible system of human relationships. This effect was particularly acute as to the role of women in Vietnamese society. Before the imposition of Chinese rule, Vietnamese women had many of the same rights as men. They were permitted to inherit family property and had more legal rights within the family than did women in China. Throughout history, many women, following the model of the Trung sisters, had distinguished themselves as intrepid warriors defending Vietnam from invasion from the north. Once Confucianism became dominant, however, women's rights in Vietnam came under severe restrictions. They were not permitted to participate in the civil service examinations, nor to serve in the bureaucracy. Within the family, their rights were equally constrained. Under the Confucian "three obediences" (*tam cuong* or, in Chinese, *san kang*), they were clearly subordinate to their husbands, who possessed all property rights and were permitted to take a second wife if the first failed to produce a son. Only males were permitted to administer the family rituals necessary to facilitate the passage of departed members to their afterlife.

A shadow of past freedoms remained, however. Under the famous Hong Duc Code, promulgated during the reign of the Confucianizing monarch Le Thanh Tong (1460–1497), women, in accordance with ancient custom, were permitted to own property and to perform limited ritual functions within the family. These rights were abrogated, however, in the nineteenth century, when the Nguyen dynasty returned to a stricter interpretation of Confucian social practice.

EDUCATION IN TRADITIONAL VIETNAM

It was above all the educational system that injected Confucian doctrine into the bloodstream of Vietnamese society. Historical records suggest that the Confucian system of education was first introduced into Vietnam during the era of Chinese rule, but it was only after the restoration of independence in the tenth century that a comprehensive system based on features used in China began to take shape. At first, the system was tailored to fit existing conditions in the new Vietnamese state. Under the Ly dynasty (1010–1200), a temple of literature was built in Hanoi to provide training in Confucian doctrine for candidates to high office. In 1075 the first examinations were held for entry into the bureaucracy. In accordance with contemporary practice, however, the competition was initially limited to members of the local aristocracy, who alone were eligible for high official positions. Eventually, however, the competition began to conform to the Chinese pattern and was opened to commoners, the most talented and ambitious of whom gradually became eligible to occupy senior positions in the bureaucracy. As we have seen, at first the content of the examinations included Buddhist and Taoist as well as Confucian texts (commonly labeled, following Chinese practice, the *tam giao*, or "three doctrines"). But by the fifteenth century, Confucianism had become the official doctrine of the state and was dominant in the examinations as well.

In theory, the Confucian educational system possessed a number of attractive features when compared to systems in existence elsewhere in Southeast Asia. The emphasis on merit provided an avenue of upward mobility for poor-but-bright young males and reduced the dominant role

Children at play. (Courtesy *Vietnam Pictoral.*)

of the hereditary aristocracy in Vietnamese society. By stressing the importance of talent and virtue, training in the classical Confucian texts also probably helped to enhance the sense of professionalism and integrity in the civil service and to promote a sense of loyalty and dedication to the community and the state.

But the system undoubtedly had its limitations. Although schools and private tutors (often failed candidates in the civil service examinations) probably existed in most Vietnamese villages, few poor parents could afford to enroll their children. In some cases, the education of talented male children from poor families might be sponsored by a well-to-do relative, but generally speaking the system favored those families with wealth and those with a tradition of education and service in the bureaucracy.

Nor was training in the Confucian classics necessarily successful in inculcating in the student high moral fiber and a proper regard for the needs of the weak. In practice, Confucian education often degenerated into formalism and a ritualistic concern for the recitation of texts rather than a comprehension of and dedication to the content. If in theory the Confucian gentleman (in Chinese, *chun tzu*, rendered as *quan tu* in Vietnamese) was wise, compassionate, and fair, in actuality he was often an arrogant pedant who paraded his learning and exhibited more contempt than compassion for his social and intellectual inferiors. Still, on balance the adoption of Confucian educational institutions on the Chinese model probably represented a net advantage to the Vietnamese state.

THE CREATIVE ARTS IN TRADITIONAL VIETNAM

If Chinese influence permeated the religious beliefs and social institutions of Vietnamese society, it was no less visible in the creative arts. In literature, art, architecture, and music, the influence of Chinese styles and techniques on Vietnamese culture was readily apparent from the original takeover by the Han empire down to the French conquest in the nineteenth century. Beyond the question of form, however, Vietnamese art often reflected local motifs. For example, although Vietnamese music followed its Chinese counterpart in the adoption of the five-tone scale and the use of instruments such as the three-stringed guitar (*tam huyen* or, in Chinese, *san hsien*), it also absorbed influence from the Indianized state of Champa, as was seen in the popularity of Cham dances and the use of the Cham rice drum.[3] Similarly, Vietnamese porcelains, highly prized throughout the region during the Tran and Le dynasties, broadly resembled their Chinese counterparts, but applied a type of green glaze not used in China.

In general, however, the similarities between Vietnamese and Chinese works of art are usually more apparent than the differences. Such is certainly the case in architecture, where civil and religious buildings erected during the traditional period often appear to be a blatant imitation of Chinese models. Unfortunately, relatively little architecture survives from the premodern period. The famous Temple of Literature in Hanoi, originally built in 1075, bears close resemblance to its classical prototypes in China. More distinctive is the so-called One-Pillar Pagoda (*Chua mot cot*), erected in the eleventh century at the order of Emperor Ly Thai Tong.

The pagoda, which arises on a single pillar from a pond filled with lotus plants, was originally part of a larger Buddhist monastic complex that has since been destroyed. The most prominent example of Vietnamese copying of Chinese classical styles during the precolonial period is probably the imperial palace of Huê, constructed in the early nineteenth century by the Nguyen dynasty in imitation of the Forbidden City in Peking.

It was in literature that the interaction between Chinese and native influence was ultimately most pronounced. Unfortunately, examples of early Vietnamese writing are fragmentary. Prior to independence, however, Chinese influence was undoubtedly paramount, both in form and content. Literary Chinese was the official written language at court and was used in all official communications. The earliest extant literary works in Vietnam show a strong imprint of Chinese models. The most common examples of literary creativity are found in historical writings and Buddhist holy texts. The most famous historical work, unfortunately not extant, was the *Dai Viet Su Ky* (History of Dai Viet), authored by the twelfth-century scholar Le Van Huu under an imperial commission. A condensed version of the work, based partly on surviving fragments, was later published in China under the title *Viet Su Luoc* (Outline of Viet History).

Still, although Vietnamese literature in the first centuries after the restoration of independence reflected a strong degree of Chinese influence, according to the respected present-day Vietnamese scholar Nguyen Khac Vien it was during this period that a truly "national literature" began to flower. During the Tran (1225–1400) and early Le (1428–1788) dynasties, several works on the history of the Vietnamese state appeared. Although the fragments still in existence show a high degree of Chinese influence—in the Chinese pattern, they consisted primarily of a chronology of official events—they nevertheless reflect a high degree of national consciousness. The officially sponsored *Dai Viet Su Ky Toan Thu* (Complete History of Dai Viet), written by the fifteenth-century historian Ngo Si Lien, traced Vietnamese history back to the semilegendary Hong Bang dynasty and was clearly dedicated to providing the state of Dai Viet with a pedigree similar to, if not equivalent to, that of China.[4]

The first centuries of independence witnessed a similar development in the field of poetry. The pacesetter in this field was the renowned scholar, statesmen, and military strategist Nguyen Trai, whose poetry combined a blend of Confucian morality and patriotic themes while he helped the rebel Le Loi to bring about the defeat of Chinese invading forces and the rise of the Le dynasty.

Although during the first centuries after the restoration of independence the dominant forms of literary creativity in Vietnam were patterned after those of classical China, an indigenous form of literature was gradually beginning to emerge. Much of this embryonic national literature was in the form of oral poetry, love songs, and popular theater and was not in-scribed, but was passed down by memory from generation to generation. Not all of this nonclassical popular literature went unrecorded, however, for it was apparently at this time that a new form of demotic script called *chu nom* (southern characters) was invented; it gradually became a popu-lar form of written communication in Vietnam. *Chu nom* (or nom, as it is often called) was an adaptation of Chinese written characters to the spo-ken Vietnamese language. The precise date of its invention remains un-known, but it was probably already in use by the time of the Ly dynasty. The earliest extent text dates from the Tran period.

At first, the new script was not generally accepted by Vietnamese scholars, many of whom undoubtedly considered it uncultured and clumsy. But eventually its value as a national form of written expression, and its superiority to literary Chinese as a vehicle to express human emo-tions, became apparent, and it came into general usage for various types of popular literature. Occasionally it was used for administrative pur-poses, and some classical texts were translated into *chu nom,* but its pri-mary function was in the writing of fiction. During the Tran and early Le dynasties, it was frequently used for the writing of poetry, but its major period of expansion took place during and after the seventeenth century, when it gave rise to the flowering of a unique national literature centered on the appearance of the novel.

With the rise of the novel form written in *chu nom,* Vietnamese litera-ture began to explore such new themes as individual happiness, sexual love, social criticism, and satire. Much of the new writing had a pervasive underlying social and political message, attacking such familiar evils of traditional Confucian society as corrupt officials, greedy landlords, and pedantic scholars. It also raised daring themes of social liberation for tra-ditionally oppressed groups like women and peasants. Significantly, a number of the new authors were themselves women, who used their satir-ical abilities like a rapier to stab at the male-oriented Confucian society around them. The most famous work of the period was the novel written in rhythmic prose, *Kim Van Kieu,* by Nguyen Du. *Kieu,* as it is familiarly called, was the poignant story of young lovers caught in the web of tradi-tional morality. Appealing to Vietnamese of all classes, *Kim Van Kieu* be-came the single-most popular and revered work in Vietnamese literature and was learned by heart by generations of illiterate Vietnamese.[5]

Side by side with the rise of the novel came the flourishing of other forms of literary writing: of poetry, rural plays, and operas such as *cheo* (a type of popular theater), of *phu* (long texts in rhythmic prose of nom), of *ca dao* (a form of lyrical song without instrumental accompaniment), and of ve (stories told in rhymed form). Such innovative forms not only explored new means of creative expression, many of them marking the transition from ordinary prose to poetry and from literature to music, they also gave visible evidence of the struggle within Vietnamese culture to transcend the limitations of Sino-Vietnamese style and social ethics. To the student of Vietnamese literature, they mark the clear emergence of a popular national literature independent of—and often in direct opposition to—the official court style introduced from China. After centuries of a sometimes suffocating cultural subordination to Chinese civilization, creative writers were beginning to declare their independence from the Confucian tradition.

Although the seventeenth and eighteenth centuries gave rise to a vast outpouring of new forms of literature, the older court literature did not entirely disappear. Historical works reflecting the classical Chinese model continued to appear throughout the period. Some of the most famous were the *Kham Dinh Viet Su Thong Giam Cuong Muc* (Imperial Historical Mirror of Dai Viet), an official history sponsored by the Nguyen dynasty, Le Quy Don's *Dai Viet Thong Su* (Complete History of Dai Viet), and Phan Huy Chu's encyclopedic biographies of major figures.

At the end of the eighteenth century, the rivalry between *chu nom* and literary Chinese took on political overtones, as Emperor Nguyen Huê, founder of the short-lived Tay Son dynasty, adopted *nom* as the official bureaucratic script for the state and ordered the establishment of a translation bureau to translate the Chinese classics into the Vietnamese script. But the Nguyen dynasty, which succeeded to the throne early in the next century, reversed the verdict and returned to the use of Chinese for all official documents.

THE CHALLENGE OF MODERNITY

The introduction of Western culture, which began in the seventeenth century and culminated in the imposition of colonial regimes throughout much of Southeast Asia 200 years later, had a traumatic effect on traditional societies throughout the region. Nowhere was this more true than in Vietnam, where Confucian institutions and values often conflicted in basic respects with those introduced by the French. Where Confucian principles emphasized the subordination of the individual to family and community, the French revolutionary trinity of liberty, equality, and fraternity focused on the bourgeois concept of individual freedom from state control as the key precept in human society. Where Sino-Vietnamese tradition preached harmony with nature and lacked a coherent doctrine of progress, the Industrial Revolution in Europe created a new set of assumptions that glorified the conquest of nature and openly promoted the value of change and the improvement of man's material surroundings. Where Confucian thought was hierarchical and asserted the dominant role of the male sex, modern Western social values contained strong egalitarian tendencies and, by the early twentieth century, progressive thinkers had begun to preach the equality of the sexes.

The imposition of French rule in the late nineteenth century, then, inevitably exerted a disintegrating impact on traditional culture in Vietnam. To some degree, this was a direct consequence of colonial policy that, in the hands of activist administrators like Governors-general Paul Beau and Albert Sarraut, took dead aim at Confucian traditions and sought the transformation of Vietnamese society through the introduction of Western values and institutions. In other cases, Western influence penetrated by more indirect means, through the growing presence of French *colons* in the cities and as the result of missionary activity, leading to the growth of the Catholic community in Vietnam to as many as 2 million believers in the late colonial period. Western influence was strongest in Cochin China, which, as a full colony and the source of much of the economic wealth of the country, was the most exposed to direct French influence. It was weakest in Annam, where the imperial court retained the formal trappings of its erstwhile authority and where, because of the lack of exploitable economic resources, there were relatively few European residents.

Above all, it was by means of the educational system that Western culture began to penetrate the minds of the Vietnamese and erode the old ways. The first generation of Vietnamese to experience French rule had been raised and educated under the traditional system. For them, Western ideas were filtered through an intellectual prism formed in the precolonial era. Beginning with the new century, however, the colonial regime gradually dismantled the traditional educational system and replaced it with a new one based at least partly on the French model. The three-tiered system of civil service examinations leading to a career in the bureaucracy was abolished, thus undermining the original purpose of the system of Confucian schools in villages and towns throughout the country. In its place arose a new Franco-Vietnamese system designed to expose the Vietnamese to Western values and culture. It operated on a two-track basis: an advanced level based on instruction in French language and culture and culminating in the newly established University of Hanoi, created for the Vietnamese elite, and a system of popular education at the elementary level, founded on instruction in the Vietnamese language, for the masses. Except in Annam, instruction in written Chinese fell into desuetude, and exposure to the Confucian classics was limited to compulsory classes in ethics. For the first generation of Vietnamese raised in the twentieth century, the Sino-Vietnamese heritage was already more a receding memory than a reality. Like their counterparts of the May Fourth generation in China, educated young Vietnamese scorned the old ways and began to seek the answers to their questions abroad, whether in Paris, London, or Moscow.

A crucial factor in the process of promoting Western knowledge was the change from the use of Chinese characters (in literary Chinese or *chu nom*) to the romanized script called *quoc ngu* (national language). *Quoc ngu*, a transliteration of spoken Vietnamese into the roman alphabet, had been invented by the Catholic missionary Alexander of Rhodes in the seventeenth century as a means of facilitating the propagation of Christianity into the country. Until the early colonial era, its use was limited to the missionary enterprise, but eventually the French (and some Vietnamese who collaborated in the colonial effort) in Cochin China soon preferred it to the aesthetically pleasing but pedagogically cumbersome Chinese ideographs. At first, use of the new script was resisted by the conservative Confucian scholar-gentry class, who considered *quoc ngu* vulgar (one is reminded of the contemptuous observation of one Chinese scholar that Western scripts moved horizontally across the page like an earthworm, rather than up and down, as a dignified script should) and a tool of the imperialists. Eventually, however, its utility became increasingly apparent. By the first decade of the twentieth century, progressive members of the scholar-gentry class such by Phan Chu Trinh began to promote its use through a new school in Hanoi, the Dong Kinh Nghia Thuc (Tonkin Free School), which also encouraged its Vietnamese students to adopt other aspects of Western civilization. Within a few years, *quoc ngu* was widely accepted as superior to Chinese ideographs and as an effective means of written expression in Vietnam.[6]

From the new school system, Western influence radiated rapidly outward into other areas of society and began to exert a corrosive impact on traditional institutions, values, and culture. It was the urban middle class above all that absorbed the new cultural currents rushing in from the West. Affluent Vietnamese in Saigon aped French eating habits and dress, entered Western professions such as engineering, medicine, and law, and lived in Western-style houses. To many, the Confucian heritage appeared totally inadequate to meet the challenge of the new century and was identified, through the effete imperial monarchy in Huê, with the French colonial regime. Some became almost entirely alienated from their native culture, sought French citizenship, and spoke French as their primary language. In such circles, the traditional Confucian principles that had for centuries defined family and personal relationships began rapidly to unravel, replaced by the more individualist values of the modern West.

Nowhere was this more visible than in relations between men and women. Women from elite or educated affluent families now began to undergo advanced schooling and to seek careers in professions previously reserved for males and "modern" youths—male and female alike—re-

jected the traditional practice of arranged marriages and sought love relationships. Western influence was slower to reach the tradition-bound villages where conservative peasants, still sheltered from the full force of
Westernization by their bamboo hedges, generally continued to honor the
old ways.

Inevitably, Western modes began to affect the arts. A growing number of artists, composers, and musicians abandoned traditional styles and
began to imitate Western trends. Literature, too, soon felt the impact of
Western influence. During the first two decades of the twentieth century, a
new journalism, influenced by developments in France, began to appear.
Much of it was written in the French language and directed at the affluent
Europeanized audience residing in the cities. Some of the new publications, like Nguyen Van Vinh's *Dong Duong Tap Chi* (Indochinese Review),
were written in *quoc ngu*. Vinh, an outspoken advocate of modern Western
ways, viewed *quoc ngu* as "a life and death issue for we Vietnamese" and
as a means of escaping the pervasive influence of Chinese feudal culture,
expressed through the Chinese written language. Vinh used the columns
of his journal to promote social and cultural reform and was a pioneer in
promoting a new role for women in Vietnamese society. In a column devoted to the needs and aspirations of Vietnamese women, Vinh criticized
them for their old-fashioned habits and urged them to imitate their progressive counterparts in the West.[7]

By the 1920s, Vietnamese journalists had become more daring, and a
number of small journals sprouted in the cities. Although few survived
for more than a few issues, they reflected a growing sense of social and political radicalism in the intellectual community and a willingness to criticize the failings of the colonial regime. Among the best known was *Phu
Nu Tan Van* (Women's News), a slick magazine published in Saigon for the
newly educated middle-class woman in Cochin China. The views expressed in the publication were moderately progressive (in a manner similar to *New Yorker* in the United States), but were relatively conservative
on women's issues. Support for female education was combined, for example, with an emphasis on home and family and opposition to free marriage.[8]

Not all the new journalism, however, was so modernist in tone.
Some conservative writers, such as the scholar-journalist Pham Quynh,
defended the continued relevance of Confucian community-oriented
values and called for a careful synthesis of modern Western and traditional cultural elements as the most effective means of enabling the Vietnamese to meet the challenges of the twentieth century. In his journal *Nam
Phong* (Wind from the South), which was sponsored by the colonial regime, Pham Quynh published essays on Eastern and Western culture as
well as translations of the French classics. He attempted to encourage the

growth of a new Vietnamese literature based on *quoc ngu* and on a fruitful collaboration of Asian and Western elements.

Western influence was as strong in the realm of fiction as it was in journalism. After World War I, a new generation of Vietnamese novelists influenced by literary trends in France began to sprout. At first, advocates of the new form shunned sensitive political and social themes that might arouse official displeasure, and authors sought refuge in escapism and literary romanticism. Common themes were unrequited love and tales of mysticism and derring-do. In the early 1930s, however, several younger writers banded together in a literary group called the Tu Luc Van Doan (Self-Reliance Literary Group) and began to use the novel to criticize the political and social inequities in colonial society. In novels and short stories, such progressive writers as Nhat Linh, Khai Hung, and Hoang Dao criticized arranged marriages, promoted social reforms, and described sympathetically the conditions of the urban and rural poor. Most new writers stayed within the bounds of moderate reformism, but a few, such as Ngo Tat To, followed the path of social revolution and opposed "art for life" to the bourgeois attitude of "art for art's sake."[9]

The influx of Western culture and ideas did not entirely staunch the flow of Chinese culture and ideas into Vietnam. Translations of the works of such Chinese reformist writers as K'ang Yu-wei, Liang Ch'i-ch'ao, and Lu Hsün appeared in Vietnam during the first decades of the new century, and some conservative intellectuals continued to voice their support for the classical Confucian tradition. But the latter had been substantially discredited by its identification in the minds of intellectuals with the effete imperial court and its shameful collaboration with the French colonial regime. As in early-twentieth-century China, there was little room in the minds of Vietnamese progressives for a fruitful synthesis of Eastern and Western ideas.

A SOCIETY AT WAR

The decade from the mid-1940s to the mid-1950s witnessed the opening stages of the long civil war that would engage the emotions and energies of all Vietnamese for the next generation. Beginning with the outbreak of the Franco-Vietminh conflict, the nation was divided, culturally as well as politically, into two separate societies. In French-controlled areas, the influence of the capitalist West intensified. In regions controlled by the Vietminh, the Communists attempted to construct a new culture based on the ideal of the "communist man" and the classless society. This ideological and cultural bifurcation of Vietnam was accentuated after the Geneva Conference of 1954 by the de facto division of Vietnam into two separate governments, one in the North and the other in the South.

The contrast was striking. In South Vietnam, the mounting U.S. presence under the regime of Ngo Dinh Diem and later that of Nguyen Van Thieu led to the growing influence of American culture and accelerated the breakdown of traditional values and institutions. For two decades the social and cultural environment in South Vietnam reflected an uneasy amalgam of Vietnamese, French, and American themes. American influence penetrated South Vietnamese society through a variety of means. U.S. economic and technological assistance stimulated the rise of an affluent middle class increasingly influenced by social and cultural trends in the United States. The educational system was re-modeled on the pattern of the U.S. system, and although the ideal of universal elementary education was not fully achieved, the literacy rate increased to levels substantially higher than during the colonial period.

In the creative arts, a subtle intermingling of indigenous and Western currents took place. In painting and the plastic arts, for example, French influence continued to predominate, along with a Vietnamese version of *chinoiserie* that interpreted traditional culture in an exotic manner to appeal to a Western audience. In literature, however, the influence of American individualism produced a rush of novels and short stories laced with satire, romanticism, and sexual love themes. Many dealt with issues raised by the war, but others were frankly escapist and somewhat reminiscent of the bittersweet era of the colonial 1920s. Popular music, too, reflected influences from the West. Popular tunes mingled indigenous themes with the rock beat of the contemporary West and, aided by the presence of a half-million U.S. servicemen, the cultural heroes of the 1960s and early 1970s in the West achieved similar popularity in South Vietnam.

While South Vietnam continued to draw its cultural models from the capitalist West, the North took its guidance from mainland China and the U.S.S.R. During the early stages of its struggle for power, the ICP had understandably devoted more attention to revolutionary strategy than to the future shape of a socialist society although, as we have seen, radical intellectuals had begun to create a socialist literature in the 1930s. Then, in 1943 the party issued a new cultural program drafted by General Secretary Truong Chinh calling for the creation of a new society based on the themes of national independence, people's democracy, and socialism. The promulgation of the program had, however, an immediate objective as well—to win intellectuals over to the party's cause in the struggle for national liberation.

After the August Revolution, the party created a Cultural Association for National Salvation with the goal of building a new culture (*mot nen van hoa moi*). During the long Franco-Vietminh struggle, the Communists attempted to put support from many progressive intellectuals to good use, calling on them not only to serve in the revolutionary armed forces, but also to put their creative talents to work in persuading others to serve as well. Vietminh leaders convened conferences for writers and artists in the liberated areas. The primary focus of the movement's cultural work was to link the world of culture to economic and political realities and to create a popular literature based on the ideal of the communist man. As Ho Chi Minh noted in a brief address to all artists in 1951: "With regard to your creative work, you must understand, get in close touch with and go deeply into the people's life. Only by so doing will you be able to depict the heroism and determination of our soldiers and people and to contribute to the development and heightening of these qualities.[10]

The party's message served as a powerful persuasive force to Vietnamese intellectuals disillusioned with Western culture and the false nationalism of the Bao Dai government. Poets like To Huu and Xuan Dieu and novelists such as Hoai Thanh, Nguyen Hong, To Hoai, and Nam Cao, fled to the *maquis* and dedicated their talents to the creation of a new literature based on revolutionary patriotism and socialist realism. Creative works focused on the glories of socialism and the sacrifice of the individual to the national cause.

With peace restored in 1954, the Communists prepared to embark formally on the construction of a socialist society in North Vietnam. The party considered cultural and ideological work to be crucial to the process and gave it equal prominence with the technological revolution and the revolution in production relations as the three cardinal objectives of the new era. The key role in this cultural struggle would be played by the educational system, for it was the children, still uncontaminated by the multiple evils of Western capitalist society, who were targeted to eventually become the pillars of the socialist state. In place of the French two-track system, which had exposed a minority of the people to Western education and the majority to little or none, the new system sought to achieve mass literacy through universal education at the elementary level. After completing nine years of compulsory elementary education, the student would either continue on to secondary or vocational school, and thus increase the ranks of the "socialist intellectuals," or enter the work force. Beyond the obvious objective of contributing to the transformation of North Vietnam into an advanced technological society, the primary goal of education in the DRV was to indoctrinate the masses with the virtues of the socialist system. This would not be an easy task, as regime spokesmen conceded, for the vast majority of the Vietnamese people, whether peasants or urban bourgeoisie, had little understanding of Marxism-Leninism.

The creative arts supplemented the educational system as a means of increasing socialist awareness among the mass of the population. To achieve this purpose, literature, music, and the visual arts were be purged of the perfidious influence of Western bourgeois culture and provided a new focus, nationalist in form and socialist in content. The importance of the dual emphasis on patriotism and ideology, an obvious reflection of the dual objectives of socialist construction and national reunification, was strongly emphasized in official statements dealing with the revolution on the cultural front. Party spokesmen went to great lengths to assert that patriotism and Marxist internationalism were not irreconcilable, but indeed were mutually compatible.

Under party rule, the creative arts were thus dedicated to two major objectives: to stimulate a sense of national identity and commitment through the encouragement of indigenous forms of art, music, and literature and to promote the growth of a socialist ethic through the creation of a new culture based on the principles of socialist realism. In order to promote national pride, traditional forms of art, music, and dance were revived and transformed to serve modern purposes. The *ca dao* and other traditional forms of literary and musical expression were transformed into a medium for serving the cause of social revolution and national reunification. In novels, plays, and poems, North Vietnamese writers portrayed in romantic terms the glorious struggle of their countrymen to bring about national independence and to achieve the goals of constructing a socialist culture in the North and achieving reunification with the South.

Nonfiction writing, as well, was provided with a new content. Sponsored by the state-run Institute of History, historians wrote biographies of great national heroes such as Nguyen Trai, Tran Hung Dao, Phan Dinh Phung, and Phan Chu Trinh. Veteran revolutionaries wrote memoirs of their activities during the August Revolution and the War of Resistance against the French and of their encounters with the quintessential national hero, President Ho Chi Minh. The DRV did not, however, deliberately create a "cult of personality" around the figure of "Uncle Ho," as Peking and Moscow had done with party leaders Mao Tse-tung and Joseph Stalin. To be sure, Ho was portrayed in the media and the arts as the founder and leader of the Vietnamese revolution, but his patriotism, his selflessness and dedication, and his matchless sense of personal ethics were stressed more than his all-knowing sagacity. It was Ho the collegial leader, the symbol of patriotism and self-sacrifice, the "Uncle Ho" kissing babies and mingling with the masses—rather than the irreplaceable, almost mythical and larger-than-life personae of Stalin and Mao—that was given prominence.

The regime's effort to build a new Vietnamese culture had mixed results during the two decades immediately following the Geneva Conference. Of the success of its efforts to promote a sense of national identity and to mobilize mass support for national liberation there can be little doubt. The campaign to wipe out illiteracy and establish a system of universal education at the elementary level was undoubtedly one of the most successful in Southeast Asia. The effort to eradicate Western influence—notably that of the Catholic church, the only well-organized religious force in North Vietnam and a potential source of resistance to the regime—was relatively successful, for the church was placed under severe restrictions without a formal break in relations with the Vatican.

Less successful, however, was the regime's plan to produce a new culture based on socialist ideals. Remolding the character of the tradition-bound and family-oriented Vietnamese peasant was a major task and undoubtedly more difficult than mere statistics would indicate. Although the vast majority of the rural population was successfully enrolled in collectives, the stubborn resistance of the Vietnamese peasant to the collective mentality—like that of his counterpart in China and the Soviet Union—was difficult to break. Traditional habits, prejudices, and rituals proved equally resistant to the blandishments of the cadres of the revolution. Press reports confirmed that "feudal attitudes" (often a euphemism for male chauvinism) continued to thwart the efforts of the regime to promote the birth of a new egalitarian society. Although women began to play a more important role in administrative and legislative bodies at the local level, party leaders sent out subliminal signals by maintaining the Politburo as an all-male preserve.

The regime was also faced with problems in urban areas. During the war of resistance, the Vietminh movement had won considerable support from intellectuals, although relatively few fled to the liberated areas to serve in the revolutionary forces. In 1956, following the example of the Hundred Flowers campaign in China, the party briefly encouraged intellectuals to speak out in favor of its domestic programs. Some, however, were sufficiently emboldened to criticize the party's domination over politics and culture and called for a liberalization of the political system and increased freedom for creative expression. Shocked by the boldness of its critics, the regime cracked down on the dissidents and closed their most prominent mouthpiece, *Nhan Van* (Humanities).

The crackdown on dissident intellectuals silenced critics of the regime, but it did little to solve the problems that had aroused dissent in the first place. One major source of public criticism was the increasing arrogance and rigidity of the bureaucracy. Party leaders were not unaware of the scope of the problem, and periodically official statements complained that many government officials and cadres were guilty of such sins as bureaucratism, "commandism," petty corruption, rigidity, and contempt for the masses. In China, evidence that party and government elites were beginning to adopt some of the less attractive habits of traditional officialdom had led Mao Tse-tung and his radical followers to launch the Cultural Revolution in the hope of cleansing the party and government and preserving the revolution. In North Vietnam, party leaders chose a more traditional route and attempted to resolve the problem through periodic rectification campaigns designed to improve bureaucratic behavior and weed out incompetent or corrupt elements. Although such programs presumably had some success, they clearly did not resolve the problem. By the early 1970s, official concern over bureaucratic misbehavior had increased and stringent regulations were issued to rid the party and government of impure elements. To provide a standard of behavior for youths entering the ranks of officialdom, a new "Ho Chi Minh class" of exemplary youths was set up as a model of revolutionary ethics.

ONWARD TO SOCIALISM?

Victory in the South in 1975 added a new dimension to the cultural challenge that the Communist party faced in its aspiration to construct a socialist society throughout Vietnam. Although over the years many southerners had been recruited, by conviction, moral suasion, or social pressure, into the revolutionary movement, the southern population as a whole had not yet been convinced of the superiority of the socialist system. In fact, some awaited the new regime with considerable anxiety. Many South Vietnamese had been influenced by Western bourgeois culture, a fact occasionally admitted in internal documents generated by party leaders in the South. Some of those most affected were the privileged youth of the big cities, many of whom had adopted a living style characterized by rock music, drugs, prostitution, and the individualist ethic. Rock stars like Trinh Cong Son—the Bob Dylan of Vietnam—popularized the view that "heroes are bunk" and "war is hell." Although such views had served the party well during the war, they posed a potential danger to revolutionary goals during the postwar era. Even some of the political and religious groups considered hostile to the Saigon regime, such as the Buddhist Association and the sects, were viewed in Hanoi as deeply imbued with a parochial or petit bourgeois attitude. And though party directives from Hanoi instructed southern leaders to rally such elements to the revolutionary cause, in practice they were often viewed with suspicion as irretrievably tainted by their past environment.

To remove the legacy of Western influence in southern Vietnam and sow the seeds of a new socialist culture would thus be one of the most complex challenges facing the party after victory in 1975. The problem was one of considerable delicacy. Economic and political realities dictated a relatively moderate and gradualist approach to avoid provoking hostility or resistance from the indigenous population in the South. On the other hand, a good case could be made for urgency. So long as Western influence had not been eliminated from southern society, the party's program of integrating the two zones and embarking on the road to socialism throughout the entire country would be severely hampered.

The new authorities moved cautiously but with deliberation. The immediate priority was to expurgate the remnants of the American era from Saigon and other urban areas in the South. As one of its first acts, the new government attempted to close the bars and drive the prostitutes, beggars, drug pushers, and juvenile gangs off the streets. The regime instructed cadres not to be overzealous in carrying out the policy, however, and on a few occasion cadres were reprimanded for harassing local youths for their long hair or Western clothing. Training centers were established to provide reeducation for addicts, delinquents, and streetwalkers, and orphanages were created for the homeless. There were some poignant exceptions, however. Children born of Vietnamese mothers and American fathers during the war were given no attention and were often viewed as pariahs by the local Vietnamese population. Many were reduced to living in the streets.

The new revolutionary authorities did their best to remove the remaining sources of U.S. influence. Within weeks of victory, all schools in the South were closed, and teachers were compelled to attend retraining sessions before being permitted to return to the classroom. When the schools were reopened, new textbooks with a Marxist orientation, hastily sent down from the North, replaced those that had been in use under the Saigon regime. A campaign to confiscate books, tapes, and records reflecting Western bourgeois decadence was launched, and newspapers that had published under the Saigon regime, except for the moderately critical *Tin Sang*, were ordered to close their doors.

The fears of party leaders that the population in the South would not be easily assimilated into the emerging socialist culture in the North were well-founded. Habits developed over a period of two decades of U.S. influence were not to be erased even by a regime as determined and well disciplined as the one in Hanoi. Despite the stringent efforts of the authorities, the southern population proved stubbornly resistant to the blandishments of the revolutionary regime. Foreign journalists reported that Ho Chi Minh City was still the old Saigon in disguise. As a report in *Time* magazine put it shortly after victory: "Good food and excellent wines are still available at the Hotel Caravelle, a favorite hangout of foreigners in the old days. Lissome Saigonese women wore hip-hugging jeans and colorful ao-dai's; although the PRG frowns on prostitution, streetwalkers and bar girls were still hawking their charms. American pop songs blared out from the jukeboxes of cafes and bars, and the old Thieves' Market on Bac Si Calumette Street was jammed with TV sets, cameras, and transistor radios taken from abandoned American PXs." *Time*'s judgment was confirmed by the authorities in Hanoi. An official report written in 1979 noted: "Some of the youths who are influenced by neocolonialism and the old social system have been infected with such bad habits as laziness, selfishness, parasitism, vagabondism, pursuing a good time, etc." Another official bemoaned the continuing influence of Western music over young people in the South, complaining that such music enticed listeners to "shirk obligations, detach themselves from reality, turn their backs on our people's life of labor and combat, regret the past and idolize imperialism."[11]

To make it worse, the easygoing lifestyle in the southern provinces was beginning to erode the spirit of revolutionary puritanism and self-sacrifice of northern soldiers and cadres serving there. For inexperienced and socially innocent northerners, the manifold temptations of southern culture must have been hard to resist. According to press accounts, cadres from the North, many of them housed in the old Hotel Continental (now renamed the Hotel of the People's Insurrection), were too often seduced by the glittering temptations of city life in Saigon. Bribery, embezzlement, black market activities, and the shirking of obligations became increasingly common among officials stationed in the South and began to occur in the North as well.

By the end of the decade, the regime had grown sufficiently concerned about the situation to launch a major campaign against "decadent" influences in Vietnamese culture. Literature, music, and art that were considered harmful to the struggle to build a socialist society were banned. Books and printed songs that portrayed such alleged Western bourgeois attitudes as individualism, selfishness, sexual license, and mysticism were confiscated and burned. In their place, stories and folk songs reflecting "the genuine spirit of the people" were revived and propagated, and new creative works were produced to meet the standards of socialist idealism and help to create the new citizen. Such views were incorporated in the 1980 constitution, which stated in Article 38:

> Marxism-Leninism is the ideological system guiding the development of Vietnamese society.
>
> The state broadly disseminates Marxism-Leninism, the line and policies of the Communist Party of Vietnam. It preserves and develops the cultural and spiritual values of the nation, absorbs the best of world culture, combats feudal and bourgeois ideologies and the influences of imperialist and colonialist culture; criticizes petty-bourgeois ideology; builds a socialist way of life, and combats backward life-styles and superstitions.[12]

To promote the birth of this new culture, conferences sponsored by the Ministry of Culture were convened at all administrative levels to acquaint cadres with official guidelines.

The authorities soon discovered, however, that new standards were not always easy to apply. For example, an article written by the minister of culture and published in *Nhan Dan* conceded that it was often difficult to classify musical works. Some "normal, soft, and unharmful music" had been banned or confiscated by government officials, but some "rock music" superfically reflecting socialist themes had been spared. Moreover, the official campaign to cleanse the nation of foreign influence and create a new national and socialist literature and art was beginning to encounter resistance from within. An article by Ha Xuan Truong in the March 1980 issue of *Tap Chi Cong San* (Communist Review) noted that some "artistic creators" had become "confused" about official policies and were inclined to blame deficiencies on the general line of the party rather than on faulty implementation at the lower level. The author was particularly critical of an article by Hoang Ngoc Hien in the June 1979 issue of *Van Nghe* (Literature and Art), which complained that under the current line more attention was being paid to "conformist realism" than to artistic truth. Truong conceded that a mechanical and shortsighted application of the principle "literature and art serve politics" was a danger to be avoided, but at the same time (undoubtedly reflecting official policy), he emphasized that "we must enable everyone to clearly realize that the fierce and extremely complicated political struggle in the world and in our country demand [sic] that now more than ever revolutionary writers and artists must firmly grasp the party's political struggle goals." If it was necessary to overcome the diseases of formalism and superficiality in party directives, it was even more important to affirm that socialist realism must transform and construct life.

The remolding of the educational system, to transform it into a more effective vehicle for building the communist citizen, was similarly plagued with problems. In an article in the September 5, 1979 issue of *Nhan Dan,* Vice Premier To Huu, the party's rising ideological czar, conceded that many youths lacked discipline and socialist awareness. To deal with such problems, he referred to a recent resolution of the party Central Committee calling for the establishment of a new national educational system. The new system, according to To Huu, must devote increased attention to ideology, politics, and revolutionary ethics. It must emphasize the unity of theory and practice, combine academic studies with practical labor, and integrate the school system into the corpus of society at large in order to make it more relevant to the nation's social needs. Only thus, he argued, could a new generation of young Vietnamese begin to emerge bearing with them "the qualities and abilities of the New Man."[13]

One of the key aspects in the party's goal of creating a new and more egalitarian society was its need to integrate the national minorities more effectively into the broader population. Thousands of peoples living in tribal minority areas were resettled from their mountain villages to newly opened centers in the southern provinces; others were persuaded to give up their nomadic way of life for settled agriculture. In order to reduce discontent by Catholics and other religious minorities such as the Cao Dai and the Hoa Hao, a constitutional provision guaranteeing freedom of religious belief was inserted into the new constitution, while state-supported religious associations attempted to win over such groups to support the policies of the regime.

The regime also sought concrete measures to bring about sexual equality and strength the role of women in a society still characterized broadly by the assumption of male superiority. The 1946 constitution had called for the equality of the sexes in all aspects of society, and a decree promulgated in 1950 had promised women full legal rights in the marriage contract with their husbands. As we have seen, during the long Vietnam War, women played an active and sometimes crucial role in the conflict, but they made up less than one-third of the members of the ruling party and were not represented in its leading body, the Politburo. Attitudes of male dominance were still widespread throughout North Vietnamese society. As an article in the June 1982 issue of *Tap Chi Cong San* noted, forced marriages, concubinage, and the maltreatment of women were "still rather widespread," especially in rural areas. In an effort to deal with such problems, Article 63 of the 1980 constitution declared that "the State and society concern themselves with the raising of the political, cultural, scientific, technical, and professional level [of women] and must promote their role in society."

Yet there were signs that the struggle for full equality would continue to be a difficult one. Although women now comprised over 50 percent of the workforce in the country and held an active position in occupations such as medicine and the trade services (which in Western countries would be the preserve of males), there is still a marked tendency to view their role in the workplace as secondary to men. Working women are still concentrated in low-paying positions and represent only about one-quarter of the skilled workforce in the SRV. Although the percentage of women members of the National Assembly and lower-level governmental positions has risen in recent years, women are still a distinct minority in the ruling Communist party. There were only seven women in the Central Committee elected in December 1986 and none have yet been raised to the rank of the Politburo.[14]

VIETNAMESE SOCIETY AND CULTURE IN RENOVATION

When party leaders attending the Sixth Party Congress in December 1986 decided to launch the program of renovation now known as *doi moi,* they did not make clear what impact the new strategy would have on of social and cultural policies. Documents issued at the end of the congress indicated that there would be a more practical approach to social problems. The Political Report presented to the delegates by General Secretary Truong Chinh, for example, placed heavy emphasis on the importance of science and technology in enhancing the performance of the economy. The goal of education was described in dual terms: to form and develop the socialist personality of the younger generation and to "train a skilled workforce" capable of contributing directly to socio-economic development.

Specific goals for education included the abolition of illiteracy, the realization of universal primary education, and extending secondary education to all areas "with favorable conditions." To help improve the quality of education, the social status and material conditions of teachers and other educational workers was heightened. The role of ideology was not ignored in the political report, however. "We should oppose vestiges of feudal, colonialist, and bourgeois cultures," it said. "All plots and moves by hostile forces aimed at making cultural and art activities a means of sowing pessimism and a depraved life style must be thwarted. Superstitions and other backward customs and practices must be curbed."[15]

Yet in recent years Vietnam continues to face severe problems in achieving these educational goals. According to available statistics, only about one-half of all eligible children are enrolled in kindergarten, and almost 40 percent of adolescents have dropped out of school by the age of 14. The country still suffers from an agonizing shortage of trained personnel, and higher education is still inadequate to meets the needs of a changing society. School buildings badly need expansion and renovation, and teachers are still poorly paid and demoralized.

There are equally serious problems on the issue of health care. Outdated equipment, poorly trained personnel, and a lack of adequate concern for sanitation characterize the medical system, which is technically run by the state, but is now being increasingly affected by free market factors. With doctors earning salaries from the state of only about $50 (US) a month, many have resorted to moonlighting to make ends meet. The result is growing differences in the quality of health care, depending on the patient's ability to pay. "If you're not ready to pay for everything," remarked one woman, "you just wait." In the meantime, malnutrition among children is among the highest in the world, and according to estimates well over one-half of the population suffers from intestinal parasites.[16]

The social impact of such conditions has been significant. With unemployment, especially among the youth, at alarming levels, such social evils as crime, drug addiction, and prostitution have become endemic in

some areas of the country. News reports indicate that there are a minimum of a half-million drug addicts in Vietnam and an equal number of
prostitutes. Although officials routinely blame such problems on the
growing presence of Westerners in the SRV, it is undoubtedly more complicated than that. According to statistics, for example, about 90 percent of
red-light clients are Vietnamese.[17]

It was at least partly for that reason that many party leaders were reluctant to abandon the effort to indoctrinate the Vietnamese people in the
virtues of socialist morality. Many students have complained that courses
on Marxism-Leninism often take precedence over those dealing with
practical subjects, even as opportunities for advancement and enrollment
in institutions of higher learning remain affected by class background (an
affirmative action program favoring sons and daughters of workers and
peasants known officially as "classism"). There are signs, however, that
party leaders have finally begun to recognize the fact that ideological purity and economic development are not always mutually compatible. In
its section on culture and education, the revised constitution of 1992 de-
leted most references to Marxism-Leninism and remarked only that

> the aim of education is to form and nurture the personality, moral qualities,
> and abilities of the citizen; to train working people and equip them with
> skills, to imbue them with dynamism and creativeness, national pride, good
> morality, and the will to strive for national prosperity, so as to meet the need
> to build and defend the country.[18]

The regime has followed up on this new approach by displaying a
more tolerant attitude toward the social, religious, and cultural practices
and beliefs of citizens, perhaps in the hope that this will help stem the
moral rot now festering in Vietnamese society. Party chief Do Muoi signaled the new attitude in the spring of 1993 by making official visits to the
Tran Quoc pagoda and the Catholic cathedral in Hanoi. Official con-
straints on religious activities such as social work, the renovation of
churches and temples, and the training of priests and monks have been re-
laxed. Vietnamese Buddhists and Catholics are now less afraid to attend
religious services, and some observers contend that popular interest in religion is on the rise because of growing disillusionment with the official
ideology of communism. Local communities are beginning to rebuild
their village *dinh* (communal houses) and Buddhist temples, and the popularity of such "feudal reactionary practices" as fortune-telling, expensive
weddings, and spirit healing is on the rise.[19]

The decline in revolutionary idealism, combined with the growing
tolerance of the regime, has been reflected in the changing character of
Vietnamese literature. During the first years after the end of the Vietnam

War, most Vietnamese writers tended to follow the accepted guidelines for creative work, restricting themselves to portraying the sacred struggle for national reunification and the building of socialist society in glowing tones. But by the mid-1980s, inspired partly by the permissive attitude ushered in by the Sixth Party Congress, writers and film producers began to broach new and politically explosive themes. Novelists like Duong Thu Huong, Nguyen Khac Phung and Le Luu laid bare the cruelties of the land reform program and the corrupt practices of party cadres. Duong Thu Huong's fictional account of the ruination of a rural family during the height of the 1955–1956 land reform program at the hands of an ideologically minded relative is especially moving. In an eerie replay, Nguyen Manh Tuan, in his recent novel *Mangrove Island,* has portrayed the heavy-handed treatment of southern supporters of the revolutionary movement by doctrinaire Viet Cong cadres after the end of the war in the South.[20]

Other writers like Bao Ninh in *The Prize of Love* and Xuan Thieu in *Huê's Red Apricot Season* turned a critical eye to the Vietnam War, portraying it not as a heroic struggle but as a savage war between brothers, marked by cruelty on both sides. Nguyen Huy Thiep, perhaps the most popular of the new generation of writers, describes in his short story "The General Retires" the disillusionment of an army officer with conditions on the home front after his return from the battlefield. Thiep has also dared to question the tendency of the regime to divide Vietnamese history into a chronicle of villians and heroes, portraying Tay Son leader Nguyen Huê and his rival Nguyen Anh (the future Emperor Gia Long) not as symbols of good and evil, but as ordinary human beings, each with a full quota of human frailties. The characters in his stories are not one-dimensional figures reflecting the morality play of the Vietnamese revolution, but ordinary people, with ordinary human frailties and concerns.[21]

Shaken by the sharpness of such criticism, party chief Nguyen Van Linh retreated from his initial attitude of encouragement to writers and artists and began warning intellectuals to refrain from criticizing the party, the socialist system, and the concept of the dictatorship of the proletariat. Prominent writers such as Duong Thu Huong, Nguyen Huy Thiep, and Doan Quoc Sy were harassed and even arrested on charges of smuggling, corruption, and even treason; editors who published their work were relieved of their positions. So far, such heavy-handed efforts by the regime have managed to silence the most outspoken of its literary critics—if only temporarily—but have not put out the fire.[22]

In other areas of Vietnamese culture, the expression of political dissent has been much more muted. Vietnamese painters have taken advantage of the new tolerance to experiment with recently popular Western styles, but none have used the palette and brush as political weapons.[23] In the field of popular music, the rock singer Trinh Cong Son—once the *en-*

fant terrible of the Saigon art world—continues to draw audiences, but restricts his lyrics to themes of love and adolescent alienation. Slowly but surely, however, young Vietnamese are becoming acquainted with counterculture music in the West. European and American rock stars of the last three decades have become popular idols among Vietnamese youth, at least in the big cities, and many fans arrive at rock concerts borne on motorbikes and wearing that calculated air of weary detachment and worldliness so familiar among their counterparts in the West. As contacts with the outside world increase in the 1990s, it will be increasingly difficult for the regime to isolate the next generation from intellectual and cultural currents sweeping throughout the region.

Conclusions

The longtime stated objective of the Vietnamese Communist party has been to create a new Vietnamese culture national in form and socialist in content. The dream of a reunited nation, secure in its borders, true to its own unique national heritage, economically prosperous, technologically advanced, and based on the Marxist vision of an egalitarian classless society, has been at the core of the party's enduring struggle since it was first founded by Ho Chi Minh over a half-century ago.

During the Vietnam War, many observers critical of the Hanoi regime questioned whether it was possible for the party to preserve the Vietnamese national culture while at the same time carrying out the dictates of proletarian internationalism. After all, they pointed out, after the division of the country in 1954 the DRV appeared to dedicate itself to destroying all vestiges of the traditional culture, described in official sources as "reactionary," "feudalist," and "oppressors of the masses." Spokespersons for the Hanoi regime vigorously defended themselves against such charges, and asserted that nationalism and communism were not incompatible. The true spirit of Vietnamese national culture, they asserted, was in its heroic defense of the nation against foreign invaders. Many of the country's great national heroes such as Nguyen Trai, Phan Dinh Phung, and Phan Boi Chau, they conceded, were Confucian scholars by training and inclination. From their training they not only developed a strong sense of personal rectitude, but also an attitude of respect and compassion for the needs of the mass of the population. In Hanoi's eyes, then, there were two strands of Confucian tradition in Vietnam, the popular and patriotic strand and the reactionary feudal strand. Presumably, the progressive elements in the Confucian tradition would be retained in the process of constructing a united, prosperous, and technologically advanced society in the future.

The problem was, during the years following the Geneva Conference, the regime appeared to show little interest in winning the support of what was officially labeled as the "patriotic landed gentry" within the population. To the contrary, such elements were brutally suppressed during the land reform campaign and publicly charged with being the class enemies of the people. Moreover, outside of a few ritualistic references to the patriotic qualities of such historical figures as Tran Hung Dao and Nguyen Trai, the regime devoted little attention to defining the question of how the country's national heritage would be expected to contribute to the society of the future. In general, in its approach to contemporary problems the North Vietnamese regime made little effort to define a strictly Vietnamese form of socialism and appeared willing to borrow in a somewhat mechanistic fashion from the U.S.S.R. and China. If there was indeed a national culture, beyond the heroic figures of Tran Hung Dao, Nguyen Trai, and Phan Boi Chau, there was precious little to show for it.

After the seizure of Saigon in the spring of 1975, party leaders for the first time were placed in a position to instill concrete meaning to their abstract pronouncements about culture during the war years. With the return of peace and reunification of the North with the South, they could now turn from the concerns of war to peacetime reconstruction. What kind of society did they have in mind, and in what specific ways was it going to reflect a national content? Was there going to be a unique "Vietnamese road to socialism," and if so, how would it differ from the Soviet or the Chinese models?

As it happened, decisions such as these were about to be made just at a time when Vietnamese relations with China were in a state of rapid deterioration. The rising tension in Sino-Vietnamese relations not only influenced Hanoi's domestic and foreign policy priorities, but also reshaped its interpretation of the Vietnamese national culture. In this new perspective, the course of Vietnamese history became a long struggle of the Vietnamese masses against two hostile and destructive forces, the feudal reactionaries at home and imperial China to the north. The Chinese were clearly the primary villain of the piece. In the prehistoric era, the Vietnamese people had already created an advance Bronze Age culture in the Red River valley. Left to its own devices, this embryonic Vietnamese state would have developed into a prosperous society with a strong national character centuries ago. But Chinese conquest led to the transformation of Vietnam into a feudal society under Chinese political and cultural domination. The Vietnamese were able to restore their independence in the tenth century, but failed to eradicate the legacy of centuries of Chinese cultural domination. In order to retain its power and preserve the feudal form of society, the Vietnamese ruling class relied on Chinese institutions and political and social philosophy. Beset by the "three evil doctrines" of Buddhism, Taoism, and Confucianism, the masses were reduced to a position of degradation and slavery. During the eighteenth century the oppressed masses, under the lead of the Tay Son chieftain Nguyen Huê (Emperor Quang Trung), rose against Sino-Vietnamese feudal domination and began to create a unique national culture. But colonial conquest set back the process, and only with the appearance of Ho Chi Minh and the rise of the Communist party after World War I were the Vietnamese people able to resume their struggle to defeat reactionary forces within and imperialist forces without and bring about the creation of a unique national culture.

Although not totally false, this interpetation is certainly somewhat simplistic. In the first place, current evidence suggests that Vietnamese society had begun to develop recognizably feudal characteristics long before the Chinese conquest and might well have evolved further in that direction even had the ancient state of Nam Viet not fallen to Chinese invasion. In the second place, the attempt to define the past as an undifferentiated era of subjugation and oppression ignored the fact that Confucian culture in Vietnam was by no means entirely feudalistic or reactionary in its orientation. To the contrary, the power of the Confucian monarchy and the professional bureaucracy contributed significantly to many of the achievements of the Vietnamese state. Progressive rulers attempted to reverse the concentration of land by dispossessing feudal magnates and distributing the land to impoverished peasants. It is from Confucian teachings that the Vietnamese inherited their reverence for education and their sense of dignity as human beings. As for the charge of subservience to China, even party ideologist Truong Chinh had conceded that many Confucianists were "deeply imbued with a national spirit." Confucianism did not blunt the Vietnamese sense of nationhood. On the contrary, it may have sharpened it.

One unfortunate consequence of this reinterpretation of history was that as the postwar era began, the role of "national" characteristics in the future Vietnamese society shrank almost to the point of insignificance. As applied by doctrinaire elements within the party leadership in Hanoi, Stalinist policies were adopted that were almost breathtaking in their lack of relevance to conditions inside Vietnam. Local officials compounded the problem by their insensitivity in dealing with the population in the southern provinces. Although party leaders in Hanoi had not lost touch with reality as much as the radical faction in China during the Cultural Revolution, they had obviously forgotten Ho Chi Minh's instructions on how to win the hearts and minds of the Vietnamese people.

It was the intellectuals who were the most vocal in pointing out the regime's errors. Like their counterparts two centuries earlier, creative writers skewered the shortcomings of the current system and demanded a government more responsible to the needs and aspirations of the people. While historians and scientists like Nguyen Khac Vien and Phan Dinh Dieu appealed to the party to grant democratic freedoms, fictional writers like Nguyen Huy Thiep and Duong Thu Huong adopted a more oblique approach, portraying individuals who were not one-dimensional stock figures mindlessly carrying out the task of revolution, but real-life complex individuals who bore the marks of the legacy of Vietnamese history and reflected all the blemishes characteristic of the human condition. Like the kite in Thiep's short story "Lessons from the Country," the human spirit is tied to the earth by a string and will eventually fall to the ground, but yet it "dares to soar high and free," far above the suffering of life, before its destiny inevitably brings it to its end.[24]

NOTES

1. Duong Quang Ham, *Viet Nam Van Hoa Su Yeu* (An Outline History of Vietnamese Literature), cited in Truong Chinh, "The long struggle to defend our national culture," in *Tap Chi Cong San* (Communist Review), March 1979, p. 62.

2. This argument is presented, inter alia, by Nguyen Khac Vien in his "Confucianism and Marxism in Vietnam," reproduced in Nguyen Khac Vien, *Tradition and Revolution in Vietnam* (Berkeley: Indochina Resource Center, 1974), pp. 35–41.

3. According to one account, Cham music was first introduced into Dai Viet as the result of a successful punitive expedition against the kingdom of Champa by the Vietnamese ruler Le Dai Hanh in 982. To celebrate his triumph, the latter returned home with a number of Cham musicians and dancers as well as a Hindu priest living with the Cham. During the ensuing Ly dynasty, Cham music attracted considerable interest because of its exotic sonority and rhythmic qualities and achieved a high degree of popularity at court. See Thai Van Kiem, "Panorama de la Musique Classique Vietnamienne des Origines a nos Jours," in the *Bulletin de la Société des Etudes Indochinoises,* XXXIX, No. 1 (First quarter 1964), pp. 64–65.

4. For the reference to a new national literature, see Nguyen Khac Vien, *Aperçu sur la Littérature Vietnamienne* (Hanoi: Foreign Languages Publishing House, 1976), pp. 37–38.

5. Although Nguyen Du's prose novel is often seen as a triumph of the Vietnamese creative spirit over the suffocating influence of Chinese tradition, the author was himself well versed in Confucianism, and *Kim Van Kieu* is laced with allusions to Chinese classical works. For an interesting discussion, see Alexander Woodside's informative introduction in Huynh Sanh Thong (ed.) *The Tale of Kieu* (New York: Vintage, 1973).

6. One reason for the popularity of *quoc ngu* among progressives was the fact that politically conservative elements in the population, such as literary critic Pham Quynh, preferred the old script.

7. Some of the female practices that he criticized were careless nursing, female fickleness and lust, and the chewing of betel nut. Other general evils of Viet-

namese society were an addiction to gambling, fuzzy talk, and Buddhist mysticism. For a discussion, see Pham The Ngu, *Viet Nam Van Hoc Su Gian Uc Tan Bien* (A History of Vietnamese Literature), Vol. III (Saigon: Quoc Hoc, 1965), pp.

8. For a lengthy discussion, see David G. Marr, *Vietnamese Tradition on Trial* (Berkeley: University of California Press, 1981), pp. 221–224.

9. For a general overview, see Maurice Durand and Nguyen Tran Huan, *Introduction a La Littérature Vietnamienne* (Paris: Maisonneuve et Larose, 1969).

10. Cited in "To the Artists on the Occasion of the 1951 Painting Exhibition," in Ho Chi Minh, *Selected Writings* (Hanoi: Foreign Languages Press, 1977), pp. 133–134. Underlining in original.

11. To Huu, "Carry out the educational reform in order to train a new generation of socialist Vietnamese," in *Nhan Dan,* September 5, 1979; Vo Van Kiet, speech broadcast on Hanoi Radio, May 10, 1981; *Time* Magazine, February 16, 1976.

12. The 1980 constitution is available in an English-language translation in William J. Duiker, *Vietnam Since the Fall of Saigon* (Athens: Ohio University Monographs in International Studies, 1989), Appendix.

13. To Huu, "Carry out the educational reform in order to train a new generation of socialist Vietnamese," in *Nhan Dan,* September 5, 1979, p. 3.

14. Perhaps the best way to define the current attitude toward women in Vietnam is by the term "separate but equal." In the June 1982 issue of *Tap Chi Cong San,* for example, author Nguyen Thi Ngu observed that women have "special physiological and psychological characteristics" that made them appropriate for the bearing and rearing of children.

15. *6th National Congress of the Communist Party of Vietnam: Documents* (Hanoi: Foreign Languages Publishing House, 1987), pp. 88, 106, 110.

16. William Branigin, "Health Care Woes Burden Vietnam," in *The Washington Post,* February 20, 1994.

17. For references, see the *New York Times,* April 20, 1988 and the FEER, July 8, 1993.

18. *Socialist Republic of Vietnam: Constitution 1992* (Hanoi: Foreign Languages Publishing House, 1992), p. 24.

19. See the two interesting articles on the subject by Murray Hiebert in the FEER, May 13, 1993.

20. Duong Thu Huong's novel has been translated into English. See Duong Thu Huong (Phan Huy Duong and Nina McPherson tr.), *Paradise of the Blind* (New York: William Morrow, 1988). On Nguyen Manh Tuan, cf. the *New York Times,* April 22, 1988.

21. See Nguyen Huy Thiep (Greg Lockhart tr.), *The General Retires and Other Stories* (Singapore: Oxford in Asia, 1992).

22. For references, see the *New York Times,* April 22 and July 5, 1988, and FEER, May 4, 1989, May 7, 1992, and February 4, 1993. For the cases of Dong Quoc Sy and Duong Thu Huong, see *Vietnam Update,* Vol. I, nos. 1–2 (Winter–Spring 1988) and *Indochina Journal,* Vol. 5, no. 3 (Christmas 1991).

23. For an overview of current trends in the arts, see Sally Goll, "Art in the time of *doi moi,*" in FEER, May 7, 1992.

24. Cited in Nguyen Huy Thiep, note 21, pp. 162–163.

8

Foreign Relations

With the 1975 entry of North Vietnamese troops into the beleagured city of Saigon, a generation of civil strife came to an end. Unification, however, did not bring peace, for in less than five years the new united Vietnam was again at war, this time with neighbors Cambodia and China. By 1980, Laos and Cambodia had become Hanoi's client states and tension was high between Bangkok and Hanoi as each massed troops on the Thai-Cambodian border. A new Indochina conflict had followed on the heels of the previous one.

For some observers, these events undoubtedly served as vivid confirmation of the widely publicized "domino theory," according to which the fall of one state to communism would lead quickly to political instability, revolution, and communist takeovers in neighboring areas. In fact, however, the tension that erupted in Southeast Asia as a result of the Communist triumph in Vietnam can be more accurately interpreted as a reemergence of historical trends that had been temporarily obscured during a century of European colonialism and Cold War struggle. For the conflicts that erupted in the region after the fall of Saigon were aroused not by ideological factors, but by deep-seated animosities related to history and ethnic rivalries. With the jealous eyes of the great powers temporarily distracted from the region, local forces quickly resumed patterns of behavior that had long predated the modern era.

This is not to say that Vietnamese foreign policy after the end of the war was not motivated in part by the spirit of proletarian internationalism. Official pronouncements from Hanoi in the months following the end of the war made it clear that senior party officials viewed their victory in the South not simply as the culmination of a century-old struggle for national reunification, but also as a crucial stage in the evolving struggle between the capitalist and socialist camps in the global arena. As one article put it, in the view from Hanoi the victory of the Vietnamese revolution marked the beginning of the collapse of the forces of global imperialism throughout the world.

But the events that took place in Southeast Asia in the years immediately following the end of the Vietnam War demonstrated conclusively that it was not ideology, but history and national interest, that would be the decisive factors in regional politics for the postwar period. Moreover, it was paradoxically the very states that in principle had dedicated themselves to the cause of proletarian internationalism—Democratic Kampuchea, China, and Vietnam—that most stridently adopted national interest as the touchstone of their postwar foreign policy. The specter of communist states warring bitterly with each other over issues of purely national concern surprised the world and made a mockery of the predictions of those outside observers who had feared that a Communist triumph in Vietnam would be followed by the sound of falling dominoes throughout Asia.

VIETNAM AND THE TRADITIONAL WORLD ORDER

It should come as no surprise that national interest should become the dominant theme in postwar Vietnamese foreign policy. Concern for national survival had been one of the dominant factors in the history of the Vietnamese people. Although cross-cultural comparisons are always risky, it is probably safe to say that historically no people in the region had cultivated a more acute sense of national identity than had the Vietnamese. This sense of separate existence, and the determination to maintain it, evidently took form even before the Chinese conquest, reaching its culmination in the restoration of independence in the tenth century. In our own era, the fate of the Communist movement has been intimately linked with that of the national destiny. It is no coincidence that the party's ascent to power commenced with its recognition in the early 1940s that the primary objective of the Vietnamese revolution was the cause of national independence and unification.

As we have seen, however, Vietnam's relationship with China involved more than simply the former's resistance to Chinese domination. Even after the restoration of independence, Vietnamese rulers found it prudent to accept a tributary relationship with their "elder brother" to the north. This relationship, which had its origins in Trieu Da's attitude of deference to the Han emperor in China, probably reflected above all a recognition by the Vietnamese of their neighbor's wealth and power, but it also contained an element of tacit deference to China's position as the most advanced civilization in the entire region. Vietnamese monarchs and scholar-officials were well aware of the cultural and political aspects of the tributary obligation and habitually looked to China for guidance in matters of culture, institutional development, and behavioral norms. Although on occasion Vietnamese rulers affected to reject this inherently unequal relationship, at other times they not only adhered to it, they found it useful in the practice of foreign affairs. Certainly it provided an entrée into the lucrative Chinese market and a stamp of legitimacy to the reigning dynasty in Thang Long. When necessary, Vietnamese monarchs were not averse to calling for Chinese aid in their disputes with internal and external rivals, as when Emperor Tu Duc appealed to the Ch'ing court for assistance against the French in the early 1880s.[1]

China, of course, was not the only source of concern for Vietnamese statesmen involved in the conduct of foreign affairs. After the restoration of independence in the tenth century, the state of Dai Viet soon became embroiled in disputes with neighboring societies in Southeast Asia. Its first rival was the state of Champa, an Indianized trading society located in the narrow coastal lands south of the Red River delta. No sooner had the Vietnamese thrown off the Chinese yoke than they began to clash repeatedly with their neighbor to the south. For centuries, the momentum in the struggle shifted periodically back and forth, with the armies of both sides occasionally invading and ransacking the capital of the other. But with the emergence in the fifteenth century of a strong and increasingly centralized state under the talented rulers of the Le dynasty, Dai Viet gained a clear advantage and eventually brought about the total destruction and absorption of the Cham state.

Almost contemporaneous with the Vietnamese conquest of Champa, Thai armies invaded the declining Angkor empire in the lower regions of the Mekong River valley and forced the Angkor ruling class to flee from their capital near modern-day Siem Reap to a new location east of the Tonle Sap. The stage was now set for the inauguration of a new rivalry between the Thai and the Vietnamese over the carcass of the now defunct Angkor empire.

Given their long familiarity with the Confucian worldview, which ordered the various political entities in the region into a framework of hierarchical relationships, it is not surprising that in their own relations with the non-Confucian neighboring states in Southeast Asia, Dai Viet rulers attempted to apply the principles of the tributary system that had been imposed on them by their own powerful suzerain in China. As Alexander B. Woodside has pointed out, some Vietnamese rulers even began the practice of applying the Sino-Vietnamese term emperor (*hoang de*) to themselves in their relations with the so-called kings (*vuong*, in Chinese *wang*) of Southeast Asia. As a rule, most Southeast Asian monarchs apparently rejected such presumptions. But superior power has its privileges, and by the nineteenth century the fragile kingdoms of Laos and Cambodia had been persuaded to accept a tribute status with their Vietnamese "elder brother," although the kingdom of Thailand, now based in Bangkok, in the lower Chao Phraya valley, claimed similar privileges. For Vietnamese rulers, the determination to force their neighbors to accept their suzerainty was not simply a case of *amour propre,* but a desire to provide the state, for the first time, with a fragile sense of security on its long and vulnerable western frontier.[2]

PERSPECTIVES DURING THE WAR OF LIBERATION

The French conquest of the Nguyen dynasty in the late nineteenth century temporarily arrested this process. Not only was Vietnam deprived of its independence and divided into three separate administrative regions, but Cambodia and Laos were given equal status as protectorates and provided with secure boundaries, thus probably saving them from political extinction at the hands of the Vietnamese and the Thai. In the process, the Ch'ing court was forced by the French to renounce its suzerainty over Vietnam. Under these new conditions, the issue of national survival continued to be of primary importance to the Vietnamese, but the immediate source of threat had changed. The historic danger from the north was replaced by the more tangible threat of national and cultural extinction at the hands of the French.

It is not surprising that several of the first-generation Vietnamese nationalist leaders, virtually all of whom had been educated within the Confucian educational system, were inspired to turn to China for assistance against the French colonial regime, much as the Nguyen dynasty had turned to the imperial court in Peking for similar protection against a French invasion a generation earlier. One of the first to do so, the scholar-patriot Phan Boi Chau, had apparently been inspired by a vision of the "lips and teeth" relationship that in principle had existed under the tribute system of the past. Others turned not to the Ch'ing court for military assistance, but to reformist Chinese intellectuals for ideas on how to resolve the problem.

For the next generation of Vietnamese, which emerged into maturity after World War I, China did not exercise the cultural or political influence that it had in the past. But it is striking to note that even though many of the nationalist leaders in the 1920s and 1930s had received their education in the new system established by the French, many of them followed Phan Boi Chau's example and turned to China for help against the French. For the VNQDD, it was the Kuomintang and the "three people's principles" of Sun Yat-sen. For Ho Chi Minh and other members of his revolutionary movement, it was the Chinese communist party. Ho, like many of his colleagues, may have harbored lingering suspicions of the ultimate intentions of the fraternal comrades in China, but was willing to rely on them for advice and material assistance.

At first, Vietnamese nationalist leaders devoted relatively little attention to the question of the western frontier. When Ho Chi Minh founded the first formal Communist party in February 1930, he selected the name Vietnamese Communist party (Dang Cong San Viet Nam) in the conviction that a focus on national independence would appeal to a broad spectrum of the Vietnamese population. Before the end of the year, however, the new organization was instructed by Moscow to change its name to the Indochinese Communist party because Comintern strategists believed that revolutions established over a larger population base were more likely to succeed against powerful European colonial regimes. The decision aroused some hostility among founding members of the party.

At first the issue of the geographical scope of the party was only a technicality. Although party documents written in the 1930s made periodic reference to the possible formation of a future "Indochinese Federation" (Lien Bang Dong Duong) under Vietnamese guidance, most party leaders were convinced that social revolutions would be long delayed in the politically backward and isolated protectorates of Laos and Cambodia and made few efforts to carry on organizational activities there. The first party cells to be formed in Laos and Cambodia were composed primarily of urban workers and intellectuals of Chinese or Vietnamese origin.

During the Franco-Vietminh war, however, party leaders began to realize the strategic importance of Cambodia and Laos to the success of the Vietnamese revolution, and by 1950 recruitment among the local population in both areas was on the rise. But success brought new problems, as ICP party members of Cambodian and Laotian extraction became restive under the direction of Vietnamese leaders who understandably thought first and foremost of their own national interests. At the Second National Congress in 1951, Cambodian and Laotian members were granted the right to form their own people's revolutionary parties, which would then wage social revolutions in concert with the newly established Vietnamese Workers' party, the linear successor of the ICP. It was reportedly at this time that the prewar concept of the Indochinese Federation was likewise abandoned, but party documents dating from the period make it clear that the VWP still planned to play a leading role in directing the revolutionary effort in all three countries and had not ruled out the possibility that at some future date the three fraternal states might be reunited in a single Vietnam-Lao-Khmer Federation.[3]

The crucial importance of Laos and Cambodia to the Vietnamese revolution was demonstrated during the struggles against the French and the United States, which undoubtedly served to strengthen the conviction in Hanoi that the three countries must be linked together in a militant alliance after the eviction of the imperialists. During the Vietnam War, Hanoi used both countries as a conduit for troops and supplies into South Vietnam as well as a sanctuary and staging area for its revolutionary forces. In turn, the Vietnamese helped Cambodian and Laotian comrades carry out their own revolutionary activities in concert with the struggle in South Vietnam.

But there is ample evidence that Hanoi was careful to guarantee that the needs of the struggle in South Vietnam took precedence over those in Cambodia and Laos. In fact, party leaders in both countries were firmly instructed to restrict their own revolutionary operations in order to avoid provoking the United States into a deeper involvement in the region. Shortly after the end of the Vietnam War in 1975, the new Pol Pot government in Phnom Penh bitterly charged that during the 1950s and 1960s the VWP leadership had advised the Khmer Rouge not to launch an armed struggle against the Sihanouk regime in order to avoid giving the latter a pretext for attacking Vietnamese sanctuaries along the common border. Captured documents confirm that North Vietnamese leaders had indeed sought to prevent the insurgency in Cambodia from interfering with the course of the war effort in South Vietnam. Although communist sources in Laos have not made a similar charge along these lines, it is clear that Hanoi took pains to ensure that the revolutionary movement in Laos did not cause difficulties for the party's struggle in South Vietnam.[4]

Irritation over the self-serving character of Vietnamese war strategy fed latent suspicions about long-term Vietnamese intentions within the Cambodian revolutionary movement and eventually contributed to the rise of a new leadership of the Cambodian People's Revolutionary party. In the early 1960s a faction under the leadership of the Paris-trained radical communist Saloth Sar (later to be known as Pol Pot) seized power over the party and proceeded to relabel it the Kampuchean Communist party, or KCP. One factor behind the decision to adopt a new name for the organization may have been the desire to declare its ideological independence from Hanoi and the determination to follow a separate path to a communist society.[5]

In 1968 a popular revolt against the Sihanouk regime broke out in rural districts in the northwestern part of the country. Whether the KCP was involved in the decision to launch the uprising is not clear, but it is evident that Pol Pot and his supporters were opposed to the moderate line foisted on the party by the North Vietnamese. Ironically, Sihanouk placed the blame for the insurrection on Hanoi and reportedly signaled to Washington his willingness to tolerate U.S. actions to reduce the Vietnamese presence in Cambodia's eastern provinces. He also ordered his armed forces to intensify their efforts to suppress communist activities inside the country.

It was the overthow of Prince Sihanouk by a military coup under General Lon Nol in March 1970 that provided Pol Pot with his first real opportunity to seize power. Hanoi responded to the coup by reversing its instructions to the KCP and encouraging efforts by the Khmer Rouge (or "red Khmer" as the KCP's forces had long been known), to promote the cause of revolution inside Cambodia. At the same time, it attempted to re-assert its control over the KCP by sending back to Cambodia several hundred party members of Cambodian extraction who had lived in North Vietnam since the close of the Geneva Conference of 1954. Pol Pot un-doubtedly recognized the tactic, however, and purged most of these new arrivals on the suspicion that they might be tools of the North Vietnamese. During the early 1970s, Vietnamese forces gave active assistance and training to Khmer Rouge units in Cambodia, but by the end of the war in 1975, relations between the two parties had become seriously strained.

MARCH TO THE WEST

Within days following the fall of Saigon, these latent tensions broke into the open. The DRV immediately contacted the new revolutionary government in Phnom Penh, which had come to power two weeks prior to the end of the war in South Vietnam and offered to establish a "special relationship" (Hanoi's new name for the Indochinese Federation) with the three Indochinese states. However, the latter bluntly rejected the offer and demanded the complete withdrawal of Vietnamese troops from Cambo-dian territory as well as the return of territories lost to the Vietnamese during the latter's expansion into the Mekong delta centuries earlier. To punctuate its demands, Phnom Penh launched armed incursions into South Vietnam and seized islands previously controlled by the South Vietnamese government in the Gulf of Thailand.

Vietnamese leaders, apparently taken aback by the audacity of Pol Pot's behavior, offered negotiations to settle the territorial issue, but con-tinued to insist on the need for a militant alliance among the three Indochinese countries. But the Phnom Penh regime, contending that the "special relationship" was simply a fig leaf for the old Indochinese Feder-ation and a disguised effort by Vietnam to establish dominance over its neighbors, continued attacks along the common border. Hanoi vigorously denied any desire to dominate its neighbors and declared that the concept of an Indochinese Federation had long since been abandoned. Yet it reiter-ated that the shared experience of the struggle of national liberation and the continuing threat from world imperialism created the need for alliance between the three Indochinese countries.

By early 1978, party leaders in Hanoi had lost faith in the possibility of a peaceful solution to the dispute and decided to resolve the problem by military force. In the fall, anti-Pol Pot elements operating in eastern Cambodia announced the formation of a new Kampuchean National

United Front for National Salvation (KNUFNS) to oppose the regime in Phnom Penh. Formed under Vietnamese sponsorship, it was undoubtedly created to provide political cover for a forthcoming Vietnamese invasion of the country and the nucleus of a new pro-Vietnamese government in Phnom Penh.

In late December, Vietnamese troops, supplemented by Khmer guerrillas recruited from among the thousands of refugees who had fled to Vietnam to escape the cruel policies of the Pol Pot regime, launched a massive attack directly across the border. After a series of short but bitter battles, the Pol Pot regime was forced to abandon the capital and seek refuge in the Cardamon Mountains west of the city, where it attempted to continue resistance. In Phnom Penh, a pro-Vietnamese regime under the little-known Cambodian leader Heng Samrin announced the replacement of Pol Pot's state of Democratic Kampuchea with a new Democratic People's Republic of Kampuchea (DPRK). The radical policies followed by the Pol Pot regime were reversed, a treaty of friendship and cooperation was signed with neighboring Vietnam and Laos (in December 1976, the neutralist government of Prince Souvanna Phouma in Vientiane had turned over power to the Pathet Lao), and Vietnamese occupation forces estimated at over 200,000 attempted to mop up the remnants of Pol Pot's army in the mountains and jungles along the Thai border.

The Vietnamese invasion of Cambodia was intended to provide the SRV with the long-sought security of its western flank, but true security was elusive. Global reaction to the invasion was generally hostile, not only among nations such as the United States that had been persistently antagonistic to the Communist regime in Hanoi, but also among neutrals and the members of the Association for the Southeast Asian Nations (ASEAN) within the region. The strength of world reaction against the Vietnamese occupation of Cambodia reached measurable levels when a large majority at the U.N. General Assembly condemned the invasion, demanded a Vietnamese withdrawal, and refused to grant recognition to the new Heng Samrin regime in Phnom Penh.

Public condemnation of its actions by a substantial segment of the world community could be tolerated in Hanoi, of course, if the interests of national security appeared to require it. Party leaders were too wise in the ways of world politics to allow the evanescent force of global public opinion to deter them from adopting measures they felt were required to protect the survival and basic interests of the Vietnamese nation. Yet there was a more tangible and painful price to pay. Although Hanoi had achieved temporary stability on its western flank, a major new threat now loomed from the north, as China massed troops on the Sino-Vietnamese border and publicly declared its intention to take action to punish the Vietnamese for their arrogance.

THREAT FROM THE NORTH

Before 1975, the signs of incipient difficulties between Peking and Hanoi were visible only to the most discerning eye. Virtually from the moment of communist victory on the mainland in 1949, the PRC had provided substantial military and economic assistance to the Vietminh in their struggle against the French. Some foreign observers speculated (and Peking sources explicitly claimed) that the Vietminh victory at Dien Bien Phu in 1954 had been engineered largely with Chinese advice and material assistance. After Geneva, China gave substantial support to the DRV in its struggle to bring about the reunification of the country. In turn, Hanoi publicly declared its gratitude for the fraternal assistance provided by China during a generation of conflict. Significantly, however, it never publicly sided with Peking in the bitter Sino-Soviet dispute. Up to the late 1960s, the DRV had attempted to maintain a posture of neutrality in the dispute, maintaining good relations with both countries. In fact, in the evident belief that the split was disadvantageous to the Vietnamese revolution, Ho Chi Minh had frequently attempted to use his considerable diplomatic skills to bring the two sides together.

When necessary, however, the North Vietnamese were not unwilling to play one rival against the other. This was particularly evident in the early 1960s when Hanoi, visibly irritated by Moscow's reluctance to approve its new policy of escalated struggle in the South, adopted a pro-Peking stance, also criticizing Soviet "revisionism," the signing of the Nuclear Test-Ban Treaty with the United States, and Moscow's strategy of peaceful coexistence with the West.

After the fall of Nikita Khrushchev and the rise of the new leadership of Leonid Brezhnev and Alexei Kosygin in the fall of 1964, the Soviet Union appeared to adopt a more tolerant attitude toward Hanoi's strategy in South Vietnam, and relations between the two countries began to improve. In the meantime, however, Hanoi's ties with China began to deteriorate when Peking offered to increase its aid to the DRV, but only on condition that the latter refuse further assistance from Moscow. Vietnamese leaders, now increasingly dependent upon the U.S.S.R. for advanced military technology needed to resist U.S. military pressure against the North, rejected the offer to the discomfiture of the PRC.

For the remainder of the war, Hanoi sought to retain amicable relations with both China and the Soviet Union. Behind the facade of amicable relations, however, trouble was brewing in Sino-Vietnamese relations. Fearful of being dragged into the spreading conflict in Indochina, Peking became increasingly irritated at Hanoi's aggressive strategy in South Vietnam and periodically advised Hanoi to adopt a cautious strategy of guerrilla warfare until China was strong enough to provide massive assistance. In turn, Vietnamese leaders were visibly angered in the early 1970s when China began to improve relations with the United States. They especially resented Peking's invitation to President Richard Nixon to visit China at a time when Washington had just resumed its heavy bombing raids on North Vietnam during the 1972 Easter Offensive.

Below the surface, other potential trouble spots loomed. One was in Cambodia. According to a White Paper issued by the SRV Ministry of Foreign Affairs in 1979, Vietnamese party leaders had begun to harbor suspicions about China's long-term intentions in Southeast Asia as early as 1949, when Mao Tse-tung and his colleagues first rose to power in Peking. To the skeptical eye of the Vietnamese, the ultimate objective of Peking's foreign policy in Southeast Asia was to keep Vietnam divided and weak in order to facilitate eventual Chinese domination of the entire region. It was for that reason, contended the White Paper, that Chou En-lai had pressured the DRV delegation to accept the partition of Vietnamese territory at the Geneva Conference in 1954. For the same reason he had conspired with delegates of the imperialist powers in refusing to concede the legitimacy of the revolutionary movements in Laos and Cambodia, thus preventing their presence at the conference. According to Hanoi, similar motives were behind Chinese policy after Geneva when, despite China's ostensible support for the liberation struggle in South Vietnam, it became increasingly clear that the ultimate goal of Chinese policy was to keep Vietnam weak, divided, and under Peking's domination.[6]

Whether or not such charges are valid is not an issue that will be discussed here. What is clear is that throughout the long conflict in Indochina, Vietnamese party leaders harbored a deep distrust of China's motives despite its "fraternal assistance" and frequent protestations of friendship to the DRV. With the end of the war in 1975, such underlying tensions quickly rose to the surface. As has so often been the case in relations between communist states, the first clear indication came in the form of a territorial dispute. The common border had been formally delineated as the result of agreements between France and the Manchu empire in the late nineteenth century and during the remainder of the colonial period had rarely been an issue in Sino-French relations. After the Communists seized power in North Vietnam in 1954, a number of minor disagreements over the location of the border surfaced among the local population on both sides of the frontier. For the most part, the disputes concerned such issues as land use, the precise demarcation of the boundary along rivers, and so on. Eventually the issue was referred to the two communist parties for resolution, and in 1958 the two governments agreed to postpone the settlement of border disputes until the end of the Vietnam War.

A second area of territorial disagreement was the delineation of territorial waters in the Gulf of Tonkin and the ownership of two small island groupings in the South China Sea, the Paracels and the Spratlys. Here the historical record was ambiguous. Earlier agreements between France and China over the territorial demarcation of the Tonkin Gulf, in accordance with existing practice, had gone no further than the three-mile limit. Beyond that limit was open sea. As for the ownership of the Paracels and the Spratlys, China and France, as well as the Philippines and the island of Taiwan, had registered conflicting claims based on somewhat imprecise historical records. But because they lacked any recognizable economic importance, the islands had been occupied only sporadically. In 1974, Chinese communist troops, perhaps in anticipation of future problems with Hanoi, seized the major islands of the Paracel group, driving off a small South Vietnamese occupation force.

Shortly after the end of the Vietnam War in 1975, armed clashes provoked by the local population erupted at various points along the border. In the meantime, lured by the possibility of offshore oil deposits in the Gulf of Tonkin and the South China Sea, both countries now asserted ownership over both sets of islands in the South China Sea and presented conflicting claims in the Tonkin Gulf. To underline its own claims, Hanoi seized several small islands in the Spratly group; others were occupied by the Philippines and Taiwan.

A new issue now emerged: As tensions between the two countries intensified, Vietnamese leaders began to harbor a growing distrust of the loyalty of the ethnic Chinese population living in Vietnam. Beginning in 1977, many overseas Chinese began to suspect that the regime was deliberately seeking to break the economic influence of the local Chinese population and perhaps to drive them out of the country. The crackdown on private commerce in March 1978 was perceived in Peking (as well as many foreign observers and the *Hoa* themselves) as directed specifically against Chinese merchants in Saigon-Cholon and resulted in the flight of thousands of people of Chinese descent, either across the border into South China or by ship to other countries in Southeast Asia.

Peking protested that Hanoi was persecuting its ethnic Chinese population, thus breaking a 1955 agreement between the VWP and the CCP that had called for the gradual and voluntary integration of Chinese nationals into Vietnamese society. In May, the PRC dispatched two ships to Vietnam to pick up thousands of overseas Chinese who were clamoring for permission to leave the SRV, but Hanoi claimed that the Chinese action represented interference in Vietnamese internal affairs and would not permit the two ships to dock at Vietnamese ports. Chinese diplomatic officials were accused of stirring up trouble among the local Chinese population, and Peking's consular office in Ho Chi Minh City was shut down.

The territorial issue and the question of Vietnamese treatment of its local Chinese residents were clear indications of growing strains in Sino-

Vietnamese relations, but they were by no means the prime cause of the breakdown that led to war in 1979. Indeed, they were only a minor irritant compared to the broader strategic question raised by the Cambodian dispute and its impact on great power rivalries in the region. For Peking, the Vietnamese occupation of Cambodia not only resulted in a decline of Chinese influence in the area; by extension it also raised the specter of a growing Soviet presence in an area vital to Chinese national security.

The prospect that Cambodia might become a major focus of Sino-Vietnamese rivalry had appeared reasonably remote at the close of the Vietnam War. Pol Pot had maintained friendly relations with a number of the more radical Chinese leaders such as Mao Tse-tung and K'ang Sheng and was an outspoken admirer of the Cultural Revolution. After the end of the Vietnam War, China began to provide a modest amount of economic and military aid to the new regime in Phnom Penh, but Peking by no means appeared anxious to commit its prestige in the area to such a slender reed. The relatively moderate leadership that took power in Peking after the death of Mao Tse-tung in September 1976 took a dim view of Pol Pot's radical prescriptions for building a communist utopia. The events of the late 1970s, however, soon foreclosed China's options and forced it to back the Pol Pot regime as its main ally in Southeast Asia.

By early 1978, Peking was providing increased military aid to Phnom Penh and had warned Hanoi that Vietnamese military action might trigger a response from China. As the crisis in Cambodia worsened and Sino-Vietnamese recriminations over Hanoi's treatment of its ethnic Chinese reached a boiling point in late spring, China reduced and then canceled its remaining aid projects in the SRV. Hanoi responded by accepting a Soviet invitation to join the Soviet-dominated Council of Mutual Economic Assistance, thus agreeing to tailor its economic planning to that of the U.S.S.R. and its allies. Vietnamese leaders also began to talk to Moscow about a mutual security pact. In November, in the aftermath of intensifying Chinese threats against Vietnam, Hanoi signed a treaty of friendship and cooperation with Moscow. Although the pact did not call for an automatic response in case of an attack on either party, it did call for mutual assistance and consultation.

To Chinese leaders, the Soviet-Vietnamese agreement was a final confirmation that Hanoi had become Moscow's puppet, an "Asian Cuba" that would serve the objectives of the Soviet Union in Southeast Asia. Vietnamese officials retorted angrily that the pact with Moscow did not infringe upon Vietnamese independence and had been signed only to demonstrate that the SRV had powerful friends who would help it to defend itself against the arrogant and domineering Chinese. Whether or not Peking's charges that Hanoi had signed away its independence of action were justified (in light of Vietnamese past behavior, an unlikely occurrence), it had indeed been a fateful step, and in China's eyes a final provocation that made reconciliation highly improbable, short of a major shift in global relationships. In that sense, it was a tragic development for both countries and for the prospects of reduced tensions in the area as a whole.

For the Vietnamese, the treaty clearly represented a gamble. Although later events validated Hanoi's assertion that it had not signed away its capacity to adopt an independent foreign policy, there is little doubt that the pact severely restricted Vietnamese freedom of maneuver in foreign affairs at a time when such freedom was patently in Hanoi's interest. One consequence of the Soviet-Vietnamese agreement was an increasing Soviet use of Vietnamese airfields and port facilities. Hanoi vigorously denied Peking's charges that the Vietnamese ports of Da Nang and Cam Ranh Bay (the latter a massive naval facility built by the United States during the Johnson administration) had been transformed into Soviet naval bases, retorting that Vietnam was doing no more than other Southeast Asian states were doing when they opened their port facilities to U.S. ships in the area. Later, when Soviet-Vietnamese relations soured, Vietnamese sources privately conceded that the Moscow would not even permit Vietnamese officials access to Soviet military bases in the SRV.

In any event, Hanoi's reassurances that it had retained its freedom of action were hardly reassuring to Peking. Chinese leaders interpreted the Vietnamese invasion of Cambodia in December 1978 as the final provocation. The following February, China launched an invasion across the border into Vietnam's northern provinces to "teach Hanoi a lesson." During a bloody three-week attack, Chinese forces penetrated several miles into Vietnamese territory in a variety of locations, destroying bridges, roads, and military and civilian installations. According to Vietnamese sources, even the cave at Pac Bo, an isolated location near the Chinese border where Ho Chi Minh and his colleagues had established the Vietminh Front in 1941, was destroyed. Moscow responded to the attack by announcing its willingness to come to the aid of its new ally, and Soviet units stationed along the Chinese border were placed in a state of military readiness, but sources in Hanoi proclaimed that the SRV was capable of handling the invading forces without massive assistance from the Soviet Union.

Events showed that Hanoi's brave words were more than bravado. Resistance to the invaders by Vietnamese military units, many of them local forces under district command, was unexpectedly stiff. And although Peking may have achieved its minimum objectives of diverting some Vietnamese main force units from Cambodia to the Red River delta and demonstrating China's will to back up its threats, the invasion also displayed the military weaknesses of the Chinese People's Liberation Army (PLA). If official sources in Hanoi are to be believed, the war also served to unify

Vietnamese public opinion against the invaders. Indeed, one official source contended that party leaders had found it easier to mobilize public resistance to Vietnam's historic enemy to the north than to the United States during the previous conflict in South Vietnam.

CONFRONTATION OVER CAMBODIA

Peking had maintained virtually from the outset that its war aims were limited, and in mid-March the PLA withdrew back across the frontier. Peace talks began soon after but broke down when it became clear that the issues that had led to the conflict had not been resolved. As the price of settlement, China demanded a Vietnamese withdrawal from Cambodia, renunciation by Hanoi of its alliance with the U.S.S.R., an end to the persecution of the *Hoa* population in the SRV, and a Vietnamese recognition of China's territorial claims along the border and in the South China Sea. As Vietnam had not in fact been militarily defeated, such peace terms were clearly unreasonable. In fact, the war had changed little except to strengthen Vietnamese distrust of China and persuade party leaders to devote increased attention to preparations for a possible resumption of hostilities.

Still, the border war had put Hanoi on notice that China had the power to make Vietnam pay a high price for its decision to pursue a special relationship with the other states in Indochina. Vietnamese leaders were clearly willing to pay that price, but they soon discovered that there were additional costs. For years North Vietnam had enjoyed a measure of support and sympathy from countries around the world for its courageous and tenacious struggle against the French and the United States. After 1975, such sympathy was transformed into practical gestures of support, as several Western European countries agreed to provide limited amounts of economic assistance to the new united Vietnam. Similar aid was soon forthcoming from international agencies. After the Vietnamese invasion of Democratic Kampuchea (as the Pol Pot regime had styled itself), however, several countries cut back or canceled their aid programs to the SRV.

A final consequence of the Vietnamese invasion was its effect on relations with the United States. On coming into office in 1977, the Carter administration had displayed a cautious willingness to consider opening diplomatic and trade relations with Vietnam. Negotiations had stalled, however, when Hanoi, citing a 1973 letter from President Nixon to Prime Minister Pham Van Dong promising $3.25 billion to Vietnam for postwar reconstruction "without any political conditions," insisted on a U.S. commitment to provide such aid as "war reparations" prior to the normalization of relations.[7] This demand was rejected by Washington. In September

1978, Vietnam implied that it was willing to drop its precondition, but by then the growing crisis in Cambodia and the prospects of an improvement in Sino-U.S. relations had severely reduced Washington's interest in establishing diplomatic ties. When Hanoi signed its security agreement with Moscow in November, the Carter administration broke off its trade talks with Hanoi and imposed an embargo on U.S. trade with the SRV.

The invasion had equally disruptive effects on Vietnam's relations with its neighbors in the region. Since the end of the war, Hanoi had been engaged in sporadic and delicate contacts with the members of ASEAN, the regional alliance then composed of Thailand, Indonesia, Malaysia, Singapore, and the Philippines. Soon after the fall of Saigon, rumors circulated that the new communist governments in Hanoi, Vientiane, and Phnom Penh might be invited into ASEAN and thus usher in a new period of peace and stability in Southeast Asia. At first, it appeared that Hanoi would not welcome such overtures, as Vietnamese sources—still locked into a Marxist-Leninist outlook on the international scene—openly predicted the rise of a wave of revolution throughout the region and publicly labeled ASEAN a "tool of the imperialists." Later, however, as the rosy glow of victory began to give way to harsh postwar realities, Hanoi became more receptive to holding talks with its neighbors on improving the regional climate, but it nonetheless posed the unacceptable condition that the ASEAN states renounce their military ties with Western nations. Still, some observers hoped that as the tensions resulting from the long Indochinese conflict subsided, Southeast Asia might yet become—in the words of the program set forth by the ASEAN alliance—a zone of "peace, neutrality, and freedom" free from the tensions of the Cold War. In the spring of 1978, as tensions with China escalated, SRV Prime Minister Pham Van Dong tested the waters by embarking on a lengthy tour of Southeast Asian capitals to hold talks on the improvement of relations.

But the Vietnamese invasion of Cambodia frightened many Southeast Asian leaders and revived their latent suspicions of possible future Vietnamese expansionism. Periodic meetings of the ASEAN foreign ministers resulted in joint calls for the withdrawal of Vietnamese occupation forces from Cambodia and the holding of national elections there under international supervision. Despite their common distaste for the now deposed Pol Pot regime, the ASEAN states continued to recognize it as the legitimate government of Cambodia and pushed U.N. resolutions condemning Hanoi's behavior.

Most hostile in its response to the events in Cambodia was Thailand, Vietnam's longtime rival for influence in mainland Southeast Asia. Thai military leaders viewed the Vietnamese action as confirmation that Hanoi was determined to dominate both Cambodia and Laos, thus destroying the historic buffer zone between Thailand and Vietnam and placing Vietnamese troops along the Thai border. And so Bangkok led the ASEAN chorus of condemnation and, in cooperation with China, provided overt support to the anti-Phnom Penh activities of rebel groups along the frontier.

Hanoi reacted with a combination of belligerence and conciliation. Adopting the diplomatic tactic of "fighting and negotiating" that it had applied so successfully during the Vietnam War, it offered to withdraw its forces from Cambodia, but only on condition that hostile elements supported by world imperialism stop supporting rebel activities led by the Pol Pot regime and that the ASEAN states recognize the legitimacy of the new regime in Phnom Penh. It also offered to withdraw its troops from the Thai border and sign a mutual nonaggression pact with Bangkok on condition that the latter refrain from assisting the guerrilla units in Cambodia. But Hanoi asserted that the survival of the current government was not negotiable, claiming that national elections were the affairs of the DPRK. To emphasize its demands, Hanoi launched punitive raids into Thai territory to clean out the Pol Pot guerrilla sanctuaries and leveled an implied threat to support insurgent activities by the Communist party of Thailand (CPT) in the impoverished northeastern provinces in the Khorat Plateau. On the diplomatic front, the Vietnamese attempted to isolate Bangkok by taking a relatively conciliatory position in discussions with Thailand's allies, Malaysia and Indonesia, both of whom were suspicious of China and inclined to view Vietnam as a potential bulwark against Chinese expansion into the region.

As the new decade dawned, the situation had temporarily reached a stalemate. The ASEAN states, supported to varying degrees by China, the United States, and a number of other Western countries, continued to refuse to recognize the fait accompli in Cambodia and reiterated their demand for a Vietnamese withdrawal and national elections. To provide an alternative to the odious Pol Pot as the basis for future settlement in Cambodia and continued pressure on Hanoi, they sponsored the formation of a united front of various political groups opposed to Vietnamese domination of the country. The new grouping, formally called the Coalition Government of Democratic Kampuchea, or CGDK, was composed of three distinct factions—one led by the noncommunist Cambodian politician Son Sann, a second by the exiled leader Prince Norodom Sihanouk, and Pol Pot's Khmer Rouge. Some observers felt that Sihanouk was the only figure who could unite the disparate factions in Cambodian politics—Sihanoukists, supporters of Pol Pot, and former followers of Lon Nol—into a political force that would represent a plausible alternative to the pro-Hanoi government in Phnom Penh. Yet the presence of the widely detested Khmer Rouge within the alliance continued to pose political and

moral problems, and observers wondered whether meaningful cooperation between the groups could really take place.

For Hanoi, the continuing disarray within the opposition camp provided a welcome opportunity to stabilize the situation in Cambodia and
resolve the problem on its own terms. To emphasize the permanent nature of the new situation and the close relations between the new regime
in Phnom Penh and the SRV, the two governments signed a mutual security treaty and began talks on the delineation of their common border. A
similar accord was reached with Laos, whose leaders viewed close ties
with the SRV as protection against neighboring Thailand and China and
agreed to permit the stationing of several thousand Vietnamese troops in
their country. Over the next few years, agreements between the three
Indochinese countries were reached to enhance cooperative efforts in all
aspects of political, economic, and cultural life. The special relationship
had indeed become an accomplished fact.

In the meantime, Vietnamese occupation forces attempted to maintain order inside Cambodia and launched sweep operations against rebel
groups operating along the western frontier as the Phnom Penh regime attempted to legitimize its authority by winning the support of the local
population. Urban residents who had been driven from their homes into
the countryside during the brutal reign of Pol Pot were permitted to return to the cities. In order to encourage an increase in production, the new
government announced that private economic activities would be tolerated; churches and temples were reopened and citizens were reassured
that they could resume normal lives. Grain was imported from abroad to
reduce the danger of mass starvation. To enhance its credibility on the international scene, the government announced that a new constitution
would soon be drafted and national elections held. The attitude of the
Cambodian people toward their new rulers was difficult to discern, but
foreign visitors reported that although few Cambodians appeared to welcome Vietnamese military occupation, they obviously preferred it to the
horrors of the previous era. For the moment, at least, Hanoi had brought
peace to Cambodia.

During the early 1980s, then, the prospects for a resolution of the
Cambodian dispute appeared dim as both sides settled into a waiting
game, confident that each could outlast their adversary. But Vietnamese
leaders were now to discover the truth in the old adage that, in a guerrilla
struggle, the guerrilla often wins if he does not lose. In fact, time was not
operating to the advantage of Hanoi. Faced with the looming menace of
Chinese troops along the Sino-Vietnamese frontier as well as continuing
insurgency in Cambodia, the SRV was forced to maintain a high level of
military expenditures, thus undermining public morale and draining precious resources from other pressing problems. In the meantime, the em-

bargo on trade and economic assistance imposed by the anti-Hanoi alliance deprived the Vietnamese economy of badly needed access to Western technology and investment opportunities. Closer economic ties with the U.S.S.R. and its socialist allies were little consolation, as worsening economic conditions in the Soviet Union led to a steady decline in the level of Soviet assistance. In 1986, the new Soviet leadership under Mikhail Gorbachëv began to pressure Hanoi to reach an accommodation in Cambodia.

Vietnamese leaders reluctantly reacted to the changing conditions. In 1986 Hanoi offered minor concessions on the Cambodian issue and announced that Vietnamese troops would leave Cambodia by 1990, whether or not there was a negotiated settlement. Hanoi was willing to withdraw its troops as part of a peace agreement, but only under a guarantee that the Pol Pot faction would not use the opportunity to return to power in Phnom Penh. Hanoi also refused to hold talks directly with representatives of the CGDK, contending that the dispute was an internal matter that had to be resolved by the Cambodians themselves. China and the ASEAN states insisted on the total withdrawal of Vietnamese occupation forces and a cease-fire leading to the creation of a neutral and nonaligned state based on the principle of free elections.

PERESTROIKA AND FOREIGN POLICY

By implication, the decision at the Sixth Party Congress in December 1986 to shift to a new economic strategy led logically to the need for a degree of "new thinking" (to use the term applied in Moscow) in foreign affairs. Some of the party leadership had reportedly argued for years that the needs of economic recovery should take precedence over the maintenance of a forward position in Laos and Cambodia, and a message to that effect was probably brought to Hanoi by Soviet delegates to the congress. The Political Report presented to the congress by Truong Chinh, however, said little about foreign affairs, simply reaffirming the importance of the "special relationship" with Laos and Cambodia and emphasizing that the alliance with the U.S.S.R. remained "the keystone of the foreign policy of our party and state."[8] In the months immediately following the congress, there were few indications of change in Vietnamese foreign policy and none in Cambodia, as both sides held esentially to the uncompromising positions they had adopted early in the decade.

In the summer of 1987, however, there were signs of movement. SRV Foreign Minister Nguyen Co Thach, widely viewed as an advocate of better relations with capitalist countries, agreed to take part in informal talks on the Cambodian dispute following a first stage of discussions among representatives of the Cambodian factions themselves. It was the first time that Hanoi had agreed to become directly involved in discussions to resolve the dispute. That December, Norodom Sihanouk, chief of state of the CGDK, met privately with PRK Prime Minister Hun Sen outside of Paris to seek a way out of the impasse. Sihanouk had become restive at the lack of progress in resolving the issue and was increasingly critical of the Khmer Rouge who, he charged, were attempting to weaken their allies in the coalition in a patent effort to dominate the alliance.

The meeting near Paris did not bring about any startling break-through in terms of defining principles for a future settlement, but it did produce a tentative outline for the future creation of a neutral and non-aligned Cambodia. Sihanouk and Hun Sen met again in Paris the follow-ing January and used the opportunity to engage in frank discussions about the process of Vietnamese troop withdrawals and the nature of a possible peacekeeping force that would replace the PAVN in Cambodia. Hun Sen rejected Sihanouk's proposal for the use of U.N. forces for that purpose, but he intimated that his government might accept an interna-tional control commission, reminiscent of the Geneva Agreement of 1954, consisting of neutralist nations like India.

From Hanoi's point of view, the meetings near Paris had produced only limited success. Sihanouk had been brought for the first time into di-rect contact with a representative of the PRK, an event that added to the latter's credibility on the world scene, but he had resisted Hun Sen's terms for a settlement and had refused to hold further meetings until Vietnam agreed to join the peace process. When Sihahouk called on Western na-tions to withhold economic aid to the SRV until it had withdrawn from Cambodia, Hanoi responded by announcing that 50,000 additional troops would depart by the end of the year. In June 1988, newly elected SRV prime minister Do Muoi informed journalists that "if possible," all re-maining Vietnamese forces would be out of Cambodia by early 1990.[9]

The following month, representatives from Vietnam, the ASEAN states, and the four Cambodian factions met at Bogor, near the Indonesian capital of Jakarta, to seek agreement on the principles for a general settle-ment of the dispute. The conference did not resolve any of the key issues, but the delegates did agree on a possible framework for a settlement, in-volving the creation of a transitional authority composed of all factions and operating under the titular leadership of Prince Sihanouk. This au-thority would assume responsibility for the maintenance of law and order in Cambodia prior to the holding of national elections and the formation of a new government.

After Bogor, attention shifted temporarily to Peking, where Chinese and Soviet officials met in late August to discuss the issue. Previously, Moscow had refused to hold direct talks on the Cambodian dispute on the grounds that it could not agree to pressure its ally to remove its troops from the PRK. In turn, Chinese leaders had declared that discussions with the U.S.S.R. could not take place until Moscow had resolved the "three great obstacles" to better relations (a Soviet military withdrawal from Afghanistan, the departure of Vietnamese troops from Cambodia, and a reduction in the presence of Soviet troops along the Chinese frontier). Hanoi undoubtedly greeted the news of the Sino-Soviet talks with a minimum of enthusiasm. Although Peking had apparently shown signs of flexibility on the Cambodian issue in recent months, Vietnamese officials were in no doubt as to China's ultimate objectives in the area. At the same time, Moscow's willingness to discuss the problem with the Chinese must have aroused bitter memories of a previous Soviet sellout of Vietnamese interests at Geneva.[10]

Hanoi need not have worried, for the Sino-Soviet talks in Peking were primarily exploratory in nature, and did not lead directly to a joint effort to impose a peace in Cambodia. But at a later meeting held in Moscow in December, the two countries did agree on the need "to bring the solution of the problem into the concluding state." Shortly before that, Chinese Prime Minister Li Peng during on an official visit to Thailand had already announced that the PRC was amenable to the creation of a new government in Cambodia under the leadership of Norodom Sihanouk, the neutralist politician whom Peking had cultivated to protect its interests in Indochina since the early years of the Vietnam War.[11]

The Road to Peace in Cambodia

The flurry of diplomatic talks on the Cambodian dispute, combined with the momentous and disturbing changes taking place in the Soviet Union, undoubtedly had an impact in Hanoi. At a meeting of the Politburo dealing with foreign policy issues held in August 1988, party leaders reportedly concluded that the Cold War balance of power that had characterized the international scene for the past generation was now coming to an end, thus creating the need for a new set of principles on which to base Vietnamese foreign policy. With Moscow no longer to be relied upon to serve as the "foundation stone" of Vietnamese foreign policy, Hanoi now recognized that it was necessary to look elsewhere for the means to protect its national security interests. Clearly, the primary obstacle to such a development was the imbroglio in Cambodia. In the hope of facilitating a settlement in Phnom Penh, party leaders decided to downplay the special relationship with Laos and Cambodia, simultaneously adopting a more independent posture in foreign affairs.

Two months previously, the regime had sent peace signals to Peking, announcing that an amendment had been introduced to remove statements critical of China from the revised state constitution then under consideration in the National Assembly. It also publicly offered to seek a peaceful settlement of the Sino-Vietnamese dispute over ownership of the islands in the South China Sea. To grease the wheels for improved relations with Washington, Hanoi announced the release of several thousand prisoners from reeducation camps, also agreeing to the creation of joint U.S.-Vietnamese teams to carry on the search for Americans missing in action during the Vietnam War (MIAs).[12]

In May of 1989, the series of Sino-Soviet talks over a resolution of the Cambodian conflict adjourned without achieving any concrete results. But new parties now entered the scene. Three months later, the governments of France and Indonesia convened an international conference in Paris to discuss the issue. The talks collapsed when PRK Prime Minister Hun Sen contended that his government would not agree to a final departure of Vietnamese forces without a guarantee that the Khmer Rouge— still technically an ally of the noncommunist factions within the CGDK— would be excluded from any role in governing the country.

Despite the failure of the conference, however, a new sense of momentum had been created, and international pressure on the various parties directly involved to agree to a settlement intensified. In September 1989, Hanoi, now under heavy pressure from Moscow to end the conflict, announced that the withdrawal of its remaining troops from the PRK was complete. Three months later, the PRK agreed to a role for the United Nations in bringing about a cease-fire and the holding of national elections to create a new government. During the summer, the five permanent representatives of the U.N. Security Council drew up a draft agreement calling for the creation of a United Nations Transitional Authority in Cambodia (UNTAC) to bring about a cease-fire and maintain law and order until the holding of national elections for a new government. They then prodded the four Cambodian factions to sign it.

After extensive discussions in world capitals, supplemented by private consultations between Hanoi and Peking, a new international conference was convened in Paris in the fall of 1991, and the final agreement was signed on October 23, 1991. To help bring about settlement, the ruling party in Phnom Penh announced that it had decided to drop its previous commitment to communist ideology and operate on the principles of multiparty democracy and a free market economy. To mark the transition, it renamed itself the Cambodian People's party, or CPP. Prime Minister Hun Sen also declared his support for Norodom Sihanouk as a possible future president of the country.

After lengthy preparations, the U.N. peacekeeping force was in place, and a fragile cease-fire was patched together in Cambodia. The long-awaited national elections were held in May 1993. To the surprise of many observers, Sihanouk's party, now known as Funcinpec and under the chairmanship of his son Norodom Ranariddh, received a plurality in the elections; the Khmer Rouge refused to take part in the process and launched sporadic attacks on U.N. forces operating inside the country. Disgruntled at the results of the elections, the ruling CPP charged that the voting had been fraudulent, threatening to remain in office. Some members of the party even implied that they might set up an autonomous region along the Vietnamese border, but were reportedly advised against it by the Vietnamese. In August, Norodom Ranadriddh and Hun Sen held talks with Vietnamese officials in Hanoi and agreed on a temporary power-sharing arrangement, with Sihanouk serving as president of the new State of Cambodia, and his son and Hun Sen accepting positions as cochairmen of the Council of Ministers. In late September, the newly created Constituent Assembly voted overwhelmingly to declare a new constitutional monarchy, with the irrepressible Norodom Sihanouk as king. Although under the new charter Sihanouk technically did not possess executive powers, he made it clear that in practice he intended to play an active role in the making of foreign policy.[13]

The final agreement to bring about a cease-fire in Cambodia must have been greeted in Hanoi with mixed feelings. By bringing an end to the war, the agreement promised to reduce the burden of high Vietnamese defense expenditures, at the same time opening the door to improved relations with China and the United States. But from the point of view of national security it also represented a major retreat from the privileged "special relationship" that had been set up in 1979. Hanoi's ability to influence events in Cambodia was now severely reduced, even though the Khmer Rouge, clearly less a threat than they had been a few years earlier, had still not been entirely eliminated as a factor in the equation. To soothe ruffled feathers in Hanoi, Sihanouk declared that he would defer to Vietnamese concerns prior to making a decision to join ASEAN, but he also announced that his government would adopt an independent and neutralist policy in foreign affairs.[14]

There were soon disquieting signs that the new government in Phnom Penh would do just that. For several years, Sihanouk had been intimating that he would demand new talks with the SRV to readjust the common border between the two countries. During the 1960s, Cambodia had reached an agreement with the DRV to respect the border that had been delineated during the colonial era by the French, but Sihanouk claimed that the Vietnamese had unilaterally moved many border markers westward after his fall from power in 1970. A new territorial agreement had been signed between Hanoi and the PRK in the early 1980s, but Sihanouk contended that the new agreement operated to the disadvantage of the latter. In October 1993, there were reports in the press that Sihanouk would demand a return to the border agreement signed in the 1960s.[15]

Hanoi also had reason to be displeased by the treatment of ethnic Vietnamese in the new Cambodia. The size of the Vietnamese presence in Cambodia has long been in dispute. Khmer Rouge sources have claimed that there are at least 2 million ethnic Vietnamese in the country and that many of them are soldiers operating in disguise. Most observers, however, put the size of the Vietnamese community at about half a million and believe that the vast majority of them immigrated on their own initiative after 1979 to seek better job opportunities than existed in the SRV. Whatever the truth of the debate over statistics, few deny the existence of tense relations between Vietnamese residents and the local Cambodian population. Attacks on ethnic Vietnamese by native Cambodians have occurred with increasingly frequency in recent years, and the failure of Cambodian political figures to speak out on the issue has led some outside observers to remark that a form of ethnic cleansing is currently taking place. Significantly, the recently promulgated constitution reportedly makes no reference to the protection of Vietnamese residents in the new State of Cambodia. The issue threatens to become a major source of acrimony between the two Indochinese states in coming years.

Mending Fences with China

A major reason for the willingness of Vietnamese leaders to withdraw from Cambodia was the promise of improving ties with China. Sino-Vietnamese relations had shown signs of mellowing in the late 1980s, the product of a number of factors. One was undoubtedly the changes taking place in the Soviet Union as Vietnamese leaders began to realize that, with the "new thinking" taking place in Moscow, the U.S.S.R. no longer provided a persuasive deterrent against a possible Chinese attack. Many veteran leaders had undoubtedly been uncomfortable with Le Duan's brusque shift toward Moscow after the end of the Vietnam War and sensed that, in the long run, Vietnam had no choice but to get along with its powerful neighbor.

The shift back toward China intensified at the end of the 1980s, when the collapse of communist governments throughout Eastern Europe brought heightened awareness in Hanoi of the risks of rapid political change. Vietnamese leaders silently approved of Peking's tough line to suppress the popular demonstrations in T'ien An Men Square in June 1989, and began to feel a growing kinship with China as one of the few remaining Marxist-Leninist states in the world. Vietnamese officials went out of their way to stress the "historic solidarity" between the two countries, adding substance to the new policy by moderating their treatment of the Hoa population in the SRV.

In September 1990, a high-level delegation led by General Secretary Nguyen Van Linh visited Peking and apparently reached agreement on a framework for a compromise settlement of the Cambodian dispute. During the next two years, commercial relations between the two countries rapidly improved. But the territorial issue remained unresolved. In July 1988, despite recent clashes between Chinese and Vietnamese naval vessels in the South China Sea, Hanoi had expressed a desire to seek a peaceful resolution of the dispute over ownership of the Spratly and the Paracel islands. China did not respond, however, and in succeeding years, clashes between naval vessels of the two countries continued with regularity. A state visit to Vietnam by Li Peng in December 1992 failed to resolve the issue, although the Chinese prime minister did assure his hosts that his country had no expansionist aims in Southeast Asia. At the close of the conference, new agreements on economic, scientific and technical, and cultural cooperation were signed, and a treaty was signed that settled differences over the land border on the basis of agreements reached by the Qing dynasty and the French in 1887 and 1895. Vietnamese sources indicated their pleasure at the results of the talks, but some officials privately expressed skepticism that the leopard had changed its spots.[16]

Vietnam and the United States

The breakup of the Soviet Union and continuing problems with China have made it doubly important for Hanoi to improve relations with the United States. Bilateral talks began during the late 1970s, but had been aborted due to a number of factors, including Hanoi's sudden announcement of the signing of a mutual security treaty with Moscow and the Carter administration's decision to seek better relations with Peking. Washington was also not convinced that Vietnam had done all it could to resolve the MIA issue, and some contended that Americans were still being held in Vietnam as prisoners of war (POWs).

During the 1980s, relations lapsed into the posture of mutual animosity and suspicion that had characterized the era of the Vietnam War. Vietnamese leaders placed most of the blame for the anti-Hanoi economic embargo on the United States, and though that was somewhat of an overstatement—Washington had originally applied the embargo in part to satisfy the desires of China and the ASEAN nations—it was true that U.S. officials often tended to echo Peking in labeling Hanoi a puppet of Moscow and continued to apply trade restrictions long after many of its partners had ceased to do so. The Reagan admnistration took the position that trade and diplomatic relations could not resume until Vietnam had both withdrawn its troops from Cambodia and cooperated with the United States in resolving the issue of U.S. soldiers missing in action during the Vietnam War.

Beginning in 1988, Hanoi began to display a more cooperative attitude with respect to both issues, inviting U.S search teams to the SRV to hunt for MIAs and also withdrawing its remaining troops from the PRK in the hope of stimulating a settlement in Cambodia. But the United States was not to be rushed. With White House officials perhaps taking some satisfaction in watching Hanoi squirm the way Washington had during the Vietnam conflict, the Bush administration set up a "road map," which involved a series of steps that the Vietnamese would have to take prior to the resumption of full economic and diplomatic ties between the two countries.

Some observers expected the Clinton administration to move rapidly toward normalization after occupying the White House in January 1993. But the new president was politically vulnerable on the issue because of his avoidance of military service during the Vietnam War, and veterans' groups, many of them convinced that Hanoi was still hiding information relative to the question of the MIAs, pressured the White House to maintain the embargo. But other voices argued that the policy of isolating Vietnam only encouraged suspicions of Western imperialism in Hanoi and made it easier for ideologues within the party leadership to resist appeals for political reforms. In their view, a policy of "constructive engagement" was most likely to encourage the trend toward liberalization in the SRV and elicit a cooperative attitude by Vietnamese officials on resolving the human legacy of the Vietnam War.

In early February 1994, against a backdrop of Vietnamese cooperative efforts on the issue of the MIAs, the Clinton administration formally abandoned the U.S. trade embargo against the SRV, and preliminary talks began on opening up liaison offices in both capitals. Proponents of normalization would now have the opportunity to test their assumption that a more conciliatory attitude toward Vietnam would accelerate the pace of change in the SRV and induce its leaders to follow the path of development adopted by most other countries in the region.[17]

THE VIETNAMESE REVOLUTION IN WORLD CONTEXT

It is one of the shared characteristics of modern revolutions that each exerts a powerful impact on the world scene, sometimes far beyond the borders of their country of origin. The French revolution of 1789, the upheavals in Russia and China earlier in the twentieth century, and the recent revolution led by the Ayatollah Khomeini in Iran are cases in point, each shooting out shockwaves that reverberated throughout the region and affecting the course of international politics for a generation or more.

Two primary factors help to account for this phenomenon. One is the fact that revolutions represent a vehicle for projecting a powerful new idea that often wins thousands of adherents in other societies far beyond their original frontiers; all great revolutions have ideological effects that are as strong as their political consequences. A second is that revolutions often arouse irredentist ambitions among their supporters, many of whom see the instability inherent in a revolutionary situation as an opportunity to recover lost territories or to become an influential position on the regional or the world scene.

It is clear in retrospect that both of these factors were at work in the Vietnamese revolution. The war carried twin visions of national liberation and social revolution that aroused fears of falling dominoes in many world capitals and heartened radicals to predict that the future would hold "one, two, many Vietnams." The political instability that emerged in the 1960s throughout Asia, Africa, and Latin America (with ripple effects in France and the United States) was inspired in no small measure by the conflict in Indochina. And although the domino theory that had been predicted by many observers was not borne out in reality, after the fall of Saigon in 1975 the Hanoi regime briefly aroused widespread concern by setting out to fulfill the old Vietnamese dream of becoming the suzerain power in Indochina and a dominant force on the mainland of Southeast Asia. Unquestionably, the Vietnam War was one of the most significant events of the last half of the twentieth century. It is hardly surprising that Vietnamese leaders saw their triumph as the first stage in the final collapse of world imperialism.

From a vantage point twenty years after the fall of Saigon, however, it is striking how quickly the impact of the Vietnam War has subsided in recent years. Despite the apocalyptic warnings of Cold Warriors in Washington, the vision of falling dominoes turned out to be widely inaccurate (except for the two predictable cases of Laos and Cambodia), and the dreaded "ripple effect" that would encourage copycat revolts elsewhere in the world turned out to be equally overstated. So is the vision of a Southeast Asian mainland dominated by a military powerful Vietnam: It has been forced to withdraw from Cambodia and the ASEAN alliance has gradually become a powerful force for political stability and the status quo throughout the region. Today, Vietnam is viewed in many world capitals not as a threat to regional stability, but as a potential bulwark against possible Chinese expansion into the area.

What explains the rapid decline of the revolutionary wave in Asia? Perhaps the most persuasive explanation is that the end of the Vietnam War coincided with the arrival of an era of political stability and economic prosperity elsewhere in the region, which was followed in a few short years by sudden changes in the world balance of power and the end of the Cold War. By the late 1970s, communist movements were in a state of decline or disintegration in much of Southeast Asia, and both China and the Soviet Union were backing away from their previously stated objectives of providing active support to the cause of world revolution. By the early 1990s, the U.S.S.R. had collapsed and the Cold War was declared to be history. To place the issue in a Leninist perspective, the world revolutionary situation of the 1960s had subsided, giving way to a new era of stability for the capitalist nations.

Whereas much of the world undoubtedly greeted the end of the Cold War with a sigh of relief, the news must have been received in Hanoi with some misgivings. For two generations, the veteran members of the party leadership had predicated their actions on the assumption that the Vietnamese revolution was an integral part of the world revolution, a parallel first pointed out by Ho Chi Minh in his pamphlet, *The Revolutionary Path*, and that Vietnamese radicals could count on the sympathy, if not always the active support, of comrades in the Soviet Union and other members of the socialist community. The U.S.S.R. was seen as a reliable if sometimes cautious patron for Vietnamese national interests and a powerful deterrent against possible attacks by hostile forces, whether from the United States and its imperialist allies or, more recently, from "international reactionary" forces in China.

The fact is, Ho Chi Minh and his colleagues, like their royal predecessors in the imperial city of Huê, saw their country as a small nation living in a dangerous world, and thus badly in need of a powerful sponsor to fend off potential enemies. The U.S.S.R., far enough away not to be a threat in itself, served that need. But in a new world without a Soviet Union or a Cold War balance of power, the international situation was laced with uncertainty, and relatively small nations such as Vietnam were potentially much more vulnerable to external threats to their national security.

In the short run, Hanoi has reacted by making peace gestures to two of its recent enemies, China and the United States. Neither country, however, can be viewed as a possible replacement for the Soviet Union as a "foundation stone" of Vietnamese foreign policy—China because of its age-old expansionist ambitions in Southeast Asia, the United States because of its ideological hostility to the Marxist-Leninist system of government. To the contrary, both are viewed as potential threats to the SRV in the near or distant future. In the eyes of many party leaders, then, gestures to Peking and Washington are aimed primarily at defusing potential sources of trouble while the regime awaits further changes in the tortuous course of international politics.

Future events, of course, cannot be predicted with any degree of certainty. Should the current situation continue, however, the Vietnamese may eventually find that their best guarantee of national security is to join with the ASEAN nations in an expanded regional security organization. Although disputes among the Southeast Asian states continue to exist, none are of sufficient importance to justify military action, and their common interest in protecting the region from a powerful external threat should provide a strong incentive to cooperation. After all, Southeast Asia has always been a power vacuum that has made it so often the focus of great power competition. The opportunity now exists for the nations of the region to take charge of their own destiny.

NOTES

1. Vietnam's historical relationship with China is a highly complex one and begs for additional scholarly research. For the moment, the standard reference is Truong Buu Lam's short but useful piece entitled "Intervention versus Tribute in Sino-Vietnamese Relations, 1788–1790," in John K. Fairbank (ed.), *The Chinese World Order* (Cambridge: Harvard University Press, 1968). For a brief discussion of Nam Viet's acceptance of a tributary relationship with the Han, see Mark Mancall, "The Ch'ing Tribute System: An Interpretive Essay," in ibid., pp. 66–68.

2. For a discussion, see Alexander B. Woodside, *Vietnam and the Chinese Model* (Cambridge: Harvard University Press, 1971).

3. After the end of the Vietnam War, party sources in Hanoi firmly asserted that all thoughts of an Indochinese Federation had been abandoned in 1951, but the documentary evidence is inconclusive and suggests that the decision might have been made a few years later. For scholarly treatments of the early years of the revolutionary movements in Laos and Cambodia, see Joseph J. Zasloff and MacAlister Brown, *Apprentice Revolutionaries* (Stanford: Hoover Institution Press, 198b), and Ben Kiernan, *How Pol Pot Came to Power* (London: Verso, 1985).

4. For an explicit example of North Vietnamese efforts to keep the Laotian revolution from interfering from the primary battlefield in South Vietnam, see Le Duan's letter to Nguyen Van Linh in July 1962, contained in Le Duan, *Thu Vao Nam* (Hanoi: Su That, 1985).

5. In a recent biography of Pol Pot, David Chandler states that the party was first renamed the Kampuchean Workers' party (in obvious imitation of the VWP), and that the decision to title it the Kampuchean Communist party was not made until after Pol Pot's visit to China in the mid-1960s. Party leaders continued to use the former name in communications with Hanoi. See David Chandler, *Brother Number One: A Political Biography of Pol Pot* (Boulder: Westview Press, 1992), pp. 74–75.

6. SRV Ministry of Foreign Affairs, *The Truth about Vietnamo-Chinese Relations over the Last Fifty Years* (Hanoi, 1979), *passim.*

7. According to Gareth Porter, Vietnamese leaders adopted a tough posture on the issue because they assumed that the United States would need Hanoi's sup-

port to help stabilize the region to obtain access to newly discovered oil reserves in the South China Sea. Later, Vietnamese officials would admit privately that the demand had been a tactical mistake. See Porter, *Vietnam: The Politics of Bureaucratic Centralism*, p. 199.

8. *6th Congress,* Political Report, pp. 120–21.

9. FBIS (Asia and the Pacific), June 23, 1988.

10. For a news report of the Sino-Soviet discussions in Moscow, see the *New York Times,* December 5, 1988.

11. Li Peng's comment in Bangkok is reported in the *Beijing Review,* November 21, 1988, p. 9.

12. Hanoi indicated that those released from the camps could emigrate to the United States if they wished. In return, the Reagan administration reportedly promised not to permit such individuals to engage in political activities hostile to the SRV. See the *New York Times,* July 18, 1988. Hanoi's moves to improve relations with Peking are chronicled in the *New York Times,* July 15, 1988. The reference to the proposed amendment to the SRV constitution is in Kyodo News Service in English, June 26, 1988, in FBIS, June 28, 1988. On Hanoi's decision to pursue a more independent foreign policy, see FEER, September 29, 1988, p. 15.

13. On the meeting in Hanoi, see Murray Hiebert's "First Steps" in FEER, September 9, 1993. On the new Cambodian constitution, see ibid., September 30, 1993.

14. FEER, October 28, 1993.

15. See FEER, October 28, 1993. For an analysis of previous discussions regarding the territorial boundary, see William J. Duiker, *Vietnam Since the Fall of Saigon,* second revised edition (Athens, Ohio: Ohio University Monographs in International Studies, 1989), pp. 151–52.

16. See FEER, December 17, 1992.

17. For an evaluation of the possible consequences of the end of the U.S. embargo on Vietnam, see Murray Hiebert and Susumu Awanohara, "Lukewarm Welcome," in FEER, February 17, 1994.

9

Conclusion

If a revolution, as commonly defined, consists of the violent over-throw of an existing order and the rise of a new ruling class accompanied by a new governing ideology, then the recent conflict in Vietnam clearly qualifies as a prime example. Although the war in Indochina was not sim-ply a social revolution—among other things, it was also a struggle for in-dependence and national reunification and a Cold War confrontation among the major world powers—for millions of Vietnamese the driving force of the conflict was the effort to realize economic opportunity and so-cial justice. And it was the ability of the Vietnamese Communist party, op-erating behind its various front organizations, to portray itself as the legit-imate vehicle to achieve these objectives that above all enabled it to win the allegiance of the Vietnamese people and triumph over its enemies.

From start to finish the revolution in Vietnam was strongly influ-enced by the strategy and tactics of Marxism-Leninism, and it therefore reflects many of the particular characteristics—the existence of the van-guard party, the concept of the united front, the emphasis on revolution-ary will, and the final goal of utopian communism—identified with the type. But in its strong rural component and the employment of a people's army to strike into the lair of the enemy, as well as in the central impor-tance of nationalism, it also bears close resemblance to the revolution in neighboring China. For a time, indeed, the influence of China was para-mount, until party leaders discovered that some elements of the Chinese model had little relevance in Vietnam and could not be applied without incurring heavy damage to the revolutionary cause. From that time on, party strategists became more selective in borrowing the experience of others, and it is fair to say that in the end they had crafted a brilliant revo-lutionary strategy that was uniquely suited to conditions in Vietnam.

After the seizure of Saigon in 1975, party leaders clearly felt that they had a mandate from the Vietnamese people to move directly to the con-structive stage of the revolution. But they soon learned the truth of the old adage that it is easier to seize power than to know what to do with it. By the end of the decade, the revolution was in a state of crisis, and the regime began a long and painful process to understand where it had gone wrong and what actions to take to resolve the problem. That process continues today.

What exactly sidetracked the Hanoi revolutionary express? Perhaps the regime's major mistake was to misread the mood of the Vietnamese people. The fact is, party leaders who had so astutely evaluated the state of U.S. public opinion during the war had seriously misconstrued the underlying meaning of their victory. The program of the National Liberation Front had promised a period devoted to national reconciliation, economic reconstruction, and negotiations over future reunification on a voluntary basis prior to embarking on the road to a fully socialist society. Such a policy would have given the Vietnamese people breathing space to improve their living standards and engage in a debate over their future destiny. Instead, doctrinaire leaders in Hanoi, arrogantly confident of the correctness of their own views and yet fearful of the lingering threat from enemies within and without, rigidly applied the Leninist maxim of "who defeats whom." Far from bringing about a national healing, the policy divided class against class and exacerbated the problem of postwar reconstruction. At the same time, an aggressive policy in foreign affairs alienated neighbors and led eventually to a resumption of bitter conflict. It was a recipe for disaster, and the country was quick to pay the price.

During the 1980s, the regime belatedly recognized its error and began to employ a more conciliatory approach. But the central problems remain. Can the doctrine of Marxism-Leninism, which in principle the party leadership still espouses, provide a successful developmental model for a society that is still overwhelmingly rural in composition and lacks many of the prerequisites for an economic takeoff into the industrial age? Can it be effectively blended with indigenous characteristics to create a culture both "national" and "socialist"? The record is hardly promising on either count. Yet party leaders are probably justified in fearing that an abandonment of the socialist ideal would not only betray the vision of the revolution but also risk a revival of bureaucratic arrogance, corruption, nepotism, and the mistreatment of women—each being one of the more undesirable characteristics of the Confucian past.

The Vietnamese revolution, then, is in a state of transition. In the eyes of many Vietnamese, the Communist party has served its historic function, but it no longer has a clear sense of purpose and has undoubtedly begun to lose the sense of discipline and self-sacrifice that characterized the movement in its earlier years. At best, it now serves as a bridge to the future as the Vietnamese people attempt to reach a consensus on the next step. It will not be an easy task. As current conditions in Eastern Europe attest, the passage to a postcommunist era has been an agonizing one for virtually all Marxist-Leninist systems. The challenge is even more intimidating in Vietnam, where two very different societies, divided by history, culture, and ideological proclivities, attempt to realize the task of creating a single Vietnamese identity.

For the moment, there is no clear picture of the future trajectory of the Vietnamese revolution. Because of the psychic trauma stemming from the long civil war and the dominating presence of the Communist party, no realistic alternative has yet appeared on the scene. The party may yet be able to pattern itself on the relatively successful example of its counterpart in China, where Teng Hsiao-p'ing and his colleagues have managed to defuse political discontent by bringing about an impressive level of economic growth. But if the current strategy in Hanoi fails to satisfy popular aspirations, competing factions are bound to emerge. In the long run, the answer may lie in an approach that has been adopted with some success by a number of other countries in the region: The emergence of a governing elite armed with centralized powers and dedicated to economic growth, but one that is conscious of the need to defer to the continued relevance of national cultural traditions. This path will not open up, however, until a vigorous and self-confident entrepreneurial class begins to play an active role in the political life of the country. History suggests that this likely will be a lengthy process.

Moreover, a total abandonment of the socialist system would arouse considerable popular resistance, especially in the northern provinces, where a generation of party rule and the relative lack of economic opportunity has led to widespread popular acceptance of the egalitarian ideals espoused by Ho Chi Minh and his successors. For the foreseeable future, Vietnamese leaders will be forced to seek an uneasy balance between the goals of uninhibited economic growth and a welfare society providing opportunity to all.

Annotated Bibliography

This brief bibliography is appended for the benefit of those readers who would like to undertake further exploration into various aspects of Vietnamese society. It is limited for the most part to titles in English, but I have included a few works in French dealing with Vietnamese literature, a subject that has received little treatment in English. This list is not comprehensive and fails to mention a number of noted books of considerable value to specialists. But it does include a useful selection of widely available works dealing in some detail with subjects that have been referred to elsewhere in this short volume.

VIETNAMESE HISTORY

The Precolonial Period

Buttinger, Joseph. *The Smaller Dragon*. New York: Praeger, 1958.
    A popular history of premodern Vietnam.
Coedes, George. *The Making of Southeast Asia*. Berkeley: University of California Press, 1966.
    A scholarly but readable survey of early Southeast Asian history by a renowned French cultural historian.
Hodgkin, Thomas. *Vietnam: The Revolutionary Path*. New York: St. Martin's Press, 1981.
    A detailed factual history of Vietnam from its origins to the August Revolution in 1945. Although the title suggests a concentration on the twentieth century, much of the book deals with the precolonial period.
Nguyen, Khac Vien (Ed.). *Traditional Vietnam: Some Historical States*. Vietnamese Studies No. 21. Hanoi: Foreign Languages Press, no date.
    A brief survey of traditional society by the Institute of Historical Studies in Hanoi.
Sellers, Nicholas. *The Princes of Ha Tien (1682–1867)*. Brussels: Thanh Long, 1983.
    A short but interesting look at an early Chinese settlement on the Gulf of Thailand.

Taylor, Keith W. *The Birth of Vietnam*. Berkeley: University of California Press, 1983.

> A ground-breaking account of the origins of the Vietnamese state, based on an exhaustive evaluation of the sources.

Woodside, Alexander. *Vietnam and the Chinese Model*. Cambridge, Mass.: Harvard University Press, 1971.

> A detailed investigation of nineteenth-century Vietnamese society by a respected scholar. Particularly useful for its analysis of Confucian institutions in Vietnam.

Colonial Vietnam

Bao Dai. *Dragon d'Annam*. Paris: Plon, 1980.

> Bao Dai's own account of his role in the crucial events that led up to the creation of two independent Vietnamese states.

Duiker, William J. *The Rise of Nationalism in Vietnam, 1900–1941*. Ithaca, N.Y.: Cornell University Press, 1976.

> An analysis of the evolution of the nationalist movement in Vietnam up to the beginning of Japanese occupation in the Pacific war.

Gurtov, Melvin. *The First Vietnam Crisis: Chinese Communist Strategy and United States Involvement*. New York: Columbia University Press, 1967.

> A thoughtful analysis of the road to Geneva and the U.S. attitude to the Franco-Vietminh War.

Hammer, Ellen J. *The Struggle for Indochina, 1940–1955*. Stanford, Calif.: Stanford University Press, 1955.

> A dated but still useful general study of the Franco-Vietminh War and its aftermath.

Hue-Tam Ho Tai. *Radicalism and the Origins of the Vietnamese Revolution*. Cambridge: Harvard University Press, 1992.

> A wide-ranging and provocative account of the rise of nationalist forces in Vietnam during the decade following the end of World War I.

Huynh Kim Khanh. *Vietnamese Communism, 1925–1945*. Ithaca, N.Y.: Cornell University Press, 1982.

> A detailed study of the foundation and early years of the Indochinese Communist Party.

McLeod, Mark W. *The Vietnamese Response to French Intervention, 1862–1874*. New York: Praeger, 1991.

> A short but useful study of a controversial and little-known period in modern Vietnamese history.

McAlister, John T. *Vietnam: The Origins of Revolution*. New York: Doubleday, 1971.

> An inquiry into the causes of Communist success in the early stages of the conflict with France. Concentrates on the rise of the Vietminh and the August Revolution of 1945.

McAlister, John T., and Mus, Paul. *The Vietnamese and Their Revolution.* New York: Harper & Row, 1970.

> An English-language synopsis of Paul Mus's renowned sociological treatise on the Franco-Vietminh conflict, *Sociologie d'une guerre.* Somewhat impressionistic but full of insights.

Marr, David G. *Vietnamese Anti-Colonialism, 1885–1925.* Berkeley: University of California Press, 1971.

> A ground-breaking study of the early stages of Vietnamese resistance to French rule. Particularly strong on social history.

———. *Vietnamese Tradition on Trial, 1920–1945.* Berkeley: University of California Press, 1981.

> An intensive study of the social and intellectual changes in colonial Vietnam. Written for the scholar but useful for the general reader.

Tonnesson, Stein. *The Vietnamese Revolution of 1945.* London: PRIO, 1991.

> An in-depth and provocative look at Great Power maneuvering and its impact on the rise of the Democratic Republic of Vietnam.

The Vietnam War, 1954–1975

Bui Diem (with David Chanoff). *In the Jaws of History.* Boston: Houghton Mifflin, 1987.

> A Vietnamese perspective on the Vietnam War, by Saigon's one-time ambassador to the United States.

Duiker, William J. *The Communist Road to Power in Vietnam.* Boulder, Colo.: Westview Press, 1981.

> An analysis of the evolution of Communist strategy in Vietnam from the birth of the party in 1930 to the fall of Saigon.

Fitzgerald, Frances. *Fire in the Lake.* New York: Vintage, 1972.

> A prize-winning study of the U.S. failure in Vietnam. Essentially two separate books, an analysis of the reasons for Communist success in the South and a narrative of the political musical chairs in Saigon, it provided for many Americans the reasons why U.S. policy in Vietnam did not succeed.

Goodman, Allan G. *The Lost Peace.* Stanford, Calif.: Hoover Institution Press, 1978.

> Similar in thematic treatment to Gareth Porter's *A Peace Denied,* but somewhat less critical of U.S. policy.

Halberstam, David. *The Best and the Brightest.* New York: Random House, 1972.

> A brilliant analysis of the personalities involved in bringing the United States into the Vietnamese conflict.

———. *Making of a Quagmire.* New York: Random House, 1965.

> A famous journalistic account of the last years of the Diem regime. Influential in raising questions among thoughtful Americans about the U.S. role in the war.

Hammer, Ellen J. *A Death in November: America in Vietnam, 1963.* New York: Oxford University Press, 1987.

> A sympathetic look at Ngo Dinh Diem and the forces that led to his downfall.

Harrison, James P. *The Endless War: Fifty Years of Struggle in Vietnam*. New York: Macmillan, 1981.

> A comprehensive and well-balanced account of the U.S. role in the Vietnam conflict from the formation of the Communist party to the fall of Saigon.

Herring, George C. *America's Longest War: The United States and Vietnam, 1950–1975*. New York: McGraw-Hill, 1993.

> A balanced and respected account of the U.S. role in Vietnam, by a knowledgeable diplomatic historian.

Kahin, George M. *Intervention: How America Became Involved in Vietnam*. New York: Anchor Books, 1987.

> An exhaustive study of the U.S. road to intervention in the Vietnam conflict.

Kahin, George M., and Lewis, John W. *The United States in Vietnam*. New York: Delta, 1969.

> An introductory account of the U.S. involvement in the war by two respected American scholars. Somewhat impressionistic in its treatment of the origins of the war, but useful for its overview of the U.S. role. Strongly critical of U.S. policy.

Kattenburg, Paul M. *The Vietnam Trauma in American Foreign Policy, 1945–1975*. New Brunswick, N.J.: Transaction Books, 1980.

> A thoughtful interpretation of the U.S. role in Vietnam by a former State Department official. Perhaps the best available introduction to the war from the American side.

Kolko, Gabriel. *Anatomy of a War: Vietnam, the United States, and the Modern Historical Experience*. New York: Pantheon, 1985.

> A critical interpretation of the U.S. failure in Vietnam, written by a leading radical historian.

Lewy, Guenter. *America in Vietnam*. Oxford: Oxford University Press, 1978.

> An analysis of U.S. policies in Vietnam. Considered by critics to be an apologia for the U.S. role in the war, it presents U.S. policy as miscalculated but based on honorable motives.

Nguyen Tien Hung, and Schecter, Jerrold L. *The Palace File*. New York: Harper & Row, 1978.

> A scathing indictment of the U.S. failure to keep its promises in South Vietnam, written from a Vietnamese perspective.

Pike, Douglas. *Viet Cong*. Cambridge, Mass.: M.I.T. Press, 1966.

> A definitive study of the organization and techniques of the insurgent movement in South Vietnam. Difficult reading but well worth the effort.

Porter, Gareth. *A Peace Denied*. Bloomington: University of Indiana Press, 1975.

> A trenchant study of the long struggle for a negotiated settlement in Vietnam, written by one of the most respected critics of U.S. policy.

Race, Jeffrey. *War Comes to Long An*. Berkeley: University of California Press, 1972.

> A classic study of the rise of the revolutionary movement in one province of South Vietnam. Very useful for understanding the origins of the war.

Shaplen, Robert. *The Lost Revolution: The U.S. in Vietnam, 1946–1966.* New York: Harper & Row, 1966.

> A fast-paced and readable account of the early stages of the war by an experienced journalist.

Snepp, Frank. *A Decent Interval.* New York: Random House, 1977.

> A detailed treatment of the fall of Saigon in 1975 by a young CIA analyst who was on the spot. Harshly critical of the failure of U.S. policymakers to anticipate the final debacle.

Spector, Ronald H. *Advice and Support: The Early Years.* Washington, D.C.: Center for Military History, 1983.

> A thorough evaluation of the first stages of the U.S. military program in Vietnam, sponsored by the Center for Military History.

Truong Nhu Tang, with Chanoff, David, and Doan Van Toai. *Vietcong Memoir: An Inside Account of the Vietnam War and Its Aftermath.* San Diego: Harcourt Brace Jovanovich, 1985.

> A valuable inside look at the formation and the functioning of the National Liberation Front in South Vietnam.

Turley, William S. *The Second Indochina War: A Short Political and Military History, 1954–1975.*

> A short but well-researched overview of the Vietnam War, with equal attention to both sides.

Van Tien Dung. *Our Great Spring Victory.* New York: Monthly Review Press, 1977.

> An account of the final campaign in the South by the military commander who planned and led it.

Vo Nguyen Giap. *People's War, People's Army.* New York: Praeger, 1962.

> A classical study of people's war in Vietnam by the party's foremost strategist.

Werner, Jayne S., and Luu Doan Huynh (Eds.). *The Vietnam War: Vietnamese and American Perspectives.* Armonk, N.Y.: M.E. Sharpe, 1993.

> A selection of provocative essays on various aspects of the war.

Woodside, Alexander B. *Community and Revolution in Vietnam.* Boston: Houghton Mifflin, 1976.

> A wide-ranging study of the Vietnamese people's search for community, from the colonial period to the final years of the war.

POLITICS AND GOVERNMENT

Boudarel, Georges, *et al.* (Eds.). *La Bureaucratie au Vietnam.* Paris: l'Harmattan, 1983.

> Essays by French and Vietnamese scholars and officials on the nature of politics in the Socialist Republic of Vietnam.

Goodman, Allan G. *Politics in War: The Bases of Political Community in South Vietnam.* Cambridge, Mass.: Harvard University Press, 1973.

> An analysis of the effort to build a democratic political system in South Vietnam by a respected American scholar.

Le Duan. *This Nation and Socialism Are One.* Chicago: Vanguard Press, 1976.
> A useful collection of General Secretary Le Duan's writings on the construction of socialism in Vietnam.

Nghiem Dang. *Vietnam: Politics and Public Administration.* Honolulu: East-West Center Press, 1966.
> A study of the growth of political institutions under the Saigon regime.

Nguyen Long. *After Saigon Fell: Daily Life Under the Vietnamese Communists.* Berkeley: University of California Press, 1981.
> A personal account of life in contemporary Vietnam by a disillusioned intellectual. The author, a U.S.-trained university professor, remained in South Vietnam after 1975 but left secretly four years later.

Pike, Douglas. *History of Vietnamese Communism: 1925–1976.* Stanford, Calif.: Hoover Institution Press, 1978.
> A short but useful introduction to the growth of the Communist party from its origins to the end of the war. Particularly strong on organization and party building.

Post, Ken. *Revolution, Socialism and Nationalism in Vietnam.* Three vols.
> A lengthy but provocative account of the rise of modern Vietnam, written from a Marxist perspective.

Turley, William S. (Ed.). *Vietnamese Communism in Comparative Perspective.* Boulder, Colo.: Westview Press, 1980.
> A series of articles by U.S. and French scholars on Vietnamese communism. Particularly useful on the political system.

ECONOMICS

Chaliand, Gérard. *The Peasants of North Vietnam.* Harmondsworth: Penguin, 1969.
> A survey of agricultural conditions and policies in North Vietnam by a French scholar who visited North Vietnam during the height of the conflict.

Fforde, Adam. *The Agrarian Question in North Vietnam, 1974–1979.* Armonk, N.Y.: M.E. Sharpe, 1989.
> An important path-breaking study of agricultural policy in North Vietnam by a specialist on the subject.

Moise, Edwin E. *Land Reform in China and North Vietnam.* Chapel Hill: University of North Carolina Press, 1983.
> A valuable comparative analysis of land reform techniques in two leading Asian communist states.

Murray, Martin J. *The Development of Capitalism in Colonial Indochina, 1870–1940.* Berkeley: University of California Press, 1980.
> An exhaustive study of the colonial economy in French Indochina. Deals with all phases of economic development.

Nguyen Khac Vien (Ed.). *Tradition and Revolution in Vietnam.* Berkeley, Calif.: Indochina Resource Center, 1974.
> A series of articles on various aspects of Vietnamese society. Contains an interesting description of collectivization in North Vietnam.

Nguyen Tien Hung. *Economic Development of Socialist Vietnam, 1955–1980.* New York: Praeger, 1977.

>   A scholarly analysis of the construction of socialism in North Vietnam from 1954 to the end of the war in 1975. Includes a brief treatment of postwar economic policy.

Popkin, Samuel. *The Rational Peasant.* Berkeley: University of California Press, 1979.

>   A provocative study of the effects of modernization on Vietnamese peasants during the colonial period.

Thrift, Nigel, and Forbes, Dean. *The Price of War: Urbanization in Vietnam, 1954–1986.* London: Allen and Unwin, 1986.

>   A short but rewarding study of the effects of war and socialist transformation on urban areas in Vietnam.

CULTURE AND SOCIETY

Bui Xuan Bao. *Le roman vietnamien contemporain* [The contemporary Vietnamese novel]. Saigon: Nhan-van, no date.

DeFrancis, John. *Colonialism and Language Policy in Viet Nam.* The Hague: Mouton, 1977.

>   A thorough analysis of language reform policy during the colonial era in Indochina. Concentrates on the development of *quoc ngu* as the national written language.

Durand, Maurice M., and Nguyen Tran Huan. *Introduction à la littérature vietnamienne.* [Introduction to Vietnamese literature]. Paris: Maisonneuve et Larose, 1969.

General Education in the DRV. Vietnamese Studies No. 30. Hanoi: Foreign Languages Press, 1971.

>   A survey of educational progress in the D.R.V., issued by the Hanoi regime.

Hickey, Gerald C. *Village in Vietnam.* New Haven, Conn.: Yale University Press, 1960.

>   A ground-breaking study of life in rural Vietnam during the early years of the war. Offers a detailed picture of village life.

Huynh Sanh Thong. *The Heritage of Vietnamese Poetry.* New Haven, Conn.: Yale University Press, 1979.

>   A collection of Vietnamese poetry from the traditional period down to the twentieth century.

Kunstadter, Peter (Ed.). *Southeast Asian Tribes, Minorities, and Nations.* 2 vols. Princeton, N.J.: Princeton University Press, 1967.

>   Includes a chapter on the ethnic minorities in Vietnam.

Nguyen Khac Vien (Ed.). *Mountain Regions and National Minorities in the Democratic Republic of Vietnam.* Vietnamese Studies No. 15. Hanoi: Foreign Languages Press, 1968.

Provencher, Ronald. *Mainland Southeast Asia: An Anthropological Perspective.* Pacific Palisades, Calif.: Goodyear, 1975.

>   A survey of the various peoples of mainland Southeast Asia. Includes one chapter on Vietnam.

Sully, Francois (Ed.). *We the Vietnamese: Voices from Vietnam.* New York: Praeger, 1971.

> A set of articles on various aspects of Vietnamese society for the general reader. Contains useful questions on resources, urban and rural life, religions, customs, and education. One of a series.

POSTWAR VIETNAM

Duiker, William J. *Vietnam Since the Fall of Saigon.* Athens: Ohio University Press, 1989.

> An overview of events in Vietnam since the end of the Vietnam War.

Shaplen, Robert. *Bitter Victory.* New York: Harper & Row, 1986.

> A highly readable account of postwar Vietnam by a veteran correspondent and Vietnam observer.

Sheehan, Neil. *After the War Was Over: Hanoi and Saigon.* New York: Random House, 1992.

> A short but moving tale of a nation still trying to come to terms with the legacy of a generation of war.

FOREIGN RELATIONS

Chanda, Nayan. *Brother Enemy: The War After the War.* San Diego: Harcourt Brace Jovanovich, 1986.

> A well-informed and readable account of the road leading to the Third Indochina conflict, by a veteran journalist.

Chen, King C. *China's War with Vietnam, 1979.* Stanford, Calif.: Hoover Institute, 1987.

> A persuasive study of the factors leading up to the bitter Sino-Vietnamese conflict in early 1979.

Duiker, William J. *China and Vietnam: The Roots of Conflict.* Berkeley: University of California Press, 1987.

> A concise analysis of the origins of the breakdown in Sino-Vietnamese relations after the end of the Vietnam war.

Elliott, David W. P. *The Third Indochina Conflict.* Boulder, Colo.: Westview Press, 1981.

> A trenchant analysis of the recent conflict involving Vietnam, China, and Cambodia. Contains articles by several respected specialists.

Race, Jeffrey, and Turley, William S. "The Third Indochina War." *Foreign Policy,* no. 38 (Spring 1980), pp. 92–115.

> A thoughtful and provocative article on the contemporary crisis in Southeast Asia.

Smyser, W. R. *The Independent Vietnamese.* Athens: Ohio University Center for International Studies, 1980.

> A sober and informative evaluation of Vietnamese policy toward its allies during the war.

U.S.-Vietnam Relations, 1945–1967. Washington, D.C.: Government Printing Office, 1971.

> The "Pentagon Papers." Documents dealing with the U.S. role in the Vietnam War.

Zagoria, Donald. *Vietnam Triangle.* New York: Pegasus, 1967.

> An analysis of the complicated relationship between Vietnam and its two socialist allies, China and the U.S.S.R. Dated, but still useful for an understanding of the period.

Abbreviations

ARVN	Army of the Republic of Vietnam
ASEAN	Association for the Southeast Asian Nations
ASV	Associated State of Vietnam
CCP	Chinese Communist party
CGDK	Coalition Government of Democratic Kampuchea
CMEA	Council for Mutual Economic Assistance
CPP	Cambodian People's party
CPT	Communist party of Thailand
CRAs	Committees of Resistance and Administration
DMZ	demilitarized zone
DPRK	Democratic People's Republic of Kampuchea
DRV	Democratic Republic of Vietnam
FBIS	*Foreign Broadcast Information Service*
FCP	French Communist party
FEER	*Far Eastern Economic Review*
FULRO	Front Unifié pour la Lutte des Races Opprimées
ICC	International Control Commission
ICP	Indochinese Communist party
KCP	Kampuchean Communist party
KNUFNS	Kampuchean National United Front for National Salvation
MIAs	Americans missing in action during the Vietnam War
NCLS	*Nghien Cuu Lich Su*
NEAs	New Economic Areas
NLF	National Front for the Liberation of South Vietnam
PAVN	People's Army of Vietnam
PLA	(Chinese) People's Liberation Army
POWs	prisoners of war
PRC	People's Republic of China
PRG	Provisional Revolutionary Government
PRP	People's Revolutionary party
RVN	Republic of Vietnam

SEATO   Southeast Asia Treaty Organization
SRV   Socialist Republic of Vietnam
UNTAC   United Nations Transitional Authority on Cambodia
VCP   Vietnamese Communist party
VNA   Vietnamese National Army
VNQDD   Vietnamese Nationalist party
VWP   Vietnamese Workers' party

About the Book and Author

Vietnam's Communist leaders, having gained control over the South in the spring of 1975, immediately attempted to establish socialism in the reunified country. But economic failure, foreign policy crises, and popular resistance to dogmatic programs undermined the regime's efforts, and in 1986 the Vietnamese Communist party embarked on a new era of *doi moi* (renovation). Today, the country's leadership is moving toward a more market-oriented approach while maintaining the ultimate goal of building a socialist society. Success is by no means guaranteed.

Offering an expanded and thoroughly revised edition of his successful text, William Duiker traces the course of Vietnamese history from its origins to the end of the Vietnam War. He considers the country's political structure, foreign relations, economic situation, social problems, and cultural heritage, analyzing the diverse aspects of Vietnamese society and revealing how they have been affected by a generation of conflict and socialist transformation. The author concludes with a discussion of the dynamic factors underlying the Vietnamese revolution, looking at how the changes have affected both the region and course of the global Cold War.

William J. Duiker is Liberal Arts Professor of East Asian Studies at the Pennsylvania State University.

Index